Human Rights in Africa

Human rights have a deep and tumultuous history that culminates in the age of rights we live in today, but where does Africa's story fit in with this global history? Here, Bonny Ibhawoh maps this story and offers a comprehensive and interpretative history of human rights in Africa. Rather than a tidy narrative of ruthless violators and benevolent protectors, this book reveals a complex account of indigenous African rights traditions embodied in the wisdom of elders and sages; of humanitarians and abolitionists who marshaled arguments about natural rights and human dignity in the cause of antislavery; of the conflictual encounters between natives and colonists in the age of Empire and the "civilizing mission"; of nationalists and anti-colonialists who deployed an emergent lexicon of universal human rights to legitimize long-standing struggles for self-determination; and of dictators and dissidents locked in struggles over power in the era of independence and constitutional rights.

BONNY IBHAWOH is a professor of history and global human rights at McMaster University. He has taught in universities in Africa, the United States, and Canada. He was previously a Human Rights Fellow at the Carnegie Council for Ethics and International Affairs, New York, and a Research Fellow at the Danish Institute for Human Rights, Copenhagen, Denmark. He is the author of *Imperial Justice: Africans in Empire's Court* and *Imperialism and Human Rights*, named American Library Association Choice Outstanding Academic Title.

D0162327

New Approaches to African History

Series Editor
Martin Klein, *University of Toronto*

Editorial Advisors
William Beinart, *University of Oxford*
Mamadou Diouf, *Columbia University*
William Freund, *University of KwaZulu-Natal*
Sandra E. Greene, *Cornell University*
Ray Kea, *University of California, Riverside*
David Newbury, *Smith College*

New Approaches to African History is designed to introduce students to current findings and new ideas in African history. Although each book treats a particular case and is able to stand alone, the format allows the studies to be used as modules in general courses on African history and world history. The cases represent a wide range of topics. Each volume summarizes the state of knowledge on a particular subject for a student who is new to the field. However, the aim is not simply to present views of the literature; it is also to introduce debates on historiographical or substantive issues and may argue for a particular point of view. The aim of the series is to stimulate debate and to challenge students and general readers. The series is not committed to any particular school of thought.

Other Books in the Series

1. *Africa since 1940* by Frederick Cooper
2. *Muslim Societies in African History* by David Robinson
3. *Reversing Sail: A History of the African Diaspora* by Michael Gomez
4. *The African City: A History* by William Freund
5. *Warfare in Independent Africa* by William Reno
6. *Warfare in African History* by Richard J. Reid
7. *Foreign Intervention in Africa* by Elizabeth Schmidt
8. *Slaving and Slavery in African History* by Sean Stilwell
9. *Democracy in Africa* by Nic Cheeseman
10. *Women in Twentieth-Century Africa* by Iris Berger
11. *A History of African Popular Culture* by Karin Barber
12. *Human Rights in Africa* by Bonny Ibhawoh

Human Rights in Africa

Bonny Ibhawoh
McMaster University

CAMBRIDGE
UNIVERSITY PRESS

CAMBRIDGE
UNIVERSITY PRESS

University Printing House, Cambridge CB2 8BS, United Kingdom

One Liberty Plaza, 20th Floor, New York, NY 10006, USA

477 Williamstown Road, Port Melbourne, VIC 3207, Australia

314–321, 3rd Floor, Plot 3, Splendor Forum, Jasola District Centre, New Delhi – 110025, India

79 Anson Road, #06–04/06, Singapore 079906

Cambridge University Press is part of the University of Cambridge.

It furthers the University's mission by disseminating knowledge in the pursuit of education, learning, and research at the highest international levels of excellence.

www.cambridge.org
Information on this title: www.cambridge.org/9781107016316
DOI: 10.1017/9781139060950

First published 2018

A catalogue record for this publication is available from the British Library.

Library of Congress Cataloging-in-Publication Data
NAMES: Ibhawoh, Bonny, author.
TITLE: Human rights in Africa / Bonny Ibhawoh.
DESCRIPTION: Cambridge, United Kingdom ; New York, NY : Cambridge University Press, 2018. | Series: New approaches to African history ; 12 | Includes bibliographical references and index.
IDENTIFIERS: LCCN 2017037639 | ISBN 9781107016316 (hardback) | ISBN 9781107602397 (paperback)
SUBJECTS: LCSH: Human rights–Africa–History. | Human rights–Africa–Philosophy. | BISAC: HISTORY / Africa / General.
CLASSIFICATION: LCC JC599.A36 I35 2018 | DDC 323.096–dc23
LC record available at https://lccn.loc.gov/2017037639

ISBN 978-1-107-01631-6 Hardback
ISBN 978-1-107-60239-7 Paperback

For
Osezua

Contents

LIST OF FIGURES	*page* x	
PREFACE	xi	
ACKNOWLEDGMENTS	xix	
LIST OF ABBREVIATIONS	xxi	
1 Visions and Disputes	I	
2 Elders and Sages	30	
3 Humanitarians and Abolitionists	55	
4 Natives and Colonists	90	
5 Nationalists and Anti-Colonists	130	
6 Dictators and Dissidents	173	
7 Old Struggles and New Causes	221	
INDEX	239	

Figures

4.1 British army operations against the Mau Mau   *page* 105
5.1 Blaise Diagne   140
5.2 Nnamdi Azikiwe   150
6.1 Mobutu Sese Seko of Zaire   193

Preface

We live in the age of rights. The doctrine of human rights has become the dominant language for public good around the world. It has become the language of choice for making and contesting entitlement claims, spawning what has been described as a global human rights revolution – a revolution of norms and values that has redefined our understanding of ethics and justice. From interstate relations to interpersonal encounters, there is growing academic and popular interest in the deep history of human rights. There is increasing willingness by scholars to re-examine historical events through the human rights lens. Historical contributions to human rights have been concerned primarily with questions of meaning, origin and genealogy. Although modern human rights doctrine is widely seen as a twentieth-century *invention* and an outcome of the tumult of World War II, questions remain about the origin and genealogy of the human rights idea. What are human rights and how have human rights ideas and struggles developed over time in various societies? How far back in time can and should we go to trace the genealogy of human rights? What are the defining moments of rupture and breakthrough in the evolution of the human rights idea and the development of the human rights movement?

In crafting a *longue durée* history of human rights in Africa, this book addresses some of these broad questions. But my aim is not so much to answer them conclusively as it is to engage them from a distinctly Africanist perspective. Although the past few decades have witnessed an explosion of interest in human rights history, Africanist historical perspectives have been few and far between. Much of the scholarship on the history of human rights has been framed in ways that omit or gloss over African experiences and perspectives in discussions of key episodes in the history – antislavery and abolitionism, liberalism and modernism, social movements and political revolutions, and the post–World War II international human rights movement. Yet African experiences, from antislavery to anti-colonialism, are clearly integral to the history and *pre-history* of international human rights.

This book aims at two intersecting goals. The first is to explore the place of Africa in the global history of human rights. The second is to broadly map the development of human rights as idea, discourse and struggle in Africa. In these endeavors, this book resists the presentism and essentialism that characterizes much of the scholarship on human rights, to tell a story that goes beyond twentieth-century violations and present-day activism. The story of human rights offered in these pages is not a tidy narrative to ruthless violators and benevolent protectors. It is a more convoluted story of indigenous African rights traditions embodied in the wisdom of *elders and sages*, of *humanitarians and abolitionists* who marshaled arguments about natural rights and human dignity in the cause of antislavery, of conflictual encounters between *natives and colonists* in the age of Empire and civilizing missions, of *nationalists and anti-colonists* who deployed an emergent international human rights lexicon to legitimize longstanding struggles for self-determination, and of *dictators and dissidents* locked in struggles over power in the era of independence and constitutional rights.

Writing a deep history of human rights in Africa demands confronting the dual presentism of African history and human rights scholarship. The presentism of human rights scholarship has long been recognized. The main critique is that human rights historiography appears trapped in an intellectual tradition of linear progressivism that tends to hinder proper understanding of historical continuities and ruptures. In a field that, until recently, attracted few historians, the linearity of human rights narratives is partly a consequence of a preoccupation with the here and now, and a tendency to read history backward. The traditional history of human rights has essentially been a retrospective teleology whereby contemporary vantage points are applied for a linear and causal projection into the past.[1] Reviewing

---

[1] Jean-Paul Lehners, "Pleading for a New History of Human Rights," in *The SAGE Handbook of Human Rights*, Mark Gibney and Anja Mihrand, eds. (New York: Sage, 2014), 34.

the bourgeoning human rights historiography, it is difficult to escape the impression that most accounts have been aimed at interpreting contemporary human rights through linear causality.

Beyond the presentism of human rights scholarship, this book confronts the presentism of Africanist historiography. Historical scholarship about Africa has been critiqued for being clustered in the twentieth century. This is driven by the pervasive sense that anything significantly before 1900 tells us little about where Africa is today. The result is a historiography that has privileged twentieth-century topics such as colonialism, decolonization and post-colonial state building, over all that came before. As others have noted, this prevailing presentism threatens to inhibit our comprehension of the continent's historical trajectories over the longer term.[2] This book addresses the charges of presentism in both African history and human rights scholarship by seeking to decenter the putative defining epochs in each field – the colonial moment within African history and post–World War II internationalism within human rights scholarship. This is reflected in my preference for terms such as "indigenous traditions" rather than "pre-colonial traditions," and "independent Africa" rather than "post-colonial Africa."

Given the book's goal of outlining the broad contours of the histories of human rights in Africa, one approach to organizing this book that I considered was a thematic approach, based on the generations of rights schema that has become a canon of human rights scholarship. This would require organizing the narrative around typologies or generations of human rights including first-generation civil and political rights that emphasize individualism and egalitarianism, second-generation economic, social and cultural rights that emphasize equality, and third-generation solidarity rights that demand global distributive justice. I opted against this approach to organizing the book mainly because of the limitations it imposes on constructing a narrative that does not take as its reference point the ruptures of mid-twentieth-century international politics. While the generations of rights framework might work well for analyzing the post–World War II human rights movement (and I draw on it at some points in this book), it is not very useful for understanding its local and global antecedents. The ideological impulses and social conditions that

---

[2] Richard Reid and John Parker, "African Histories: Past, Present, and Future," in *The Oxford Handbook of Modern African History*, John Parker and Richard Reid, eds. (Oxford: Oxford University Press, 2013), 10.

fostered human rights movements at various points in history cannot be neatly subsumed under these categories. Moreover, ordering the history of human rights in terms of generations that prioritize civil and political rights over social and economic rights, or vice versa, tends to privilege particular ideological and epistemological constructs of human rights. This runs against the counter-hegemonic impulse of human rights that also frames this book.

Another possibility in organizing this book was to adopt a country-specific or regional approach. The appeal of this approach is that it allows for a contained narrative framed around national and regional histories and institutions. Constructing narratives around nation-states is particularly attractive to human rights scholars because of the state-centric character of modern day international human rights systems. For legal and positivist scholars who see human rights essentially as enforceable entitlements that individuals hold in relation to the state, a state-centered approach to human rights has undeniable appeal. However, as with the generations of rights schema, the key limitation of this approach is that it negates accounts that do not take the nation-state or the post–World War II human rights regime as paradigmatic take-off points. Presuming the primacy of the national unit in thinking about human rights is, in itself, a presentist conception and it is perhaps not a durable one.[3] The modern state is a relatively recent *invention* with origins in the collapse of the great multinational empires in the early twentieth century that brought several new states into existence. The emergence of the sovereign nation-state as the dominant unit of political organization became global only with mid-twentieth-century decolonization. In Africa, where the nation-state has had the shortest history, national identities remain fragile and unsettled. Although discussions about human rights are often framed around state obligations, I have chosen not to organize this book primarily around countries or regions.

I have opted instead to organize this book around themes that cut across both human rights and African history to allow a narrative that is attentive to transnational and transregional patterns. The main themes include indigenous egalitarian morality and African notions of personhood, dignity and justice; slavery and antislavery; colonialism,

---

[3] Frederick Cooper, "Afterword: Social Rights and Human Rights in the Time of Decolonization," *Humanity: An International Journal of Human Rights, Humanitarianism, and Development*, 3, 3 (2012): 476.

anti-colonialism and decolonization; independence, democracy and state-building; and, finally, debates about localizing or vernacularizing universal human rights. To complement this thematic ordering, I have tried to present an account that is regionally representative. Conscious of the tendency to read Africa as meaning essentially sub-Saharan Africa, I have paid attention to the histories of human rights ideas and struggle in North Africa. With regard to periodization, I have resisted the temptation of framing this history of human rights in Africa primarily with the milestones of the beginning and end of colonial domination. Although colonialism marked a defining moment in the history of human rights in Africa, I have sought to decenter this narrative by treating it as one episode, among many, in the human rights story rather than the core of the story itself.

Chapter 1 examines the conceptual and theoretical framings of human rights. It explores the *vision* of human rights and the continuing *disputes* over its meaning, interpretation and scope. It asks the basic questions that every book on human rights must confront. What are human rights? How can human rights as discourse and struggle be understood and analyzed historically? How do we address the tensions between the universalist aspirations of international human rights and the challenges of cultural relativism and cultural legitimacy? The chapter also addresses specific questions about conceptualizing human rights in Africa. Rather than seeking definitive answers, the aim of the chapter is to lay bare the contending arguments and outline a guiding conceptual framework.

Chapter 2 explores what may be termed the *pre-history* of human rights in Africa. It examines indigenous humanism as expressed in moral principles and cultural practices that affirm human dignity and promote individual and collective liberties. It considers how these early humanist traditions have been invoked in contemporary human rights discourse and considers their place in the broader history of human rights in Africa.

Chapter 3 offers an Africa-centered narrative of antislavery rights discourses and struggles. It seeks not simply to reinterpret abolitionism in Africa using the lens of human rights or to fit antislavery neatly into a genealogy of human rights. Rather, it is an attempt at constructing a pre-history of modern human rights by exploring the place of antislavery in the development of ideas about human rights in and about Africa. The chapter also explores the links between antislavery and human rights in the context of abolitionism as an organized socio-political movement, and the role of Africans within it.

Chapters 4 and 5 center on discourses about and struggles for human rights within the colonial state. These range from affirmations of native rights deployed to justify and legitimize colonial rule, to the human rights impacts of colonial policies and practices. Chapter 4 examines how colonial rule changed understandings of rights at discursive and practical levels, and how it restricted or expanded the scope of liberties enjoyed by particular groups within the colonial state. Chapter 5 specifically explores the links between colonialism and human rights as they relate to anti-colonial struggles and the legacies of colonial rule on human rights. I pay particular attention to the labor question within anti-colonialism and argue the case for reading labor struggles and discourses of workers' rights as part of a nascent economic and social rights advocacy movement.

The focus shifts to independent Africa in Chapter 6 with discussions of oppositional politics, individual liberties, minority rights, state sovereignty and the challenges of state-building. The chapter specifically addresses the claim that African leaders who invoked the right to self-determination in anti-colonial struggles abandoned human rights ideals once they assumed power at independence. Did African political elites turn their backs on human rights once independence was attained? If so, what accounts for this volte-face? In addressing these questions, I explore the shifts and turns in human rights in the independent African state, juxtaposing state authoritarianism with a resurgent oppositional rights discourse. I go beyond the narrative of abandonment to examine the political, economic and social contingencies that shaped the shifts in human rights discourses and practices. I am concerned here not only with the objective human rights conditions in the independent state, but also with the contestations over the human rights in statist and oppositional rights discourses.

Chapter 7 offers concluding reflections on the history of human rights in Africa and the continuing tension between local visions and interpretations of human rights, on one hand, and the obligations of states under international human rights law and norms, on the other. It also ponders the transformative changes and underlying continuities in the history of human rights in Africa.

In writing this book, I have aimed for a narrative that appeals to audiences beyond academia. My goal from the onset was to tell a story of human rights that engages key academic questions while also appealing to a broad non-specialist audience of educators, policy-makers, field practitioners and general readers. This made it

sometimes necessary to distill complicated debates and episodes into a
few lines or paragraphs, and to focus on general themes that pull
the story together rather than the minutiae of national and regional
contexts. Admittedly, this broad brush approach does not always do
justice to the complexities of the issues discussed. While I understand
the misgivings that some might have about such an approach, I believe
that there is much to be gained from a history of human rights
undertaken from a broad transnational and comparative perspective.
After all, universality and transnationalism are defining attributes of
modern human rights. My quest to construct a history of human rights
in Africa that appeals to a general audience is also driven by the belief
that the subject of human rights is too important to be left to experts
and specialists. Human rights discourses, laws, policies and practices
affect the everyday lives of millions of ordinary people in Africa and
around the world. It is important to engage the broadest audience
possible in conversations about human rights.

Acknowledgments

I have incurred many debts in the course of writing this book. The main funding support for this project came from grants from the Social Science and Humanities Research Council of Canada and from McMaster University, for which I am grateful. The story of human rights in Africa that I tell in this book has been shaped by my occasional sojourns into the practical world of human rights advocacy and public history. This has enabled me to see beyond the sometimes esoteric debates that preoccupy human rights scholars. I am grateful to researchers and curators at the Canadian Museum of Human Rights in Winnipeg with whom I worked on constructing a "Global Historical Human Rights Timeline" for the museum. Working on this project raised new questions that challenged me to rethink old approaches and answers. The moving and compelling exhibits at the museum remind us that human rights represent human experiences and relationships, and that human rights histories are ultimately stories of human struggles. These histories, like the struggles they represent, are complex, deep and diverse. The idea of human rights is not the invention of any one particular society or culture. As the plaque that welcomes visitors to the museum proclaims: "Throughout history, people have grappled with ideas about human dignity, respect and responsibility ... [Human rights] is an idea thousands of years in the making."

This book draws on some of my arguments previously presented elsewhere. I am grateful to journals and editors for granting me permission to reproduce them in this volume. Other ideas were tested at various scholarly forums, eliciting comments, suggestions and critiques from students, practitioners and colleagues. I am indebted to the students in my undergraduate courses and graduate seminars on human rights at McMaster University, the University of Lagos and Covenant University. This book has benefited from our discussions about the meanings of human rights, the paradoxes of rights talk, the challenges of protecting human rights in Africa, and the *problematique* of constructing local and global human rights histories. A conference on "Human Rights and the Public Sphere in Africa" organized by Carleton University's Institute of African Studies provided an excellent opportunity to share my ideas with an assemblage of distinguished Africanists and human rights scholars. I am grateful to my student research assistants at various stages of writing this book: Samantha Stevens-Hall, Lekan Akinosho, Paul Emiljanowicz, Halimat Somotan and Rashida Shariff. My thanks to Martin Klein for nudging me into this project and pushing me to see it through. I am deeply grateful to friends whose interest in this project has been a constant source of motivation – Julius and Bimpe Egbeyemi, Dominic and Catherine Adesanya, John and Lisa Sainsbury, Shedrack and Nkiru Agbakwa, Bill and Christine Oates. Finally, and as always, I am indebted to my family – Omo and our boys whose love and support make all my research endeavors possible.

Abbreviations

ACHPR	African Charter on Human and People's Rights
ANC	African National Congress (South Africa)
APS	Aborigines Protection Society
ARPS	Aborigines' Rights Protection Society
ASAPS	Antislavery Society and Aborigines Protection Society
AU	African Union
BFASS	British and Foreign Anti-Slavery Society
CCPR	Covenant on Civil on Civil and Political Rights (United Nations)
CESR	Covenant on Economic and Social Rights (United Nations)
CPP	Convention People's Party (Gold Coast)
ECHR	European Convention on Human Rights
EOHR	Egyptian Organization for Human Rights
FLN	National Liberation Front (Front de Libération Nationale)
ICC	International Criminal Court
ILO	International Labor Organization
IMF	International Monetary Fund
KANU	Kenya African National Union
KPU	Kenya People's Union
MPLA	People's Movement for the Liberation of Angola
NAUK	National Archives of the United Kingdom
NCAW	National Council of African Women

OAU	Organization of African Unity
SANNC	South African Native National Council
SAPC	South African Communist Party
TANU	Tanganyika National Union
TLHR	Tunisian League of Human Rights
TRC	Truth and Reconciliation Commission
UDHR	Universal Declaration of Human Rights (United Nations)
UGCC	United Gold Coast Convention
UGTT	Tunisian General Labor Union (Union Générale Tunisienne du Travail)
UN	United Nations
UNITA	National Union for the Total Independence of Angola (União Nacional para a Independência Total de Angola)
UNHRC	United Nations Human Rights Council
UPC	Uganda People's Congress

Visions and Disputes

In his famous autobiography, written in 1789 and depicting the horrors of transatlantic slavery, Olaudah Equiano invoked human rights. Describing his torturous journey of captivity from the West African hinterland to the coast, he referred to his captors as "sable destroyers of human rights."[1] He went on to compare this passage to the coast with the terrifying and traumatic life of chattel slavery in the New World. Equiano was not alone in invoking "human rights" within nineteenth-century antislavery. In the 1830s, the American Anti-Slavery Society published two regular campaign pamphlets – *The Anti-Slavery Examiner* and *Human Rights Extra* – which framed the abolitionist movement partly in terms of human rights. In the pages of *Human Rights Extra*, slavery was challenged not only in terms of Christian ethics but also on the normative grounds of a universal humanity expressed in terms of human rights of the "negro." Soliciting contributions for the Anti-Slavery Society's campaign for emancipation resettlement in Africa, one abolitionist stated that in no part of the globe was the "colored man found in the full enjoyment of human rights except in Liberia."[2] The writer bemoaned the "sad fact" that in the United States, with its abundance of "wealth and intelligence," the negro's human rights condition was much worse than in newly settled Liberia where the resettled citizens could enjoy

---

[1] Olaudah Equiano, *The Interesting Narrative of the Life of Olaudah Equiano* (Radford, VA: Wilder Publications, 2008), 18.
[2] B. T. Kavanaugh, "Facts," *The African Repository and Colonial Journal* (1847), 23, 349.

unrestrained liberties. Slavery, another contributor proclaimed, was "an outrage on human rights."[3] These abolitionist writings have been described as some of the strongest contemporary intellectual statements that we possess on the human rights character of antislavery.[4]

***

In 1919, a group of continental and diaspora African leaders gathered in Paris for a Pan-African congress that they hoped would address varied issues of racism and exclusion, colonialism and exploitation affecting peoples of African descent globally. The congress attracted fifty-seven delegates representing fifteen countries and colonies including Liberia, several West African colonies, Haiti, the British West Indies and the United States. Two key figures behind the organization of the congress were the African American intellectual W. E. B. Du Bois and the influential Senegalese politician Blaise Diagne, who, as Senegalese deputy to the French Parliament, was the highest-ranking African in French politics. Coinciding with the end of World War I and the gathering of European and American politicians for the Versailles Peace Conference, the Congress's objective was to influence the political agenda of the Peace Conference and the fate of black people in the post-war era. A key outcome of the Congress was the adoption of a charter of rights for peoples of African descent. Delegates passed a resolution calling for a "code of law for the international protection of the natives of Africa" from abuse, exploitation and violence. The resolution called for the direct supervision of colonies by the League of Nations to prevent economic exploitation by foreign nations, and the abolition of slavery and capital punishment of colonial subjects in Africa. It also asserted the rights of black people to education within the colonies and the rights of African people everywhere to participate in government. The Congress delegates specifically demanded that "civilized" persons of African descent be "accorded the same *rights* as their fellow citizens [and] not be denied, on account of race or color, a voice in their own government, justice before the courts and economic and social equality."[5] These resolutions affirming rights and equality

---

[3] Samuel J. May, "Slavery and the Constitution," *The Quarterly Anti-Slavery Magazine* (American Anti-Slavery Society), 2 (1837): 77.

[4] Lamin Sanneh, *Abolitionists Abroad: American Blacks and the Making of Modern West Africa* (Cambridge: Harvard University Press, 1999), 278.

[5] "Pan African Congress Resolution, Pars, 1919," in *African Intellectual Heritage: A Book of Sources*, Molefi K. Asante and Abu Shardow, eds. (Philadelphia: Temple University Press, 1996), 519.

for Africans and peoples of African descent garnered a tepid response from the great powers gathered at the Versailles Peace Conference. No delegate at the Pan-African Congress was invited to address the Peace Conference, and ultimately, the resolutions were not instituted at the Conference. Undeterred, the Pan-African Congress delegates resolved to continue lobbying for their goals, and went on to hold more congresses in London in 1921, in Lisbon in 1923 and in New York in 1927.

★★★

Accused of planning acts of sabotage against the state, Nelson Mandela was tried and sentenced to life imprisonment by the South African apartheid government in 1964. In the course of the trial, Mandela appealed to universal human rights. Presenting his defense from the dock, he offered three justifications for the African National Congress's defiance of the ban imposed on it by the government, and the organization's resort to violent sabotage tactics in its campaign against white minority rule. Mandela stated that the ANC believed that the government's repressive policies made violent response by Africans inevitable. Unless responsible leadership was given to control the frustrations of the oppressed African masses, there would be outbreaks of terrorism that would produce intense bitterness and hostility between the various races in the country. Second, Mandela felt that without restrained violence, there would be no way open to the African people to succeed in their struggle against white supremacy that implied black inferiority. All lawful modes of expressing opposition to this principle, he asserted, had been closed by apartheid legislation. Then, Mandela turned to the human rights argument. "We believed," he said, "in the words of the Universal Declaration of Human Rights that the 'will of the people shall be the basis of authority of the government.'" To accept the ban on the ANC would be equivalent to accepting to "silence the African for all time." Mandela closed his speech by restating his enduring belief in the ideal of a free and democratic society in which all persons live together in harmony and with equal opportunities. "It is an ideal which I hope to live for and to achieve," he said, "but if need be, it is an ideal for which I am prepared to die."[6]

★★★

In 2008, the president of Sudan, Omar al-Bashir, became the first sitting head of state to be indicted by the International Criminal Court

[6] Nelson Mandela, *No Easy Walk to Freedom: Articles, Speeches and Trial Addresses of Nelson Mandela* (London: Heinemann Educational, 1973), 189.

(ICC) established in 1998 to prosecute individuals for gross human rights violations including genocide, crimes against humanity and war crimes. Al Bashir was accused of being personally responsible for war crimes and genocide committed against the civilian population of Darfur. The warrant issued for Al Bashir's arrest by the ICC claimed that the government of Sudan, under his leadership, was responsible for attacks against the civilian population of Darfur and subjecting them to torture, forcible transfer, murder and extermination.[7] Al Bashir and the government of Sudan promptly rejected the ICC charges and refused to cooperate with the Court, depicting the allegations as baseless and challenging the ICC's jurisdiction over the Darfur situation. The charges against Al Bashir were also criticized by African multilateral governance institutions. The African Union and the Arab League condemned the warrant of arrest as unnecessary and unacceptable. Their principal concern was that by targeting a sitting head of state, the ICC was setting a precedent that could potentially undermine the legitimacy of ruling regimes and engender political instability in already fragile African states. In contrast to this position, human rights activists and Darfur leaders welcomed Al-Bashir's incitement as a move against state impunity for human rights violations. Human rights groups described the warrant as a lifeline for victims of Sudanese government atrocities that would change the mood of frustration and helplessness.[8] In a letter to the UN Human Rights Council supporting Al Bashir's indictment, a coalition of African and international human rights non-governmental organizations urged the Council to recognize and respond to the gravity of the human rights situation in Sudan and to address the widespread violations of human rights and international humanitarian law in the country.[9]

★★★

These four episodes, spanning three centuries, exemplify the range and complexity of human rights narratives in African history and politics. They reflect the vast scope of human rights as both an idea

---

[7] International Criminal Court, Warrant of Arrest for Omar Hassan Ahmad Al Bashir, ICC 02/0501/09, March 4, 2009.

[8] Marlise Simons and Neil Macfarquhar, "Court Issues Arrest Warrant for Sudan's Leader." Available at www.nytimes.com/2009/03/05/world/africa/05court.html. Accessed January 16, 2015.

[9] NGO Letter Regarding Human Rights Situation in Sudan at the 27th session of the Human Rights Council, July 29, 2014. Available at www.hrw.org/news/2014/07/29/ngo-letter-regarding-human-rights-situation-sudan-27th-session-human-rights-council.

and a movement in the African experience. From Olaudah Equiano to Blaise Diagne, from Nelson Mandela to Omar al-Bashir, they also exemplify the varied historical moments and contexts in which the idea of human rights has been deployed by Africans and by others in relation to Africa. The theme of human rights resonates in several aspects of African history including indigenous egalitarian morality as it intersects with notions of personhood and human dignity, European Christian humanism and missionary activities, slavery and the antislavery movement, colonial conquest and domination, anti-colonialism and decolonization, and the tumult of post-colonial nation-building. Although these themes have received varying degrees of attention from historians, few studies have examined them from distinctly human rights perspectives.

Given the deep echoes of rights in African history, a longue durée history of human rights in Africa must begin with some conceptual and methodological clarification of the scope of the present inquiry. A key conceptual question relates to the meanings of human rights in varied historical contexts. For example, is there an underlying notion that links Equiano's invocation of human rights within eighteenth-century antislavery, through anti-colonial petitions for self-determination, to contemporary discourses of international human rights and transnational justice? Does the idea of human rights possess some foundational meaning outside these specific sociohistorical contexts? These are some of the conceptual and methodological questions that any inquiry into human rights history must address. For a study that aspires to tell the story of human rights in Africa over a long expanse of time and across national and cultural boundaries, these conceptual questions are amplified.

This book engages questions that are integral to human rights history from an Africanist perspective. It is as much about the history of human rights in Africa as it is about the place of Africa in human rights history. It offers an interpretative history of human rights as vision, discourse and sociopolitical struggle in Africa and within global contexts. This book does not present a comprehensive account of human rights throughout African history; that would be a task requiring several volumes. Rather, the aim here is to trace the broad contours of the history of human rights in Africa by providing chronological and thematic excursions into the key ideas, events and movements that have shaped the human rights experience in the continent. More specifically, this book investigates the complementarities and tensions between traditional African sociopolitical systems pertaining to human dignity and the more formal liberal rights regimes introduced with colonial rule and instituted in the independent state. It explores how human rights were promoted and subverted in these varied contexts. This study also examines the connections between human rights in Africa and the broader global human rights movement. Because human rights movements are essentially struggles for social and political inclusion, the human rights story becomes ultimately a narrative of ideas, events and personalities. It becomes not just the political history of oppressors and victims but also the intellectual history of visionaries and social history of movements and activists.

The story of human rights in Africa cannot fully be told outside the broader history of the global human rights movement. The contemporary meanings of human rights have come to be closely associated with global inclusion. Universalism and internationalism are the defining markers of human rights as we understand them today. The post–World War II human rights movement is premised on inalienability and a persistent universalism that posits that every human being in the world is entitled to certain basic rights simply by virtue of being human. This conception of human rights which follows from the notion that human nature is universal and that human rights are rights that one has irrespective of their membership or place in society, therefore ascribes an irreducible moral value to each individual human being.[10] This concept of human rights conveys an intrinsic entitlement to autonomy and equality that all individuals can demand from the state, and which are protected by the state as well as regional and global multilateral institutions. The universal character of modern human rights makes it essential to interpret the history of human rights in Africa from global comparative perspectives. African experiences, from antislavery through anti-colonialism to modern-day state violations, are integral to the history of the global human rights movement. Diasporic experiences, particularly those relating to slavery and antislavery, also make the African human rights story a global human rights story.

The varied sociopolitical currents that have shaped human rights as doctrine, law, policy and social movement make constructing a

---

[10] Jack Donnelly, "Human Rights and Western Liberalism," in *Human Rights in Africa: Cross-Cultural Perspectives*, Abdulahi Ahmed An-Na'im and Francis M. Deng, eds. (Washington, DC: The Brookings Institution, 1990), 35.

continent-wide account of human rights an intricately subjective exercise in historical cherry-picking. Discussions about rights occur in almost every facet of human life. Individuals are constantly asserting what they consider to be their rights in the constructions of personhood and dignity, in struggles for freedom and equality, in competition over resources, and in everyday social interactions. Many of these encounters involve questions of "liberties," broadly understood as the freedom to think or act without being constrained by force. Other encounters pertain to more formal legal and moral entitlements founded on normative rules about what is allowed of people or owed to people in specific contexts. At the most basic level, therefore, a history of human rights requires certain conceptual and contextual parameters to guide the discussion.

Ruptures and Continuities

Although the twentieth century has been described as the age of the human rights revolution, human rights remain an elusive concept. Because multiple and competing claims can and have been historically advanced in the name of human rights, several human rights stories are possible. The term "human rights" has been used to convey a broad range of ideas and practices, from notions of freedom and human dignity within antislavery to particularistic claims about political liberties, self-determination within anti-colonialism and democratic rights in independent states. Some of these human rights stories have clearly received more attention than others in the bourgeoning human rights historiography. In spite of its deep etymology and normative antecedents, human rights have come to be seen as a uniquely twentieth-century invention, with the age of the "human rights revolution" ushered in by the World War II and specific events in its aftermath.[11]

The conventional wisdom is that modern human rights, understood as universal inalienable rights that all human beings hold simply by virtue of their humanity, came into prominence only with the end of World War II, the establishment of the UN organization and the

---

[11] See generally Michael Ignatieff, *The Rights Revolution* (Toronto: Anansi, 2000); Akira Iriye, Petra Goedde and William I. Hitchcock, eds., *The Human Rights Revolution: An International History* (New York: Oxford University Press, 2012).

new international order that this era ushered. The adoption of the Universal Declaration of Human Rights (UDHR) by the UN General Assembly in 1948 was a defining moment in this process. Both the UN Charter and the UDHR challenged the principle of state sovereignty that emerged from the Peace of Westphalia three centuries earlier, which had governed the relationship between nations and empires. Human rights featured prominently in the visions of the post-war international order and in the establishment of the UN. The UN Charter expresses "faith in fundamental human rights, in the dignity and worth of the human person, in the equal rights of men and women and of nations large and small."[12] The Charter also outlines principles aimed at realizing human rights and fundamental freedoms without distinction as to race, sex, language or religion.[13]

These human rights principles are now well established in international law, primarily through the UDHR and related UN Human Rights Covenants. However, the notion of universal human rights continues to be challenged on multiple fronts. It has been challenged by proponents of varying degrees of national and cultural relativism who question universal rights claims, by *positivists* who refuse to recognize any human rights other than legally enforceable entitlements, by *essentialists* who subscribe only to a post–World War II UN-inspired definition of universal human rights, and by *evolutionists* who emphasize the historical continuities of the human rights idea rather than the paradigmatic shifts of the twentieth century.[14] To legal positivists and essentialist scholars, rights without legal remedies are no rights at all. The long-standing argument for African and other non-Western values in conceptualizing or interpreting human rights typifies the relativist position. Scholars have made the case for an African concept of human rights founded on communitarian values and distinct from "Western" human rights traditions that are premised on atomized individualism. I examine in detail the philosophical arguments for African human rights values in the following chapter.

Recent histories of human rights have sought to go beyond the twentieth-century meanings of human rights to excavate the

---

[12] United Nations, Charter of the United Nations, 24 October 1945, 1 UNTS XVI.

[13] United Nations, Charter of the United Nations, 24 October 1945, 1 UNTS XVI. Articles 13, 55.

[14] For an insightful discussion on how different scholars have approached the concept of human rights, see Marie-Bénédicte Dembour, "What Are Human Rights? Four Schools of Thought," *Human Rights Quarterly*, 32, 1 (2010).

antecedents of the human rights idea. Throughout history, people have indeed grappled with ideas about human dignity, fairness, respect and responsibility. It is fitting to describe human rights as an idea that is "thousands of years in the making."[15] But where precisely does the story of the idea begin? Accounts of human rights origins and genealogy are dominated by questions of meaning, as scholars seek to make connections between modern interpretations of human rights and their historical antecedents. Most accounts acknowledge that the norms enshrined in the UDHR that have come to define the international human rights movements have sources in prior rights traditions. There is a growing inclination toward reexamining, from human rights perspectives, key historical events including the anti-slavery movement,[16] indigenous social systems and rights traditions,[17] Enlightenment liberalism, and eighteenth-century Euro-American political revolutions,[18] colonialism[19] and anti-colonialism.[20] Key contributions on these topics have sought to chart new genealogies of human rights showing the complex links between past human struggles and a rights movement that has been cast as a uniquely twentieth-century phenomenon.

★★★

The genealogy of human rights is marked by certain defining epochs and episodes. These represent milestones in the development of the

---

[15] This quotation welcomes visitors to the Canadian Museum of Human Rights in Winnipeg, Canada.

[16] Jenny Martinez, *The Slave Trade and the Origins of International Human Rights Law* (New York: Oxford University Press, 2012); Robin Blackburn, *The American Crucible: Slavery, Emancipation and Human Rights* (New York: Verso, 2011).

[17] Francis M. Deng, "A Cultural Approach to Human Rights among the Dinka," in *Human Rights in Africa: Cross-Cultural Perspectives*, Abdullahi Ahmed An-Na'im and Francis M. Deng, eds. (Washington, DC: The Brookings Institution, 1990); Brendan Tobin, *Indigenous Peoples, Customary Law and Human Rights: Why Living Law Matters* (New York: Routledge, 2014). Timothy Fernyhough, "Human Rights and Pre-Colonial Africa," in *Human Rights and Governance in Africa*, Goran Hyden and Winston P. Nagan, eds. (Gainesville: University Press of Florida, 1993).

[18] Lynn Hunt, *Inventing Human Rights* (New York: W. W. Norton, 2007); Kate E. Tunstall, ed., *Self-Evident Truths? Human Rights and the Enlightenment* (London: Bloomsbury, 2012).

[19] Alice Conklin, "Colonialism and Human Rights, a Contradiction in Terms? The Case of France and West Africa, 1895–1914," *The American Historical Review*, 103, 2 (1998); Bonny Ibhawoh, *Imperialism and Human Rights: Discourses of Rights and Liberties in African History* (Albany: SUNY Press, 2007).

[20] Ronald Burke, *Decolonization and the Evolution of International Human Rights* (Philadelphia: University of Pennsylvania Press, 2010).

human rights idea that various scholars have identified and empha-sized. There is no agreement, however, on which of these episodes marked the most significant epoch or turning point in the develop-ment of modern human rights. At least eight of these defining histor-ical episodes stand out: ancient religious and secular humanism, classical philosophical traditions and Enlightenment liberalism, eighteenth-century Euro-American political revolutions, the antislav-ery movement, World War II and the Holocaust, the emergence of the UN and the adoption of the UDHR, anti-colonial movements, and the universalizing human rights agenda of the 1970s characterized by the rise of international human rights NGOs.[21] Although scholarly skepticism of such neat watersheds is justified, it is useful to engage them. Of particular interest for present purposes is the question of where African history fits in the broader debates on the origins and genealogy of human rights.

Most human rights histories proceed from the premise that rights ideas are as old as civilization.[22] Several accounts of the global history of human rights go as far back as the Hammurabi Code and the religious traditions of Buddhist, Hindu and Confucian texts; the Torah; the Bible and the Quran. Although few accounts draw direct connections between these traditions and the modern concept of human rights, ancient ideas and practices of justice are seen as the normative beginnings of the human rights idea. Many accounts seek the direct origins of human rights in Western legal and philosophical traditions epitomized in natural law theory. Most histories of human rights begin the story here, tracing modern conceptions of rights and liberties from natural law and ancient Greek stoicism through the medieval period to Enlightenment liberalism. Natural law philosophy characterized by a belief that laws and rules of conduct are embedded and derivable from the nature of man has become a secure place in antiquity to ground universal human rights. Since human nature is the same around the world, the laws derived from that nature are seen as

---

[21] Bonny Ibhawoh, "Where Do We Begin? Human Rights and Public History," in *Taking Liberties: Human Rights History in Canada*, David Goutor and Stephen Hea-thorn, eds. (Don Mills: Oxford University Press, 2013), 67.

[22] For example, Micheline Ishay, *The History of Human Rights: From Ancient Times to the Globalization Era* (Berkeley: University of California Press, 2008); Paul Gordon Lauren, *The Evolution of International Human Rights: Visions Seen* (Philadelphia: University of Pennsylvania, 2003).

universal and true to all humans, at all times and places. Thus, they are unquestionably inherent, objective and absolute.

Some accounts make more explicit connections between the notion of natural law and rights ideas that emerged from the sociopolitical tumult of Enlightenment Europe.[23] Enlightenment liberalism and notions of freedom and equality, particularly in the use and ownership of property, created unprecedented commitment to individual expression and world experience, reflected in varied writings from the works of Thomas Aquinas and Hugo Grotius to the provisions of the *Magna Carta*, the *Petition of Rights* of 1628 and the *English Bill of Rights* of 1689. Enlightenment thought founded on natural law theory, several scholars argue, inaugurated a new intellectual tradition in which the individual as a political actor was abstracted from the holistic totality of medieval society.

An emphasis on Euro-American political revolutions of the eighteenth century privileges Enlightenment liberalism in the discourse of human rights. These revolutions and the documents they inspired are said to be central to modern human rights because they espoused the notion of the autonomous individual endowed with certain inalienable rights. In *Inventing Human Rights*, Lynn Hunt specifically locates the origin of human rights in the American and French revolutions and the declarations arising from them. Hunt traces the impact of Enlightenment ideas on the social and political expansion of human right and argues that equality, universality and naturalness of rights gained direct political expression for the first time in the American Declaration of Independence and the French Declaration of the Rights of Man and Citizen.[24] The influence of Enlightenment liberalism is particularly evident in the American Declaration of Independence, which famously proclaims that all men are created equal and that they are endowed by their Creator with certain unalienable rights, among which are "Life, Liberty and the Pursuit of Happiness."[25] These developments, Hunt argues, underscore a "*sudden* crystallization of human rights claims at the end of the eighteenth century."[26]

---

[23] For a discussion of this conceptual debate, see Peter De Bolla, *The Architecture of Concepts: The Historical Formation of Human Rights* (New York: Fordham University Press, 2013), 2.

[24] Hunt, *Inventing Human Rights*, 20.

[25] The American Declaration of Independence (US Congress, July 4, 1776).

[26] Hunt, *Inventing Human Rights*, 20. My emphasis.

The claim is that this is the historical place and moment at which human rights were "invented."

Beyond Inventions and Watersheds

Key debates in human rights history seem to turn on when and where human rights were "invented." But the use of the language of "invention" in relation to human rights history is contentious. Privileging the Enlightenment as the origin of human rights may have gained currency in human rights scholarship, but it remains a decidedly European-centered approach. To be sure, Enlightenment liberalism marked an important phase in the evolution of the modern human rights idea, but framing it in terms of "invention" or limiting that invention to Western history constrains our understanding of human rights history. Such an intellectual approach lends credence to the claim, often advanced by opponents of human rights reforms, that human rights are a Western invention – a totalizing idea conceived in the West and exported to the rest of the world.[27] It is an argument that undermines the cause of universal human rights and one that is problematic for constructing a global history of human rights. The argument also ignores the deeper cross-cultural ideas, global networks of ideational exchange and intellectual traditions about human dignity that have shaped understandings of human rights in different societies. The notion of the "invention of human rights" gets in the way of a full understanding of the complex processes by which human rights ideas have evolved, and makes little allowance for continuity, contestation and ambiguity. Rather than a fruitless debate over the origins or definitive breakthrough moments of human rights, it is more useful to consider the multiple genealogies of human rights and the great variety of rights vernaculars that have shaped and continue to define modern human rights.[28]

The defining character of modern human rights has certainly been significantly shaped by the reformist impulse of the late nineteenth century. The abolition of the slave trade, the development of factory

---

[27] See, for example, Makau Mutua, *Human Rights: A Political and Cultural Critique* (Philadelphia: University of Pennsylvania Press, 2002).

[28] Robert Brier, "Beyond the Quest for a 'Breakthrough': Reflections on the Recent Historiography on Human Rights," in *European History Yearbook: Mobility and Biography*, Sarah Panter, ed. (Berlin: De Gruyter, 2015), 158.

legislation, mass education, trade unionism and universal suffrage all served to broaden the dimensions of individual rights and stimulate increased international interest in their protection. The rise and fall of Nazi Germany perhaps had the most profound impact on the idea of universal human rights in the twentieth century. The international community united in horror and condemnation of Nazi war-time atrocities including the state-sanctioned extermination of Jews and other minorities. Nazi atrocities, more than any previous event, brought home the realization that law and morality cannot be grounded in any purely utilitarian, idealist or positivist doctrine.[29] Certain actions are wrong, regardless of the social or political context, and certain rights are inalienable irrespective of sociopolitical exigencies. This strengthened the idea that all human beings are entitled to a level of basic rights and that it was the duty of nation-states and the international community to protect these rights.

The new post-war international consciousness of the need to protect the basic rights of all peoples by means of some universally acceptable parameters partly influenced the 1945 Charter of the UN, which affirmed faith in fundamental human rights and in the dignity and worth of the human person.[30] This commitment to human rights would be reinforced in 1948 in the UDHR, which established a common understanding of ideas and expectations about the political relationship between governments and citizens and about the socioeconomic basis of human dignity. The two main treaties derived from the Declaration, the International Covenant on Civil and Political Rights (ICCPR) and the International Covenant on Economic, Social, and Cultural Rights (ICESCR), alternatively proclaim the rights of full participation in the political processes of state and government and elevate basic welfare needs to the status of rights.[31] The UDHR and the two covenants adopted by the UN in 1966 have collectively come to be known as the International Bill of Rights and the foundations of universal human rights. Since the 1940s, the international human rights regime has expanded to include several multilateral treaties that, alongside the

---

[29] Orlando Patterson, "Freedom, Slavery, and the Modern Construction of Rights," in *Historical Change and Human Rights: The Oxford Amnesty Lectures 1994*, Olwen Hufton, ed. (New York: Basic Books), 176–177.

[30] United Nations, "Charter of the United Nations, 24 October 1945," 1 UNTS XVI. Accessed February 16, 2016. Available at http://www.un.org/en/charter-united-nations.

[31] Susan Waltz, *Human Rights and Reform: Changing the Face of North African Politics* (Berkeley: University of California Press, 1995), 15.

advocacy work of state and non-state actors, continue to define the modern human rights movement.

When the UDHR was adopted by the UN General Assembly in 1948, many political leaders welcomed it as ushering a new global order. One of the Declaration's chief architects, Eleanor Roosevelt (at that time the First Lady of the United States), hailed it as a "Magna Carta for all mankind."[32] Another architect of the Declaration, the French jurist René Cassin, described it as a "milestone in the struggle for human rights and a beacon of hope for humanity."[33] The UDHR was not simply another episode in the human rights story but an epoch-making event that defined the very idea of modern human rights. It articulated a regime of inalienable rights to which all human beings are entitled simply by virtue of their humanity. The idea of unfettered individual rights that individuals could claim against the state meant that traditional notions of state sovereignty over citizens and the Westphalian ordering of world affairs had to be reconciled with a new international obligation to protect the universal human rights of every human being.

The UDHR outlines a broad array of human rights principles, ranging from basic rights such as the right to life and the prohibition of slavery, to more contentious provisions such as the right to form and to join trade unions and the right to have rest, leisure and periodic holidays with pay. Although these rights are framed as universal and inalienable, and have been affirmed by most countries of the world, they remain largely aspirational. When the UDHR was drafted and adopted between 1946 and 1948, there were only four African members of the UN (Egypt, Ethiopia, Liberia and South Africa). The rest of continent was under colonial rule imposed by some of European powers leading the human rights debates at the UN. Thus, although most African countries have since signed on to the UN's human rights regime, the concern persists that they have had to do so on the basis of a predominately Western cultural and normative framework.[34] This remains one of the most persistent critiques of the international human rights system.

---

[32] Quoted in Randall Williams and Ben Beard, *This Day in Civil Rights History* (Montgomery, AL: New South Books, 2009), 309.

[33] René Cassin, *La pensée et l'action* (Paris: F. Lalou, 1972), 118.

[34] Abdullahi A. An-Na'im, ed., *Cultural Transformation and Human Rights in Africa* (New York: Zed Books, 2002), 33.

A key historical debate regarding modern human rights doctrine centers on its influence on social movements and rights-based struggles of the twentieth centuries. Universal human rights found appeal in the 1950s as colonized peoples in Africa and Asia drew on it to champion long-standing demands for self-determination. However, anti-colonial activists remained deeply skeptical of the transformative potential of a UN human rights agenda, purportedly affirming the rights of all human beings, drawn up by the same European imperial powers actively denying colonial subjects their right to self-determination. Nonetheless, anti-colonial struggles had a significant impact on the development of the post-war international human rights movement. The adoption of the UDHR in 1948 and the European Convention on Human Rights (ECHR) in 1950 lent the moral legitimacy of a new internationalist discourse of rights to anti-colonial struggles for independence. These national self-determination movements were among the first mass movements to draw on the post–World War II language of universal human rights. As I argue later in this book, African independence activists in the colonies not only drew on the language of universal rights in struggles for self-determination, they also shaped an emergent global human rights system.

Universalizing Human Rights

The idea that the post–World War II doctrine of universal human rights marked a paradigmatic shift from previous notions of human rights has become a canon of human rights scholarship. Human rights scholars distinguish between the concepts of *distributive justice,* or citizenship rights, and the notion of human rights. Distributive justice involves giving a person that to which he or she is legally or morally entitled (his or her rights). Unless these rights are those to which the individual is entitled simply by virtue of being human, the rights in question will not be human rights. In many pre-modern societies, rights were assigned on the basis of communal membership, family, status or achievement.[35] These would not qualify as "human rights" in the modern understanding. Historian Samuel Moyn has argued for a

---

[35] See, for example, Jack Donnelly, "Human Rights and Human Dignity: An Analytic Critique of Non-Western Human Rights Conceptions," *American Political Science Review,* 76, 2 (1982): 303.

distinction between the human rights idea as it emerged in the second half of the twentieth century and earlier iterations of rights idealism.[36] He posits that the concept of human rights, in the modern sense of the word, did not exist before the twentieth century and that the "history of human rights does not necessarily form the basis of contemporary human rights."[37] Because *citizenship rights* are distinct from *human rights*, "there were no human rights prior to World War II except those concretized domestically by the state."[38] For essentialist scholars like Moyn, human rights are rooted in post–World War II internationalism, specifically the adoption of the UDHR and the subsequent internationalization of human rights norms.

But even among essentialist scholars, there is no agreement on where exactly to place the defining twentieth-century turning points in human rights history. While many accounts privilege immediate post–World War II internationalism of the 1940s and '50s, others point to the globalizing impulses of the 1970s onward. For the latter group of scholars, the 1940s ushered the UN human rights movement, but the breakthrough moment was in the 1970s when human rights captured the global imaginary.[39] Human rights discourse marked an alternative in an age of ideological betrayal and political collapse, as new generations of visionary non-governmental activists constructed human rights outside the framework of nation-states organized through the UN.[40] Driven partly by Cold War international politics, human rights activism experienced a dramatic boom during this period with the extension of the activities of non-governmental organizations, such as Amnesty International, to areas where human rights

---

[36] The historian Samuel Moyn is a foremost proponent of this view of human rights history. See Samuel Moyn, *The Last Utopia: Human Rights in History* (Cambridge, MA: Harvard University Press, 2010); Samuel Moyn, "Imperialism, Self-Determination and the Rise of Human Rights," in *The Human Rights Revolution: An International History*, Akira Iriye et al., eds. (New York: Oxford University Press), 162; Samuel Moyn, "Substance, Scale, and Salience: The Recent Historiography of Human Rights," *Annual Review of Law and Social Science* 8 (2012): 128.

[37] Jean-Paul Lehners, "Pleading for a New History of Human Rights," in *The Sage Handbook of Human Rights*, vol. 1, Anja Mihr and Mark Gibney, eds. (Thousand Oaks, CA: Sage, 2014), 21.

[38] Moyn, "Imperialism, Self-Determination and the Rise of Human Rights," 162.

[39] Jan Eckel and Samuel Moyn, eds., *The Breakthrough: Human Rights in the 1970s* (Philadelphia: University of Pennsylvania Press, 2014).

[40] Samuel Moyn, *The Last Utopia: Human Rights in History* (Cambridge, MA: Harvard University Press, 2010), 8.

infractions occurred most frequently and violently.[41] For those who locate the human rights breakthrough moment in the 1970s, this singular development is what allowed human rights to evolve into a global movement, becoming the dominant framework for addressing systematic atrocities and injustices.

What appears common to genealogical accounts that locate defining or breakthrough moments in the 1940s or 1970s is a tendency to see human rights in the limited sense of entitlements that individuals hold against the state.[42] The history of human rights then becomes a story of the progressive restraint of state power over citizens. I am skeptical of this approach to human rights history. The goal of human rights history should not simply be to establish a causal chain of events between the different stages of the development of rights ideas over time. In privileging change over underlying continuities, essentialist readings of human rights tend to obscure the deeper philosophical and institutional foundations of modern human rights. Essentialist approaches also tend to overlook the cultural and ideological contestations of the meanings of human rights in varied locales and at different historical moments.

In this Africa-centered retelling of the human rights story, I locate atomized individualism and state-centrism as unique attributes of a particular phase of the human rights movement rather than the totalizing essence of the human rights idea. International human rights as it emerged in the mid-twentieth century was mainly a response to the crisis of nationalism in Europe and the imperative of constraining state power over citizens. As several histories of post-war internationalism at the UN have shown, the geopolitical interests of influential member states significantly shaped the visions and regimes of human rights that emerged at that moment.[43] This vision of human rights prioritized individual liberties over the collective rights of peoples. It also prioritized civil and political liberties over economic, social or

---

[41] Petra Goedde, "Review of Roland Burke, *Decolonization and the Evolution of International Human Rights*," *Human Rights Quarterly* 33, 2, (2011): 564.

[42] See Ronald Dworkin, *Taking Rights Seriously* (Cambridge: Harvard University Press, 1977), xi.

[43] See, for example, Mark Mazowe, *No Enchanted Palace: The End of Empire and the Ideological Origins of the United Nations* (Princeton, NJ: Princeton University Press, 2009); Stephen C. Schlesinger, *Act of Creation: The Founding of the United Nations. A Story of Superpowers, Secret Agents, Wartime Allies and Enemies, and Their Quest for a Peaceful World* (Cambridge, MA: Westview Press, 2004).

cultural rights. In the age of decolonization and the Cold War, this interpretation of "universal" human rights was neither settled nor paradigmatic.

This limited vision of human rights would be challenged and expanded in the 1950s and '60s as the voices of formerly colonized peoples gained notice within a more globally representative UN. With the emergence of the post-colonial UN, the scope and meaning of human rights would once again be redefined as coalitions of formerly colonized, newly independent states of the Global South, including many African countries, pushed for the expansion of human rights to include economic and social rights, the collective right to self-determination and even the solidarity right to development.[44] Human rights came to mean not just individual civil and political entitlements against the state, but also collective social and economic entitlements. Interpretations of the human rights doctrine, even at its assumed mid-twentieth-century moment of inception, were not as static or as paradigmatic as often now assumed. There is some merit in proceeding more cautiously, recognizing that the idea of human rights has been, and continues to be, a deeply contested and an evolving one.

What we can be more certain about is that the international human rights movement that emerged after World War II ushered in an important phase in human rights history. The founding of the UN and the adoption of the UDHR marked global milestones in the long struggle for human rights. The UDHR's promise of inalienable universal rights provided a framework for articulating both new and long-standing demands for fundamental freedoms across the world. But is that where the human rights story begins? I think not. Locating the "invention" of human rights within Enlightenment liberalism, Euro-American revolutionary idealism or post–World War II internationalism is akin to seeking the origins of the notion of "justice" in a specific place and time. Such narratives of human rights origins belie the divergent social and political processes by which human rights ideas have evolved in different parts of the world. The idea that all humans are entitled to certain basic rights and liberties certainly did not emerge in the 1940s and few would argue that it did. What is unique about the post–World War II human rights movement is the consensus by

---

[44] This expansion of the scope of universal human rights is evident in the UN "Declaration on the Granting of Independence to Colonial Countries and Peoples" in 1960 and the "Declaration on the Right to Development" in 1986.

nation-states on an international legal and policy regime of universally applicable rights within the framework of a global intergovernmental organization. But even this was initially a partial consensus. At the adoption of the UDHR in 1948, most African countries were under colonial rule and unrepresented at the UN. They were not party to the early UN debates that framed human rights, even though independent governments subsequently affirmed international human rights.

The concept of human rights that I employ in this book is much broader than the interpretations preferred by positivist and essentialist human rights scholars. To be clear, I acknowledge the conceptual distinction between politically contingent citizenship rights and the UDHR-inspired vision of universal human rights as rights that pertain to people simply by virtue of their humanity. It is necessary to disentangle the various vocabularies that are too often used interchangeably in the area of rights. However, claims of discontinuity are unsustainable.[45] Rather than seeing the development of rights concepts as disparate human rights stories, I prefer to focus on the connections and tensions between multiple visions of rights and the struggles to actualize them. The full story of human rights in Africa, as indeed anywhere else in the world, cannot be told without drawing these connections between rights idealism, discourses and struggles at different historical moments.

The notion of human rights deployed in this book denotes in a historical sense a range of ideas and practices relating to human dignity and liberties, both individual and collective. The concept also encapsulates notions of altruism, justice and fairness. As entitlements deemed essential for individual and collective dignity, human rights have been articulated as moral claims or more formal legal claims canonized in laws and enforced by courts. But legal codification and enforceability do not in themselves define human rights. Human rights are first and foremost representations of ideas about human dignity and human worth. Individuals *and groups* make claims upon society for their observance based on a variety of normative rules and social conventions that society is obligated to satisfy. This matrix of rights entitlements, moral/legal claims and fulfilment obligations have manifested in different ways in various societies over the course of history.

---

[45] Philip Alston, "Does the Past Matter? On the Origins of Human Rights: An Analysis of Competing Histories of the Origins of International Human Rights Law," *Harvard Law Review*, 126 (2013): 2052.

In response to World War II atrocities and the crisis of nationalism in Europe, claims pertaining to human dignity and individual liberties came to be framed as inalienable universal human rights under the auspices of the UN. Under this system of rights, the nation-state became the primary duty-bearer for fulfilling human rights entitlements. Before the emergence of the modern nation-state in the nineteenth century, however, moral and legal principles for protecting human rights existed in other forms. In the imperial age, for example, rights claims were framed more narrowly within imperial bounds of citizenship and subjecthood, with the duty of fulfilling human rights obligations resting on rulers and monarchs. In the post-imperial age of globalization and solidarity rights, the scope of universal human rights has expanded to include communities (not just individuals) as rights holders and non-state entities, such as corporations, as duty-bearers.[46] We must therefore resist the inclination to freeze the meaning of human rights at convenient historical moments and, instead, take account of the shifts and contingencies in the interpretations and practices of human rights.

Human Rights as Discourse

A major critique of human rights historiography is that it is trapped in an intellectual tradition of presentism and linear progressivism that tends to obfuscate full understanding of the development of human rights as ideas and practices. Human rights histories have mostly presented a narrative of relatively steady progress in the evolution of ideas dating even from ancient times, and the gradual uptake of these ideas in the form of legal norms.[47] The dominant trend has been to present human rights – despite frequent setbacks and many contradictions – as part of a saga of relentless human progress. Histories of human rights have tended to adopt a largely celebratory attitude toward the emergence and progress of human rights. Most accounts almost uniformly provide recent enthusiasms with uplifting backstories, differing primarily on where to locate the crucial turning points in the evolution of the human rights idea. History, one historian notes,

---

[46] United Nations, "United Nations Guiding Principles on Business and Human Rights 2011." Available at www.ohchr.org/Documents/Publications/GuidingPrinciplesBusiness HR_EN.pdf. Accessed August 14, 2016.

[47] Alston, "Does the Past Matter?," 2043.

has been used to confirm the inevitable rise of human rights as the *last utopia* rather than as an ideology, one of several utopias, shaped by conscious choices, historical accidents and convergences.[48]

Indeed, human rights scholarship has, for the most part, produced a triumphant vision of the role of the human rights movement in securing progressive and transformative social and political change. The ability to exercise one's human rights has come to be taken as an objective marker of social and political progress. The philosopher Ronald Dworkin uses the term "rights as trumps" to convey the discursive power of human rights. As foundations of modern political morality, human rights claims are meant to take precedence over other possible social goals and take priority over alternative considerations when formulating public policy.[49] Although increasingly challenged, assumptions about the absolutism of rights remain dominant in human rights scholarship. What has not been sufficiently explored in the discussion are the ways in which rights have been invoked to further more complex and sometimes contradictory agendas – progressive, reactionary and everything in between. Modern human rights doctrine has been shaped by its contentious history in terms of both positive support for it and, paradoxically, opposition to it.

This history of human rights presented in this book is not one of unremitting progress or journey toward one or several utopias. What is offered here is a more uncertain record of competing visions of rights. It is a history of rights inclusion and exclusion, expansion and contraction, at different historical moments. It is also a paradoxical history of exclusion and struggles for rights inclusion that pays as much attention to the continuities in rights discourses as it does to the ruptures brought about by rights struggles. It is a story of tensions and contradictions – of indigenous moral philosophies that validated certain exclusions, of European Christian humanisms implicated in the cultural dispossession of indigenous people, of emancipatory antislavery impulses that legitimized colonial subjugation, of European war-time and anti-Nazi rhetoric of freedom that rejected African self-determination, and of tensions between collective solidarity rights and individual-centered civil liberties in anti-colonial movements and independent state-building.

---

[48] Samuel Moyn, *The Last Utopia: Human Rights in History* (Cambridge, MA: Belknap Press of Harvard University Press, 2010), 5
[49] Dworkin, *Taking Rights Seriously*, 153.

Ideas and movements for rights inclusion have historically been confronted with counter-movements by dominant groups to prevent the expansion of rights benefits and protections to those considered outsiders. This makes the history of human rights more a narrative of tensions and paradoxes than one of certainty and teleological progress. The central tension is between movements for rights *inclusion* and *expansion*, on one hand, and counter-movements for rights *exclusion* and *restriction*, on the other. What emerges is not simply a story about the transformative power of the human rights idea but also an account of the opportunistic cooption of human rights discourses to attain or enhance power. In this respect, the history of human rights in Africa mirrors the global history of human rights.

This book offers a history of human rights defined not solely by the ruptures of the mid-twentieth-century human rights movement but also by the varied rights visions and struggles preceding the twentieth century. I examine the African human rights experience from the two related perspectives of human rights as *discourse* or idea and as *struggle* or social/political movement. This approximates to the distinction between the theory and practice of human rights. Exploring the history of human rights as discourse centers on the intellectual substance of rights claims. This includes principles and writings relating to human rights articulated in social and political spaces, as well as the rules and policies that emanate from them. The history of human rights as discourse also includes debates relating to rights legislation, regulation, legal codification and enforcement.

In interpreting human rights as discourse, I draw on the methods of critical discourse analyses popularized by social linguists, which problematize the link between epistemology and ontology. "Discourse" here is speech or writing understood from the point of view of the beliefs, norms and values that it embodies. It constitutes the organization and representation of people's thought experiences, ways of knowing, and understandings of their world. Within this framework, speech and writing are not taken at their face value but analyzed on the basis of the practices and rules that produced these texts and the methodical organization of thinking underlying them.[50] For example, rather than take for granted prevailing assumptions about the origins

---

[50] This approach to historical discourse is along the lines of colonial and post-colonial discourse analysis famously represented in the works of Edward Said. See Edward Said, *Orientalism* (London: Routledge & Kegan Paul, 1978).

and breakthrough moments in human rights, I interrogate the epistemological influences that shape these claims and ask why certain
definitions and genealogies of human rights have gained dominance
over others. Discourse analytical methods are especially useful in
human rights studies because they allow us to pay better attention to
the ways power, dominance and inequality are enacted, performed,
reproduced and resisted – through text and talk – in different social
and political contexts. Discourse analysis draws attention to the often
subtly expressed power of dominant groups as interpreted in laws,
rules, norms and habits.[51]

Attention to discourse is important because the development of
human rights is often measured in terms of the rise of rights language.
The increasing use of the terms *human rights* and *droits de l'homme* in
public discussions is taken as an indication of the relevance of human
rights in the twentieth century. Using new digital research tools, some
scholars have sought to measure the salience of human rights by
analyzing the discursive usage of the term over time, in published
documents and textual archives. One outcome of this method is the
argument that anti-colonial struggles for self-determination were not
human rights movements because anti-colonial activists rarely used
the term "human rights" in their writings.[52] However, in constructing
human rights genealogies, historians have been cautioned against the
"search engine mentality"– the tendency to celebrate every reference
of the phase "human rights" that we stumble upon in the archives as
evidence of diachronic linkages between rights ideas, or the temptation to make sweeping conclusions about the history of human rights
on the basis on how often the term shows up in database searches.[53]
In specific relation to African history, a focus on metropolitan lexicon
and databases cannot tell the full story of human rights in the age
of Empire. Such keyword-centered approaches cannot adequately
capture the experiences of non-literate indigenous peoples or the

---

[51] Teun A. Van Dijk, "Critical Discourse Analysis," in *Handbook of Discourse Analysis*,
D. Tannen, D. Schiffrin and H. Hamilton, eds. (Oxford: Blackwell, 2001), 352–371.

[52] Jan Eckel, "Human Rights and Decolonization: New Perspectives and Open Questions," *Humanity: An International Journal of Human Rights, Humanitarianism, and
Development* 1, 1 (2010): 115.

[53] Alston, "Does the Past Matter?" Alston is particularly critical of Samuel Moyn, who
in his book *The Last Utopia* emerges triumphal from electronic searches of the *New
York Times* and Google Books databases that reveal very few references to "human
rights" before 1977 and a dramatic uptake thereafter.

perspectives of colonial subjects at the margins of Empire whose voices are often missing or obscured in metropolitan archives. Critical analysis of historical discourse offers a means of going beyond human rights language and rationalities, to uncover the ideas, visions and tensions that underlie them.

Human Rights as Struggle

Beyond discourse, this book explores human rights as *struggle* or social movement. The rich and diverse scholarship on human rights is dominated by studies that conceptualize human rights as a moral regime, legal corpus or political ideology. The relational aspect of human rights tends to be ignored or overlooked. Yet, at the most basic level, human rights are about relationships and struggles, both individual and collective. The omission of people's experiences from dominant human rights founding stories is intimately related to the forces of exclusion that keep so many separated from their human rights today. This has prompted calls for a "people-centered human rights history" that reinscribes people into human rights stories.[54]

If we conceive of human rights as being primarily relational, constructing human rights histories would require paying particular attention to struggles and conflicts. Seen as struggle, human rights history becomes more than simply an account of states and regulations, individual actors or particular rights texts. It also becomes an account of human relations that emerge from conflictual encounters. Understanding rights struggles requires locating and mapping the dynamics of each encounter in relation to others. In the course of such conflicts, the word "rights" or the term "human rights" may not be explicitly stated but may be implicit in discourse and action. The participants in the conflict may not necessarily be acting in concert with one another or with shared intentionality as in a social or political movement, per se. They may not see themselves as part of an evolving human rights drama, but they are, nevertheless, operating at a meta-level as a single force directed toward similar ends and outcomes.[55] The task of the historian is to make meaning of these disparate conflicts and struggles,

---

[54] Christopher Roberts, *The Contentious History of the International Bill of Human Rights* (Cambridge, Cambridge University Press, 2015), 13.
[55] Ibid., 52.

exploring how they cohere in a broader human rights story. We need to understand the struggles that have shaped the human rights movement, for better and worse, over the centuries in varied social contexts, and to acknowledge the role of historical precedents in paving the way for change.[56]

The value of interpreting human rights as struggle is again evident in the debate over the place of anti-colonialism in the history of human rights. The arguments against reading anti-colonialism as a human rights movement privileges particular *discourses* over *struggle*. Anti-colonial activists in Africa may not have specifically referenced "human rights" in their writings, but they spoke of *uhuru* (freedom), linking it to the promise of the Atlantic Charter, the equality of peoples and races, and the debates about fundamental freedoms at the UN. Even if they did not explicitly invoke "human rights" in their anti-colonial campaigns, their actions and discussions in the local lexicon demonstrate engagement with universal human rights.

Approaching human rights as discourse and struggle allows for an alternative human rights story that is less concerned with consensus and moral progress and more attuned to relational tensions. Constructing human rights as discourse and struggle, however, does not necessarily disavow other accounts. Each story has its place. Africanists who must work often with oral histories are familiar with the benefits of multiple tellings of a story. When a story is told from several perspectives, each retelling helps the listener appreciate its inherent complexities. Human rights scholars also recognize the value of having the human rights story told from divergent perspectives, particularly those of subaltern actors. Each retelling serves as an invitation to return, more critically, to dominant versions. Alternative accounts privilege different contributions and contributors, thus expanding our knowledge of the global development of human rights.[57]

In one of the earliest works on the concept of human rights in Africa, the legal scholar Issa Shivji noted that the discourse about human rights in Africa constitutes an ideology of domination that reflects an "imperialist world outlook."[58] The dominant discourse, he argued, tends

---

[56] Alston, "Does the Past Matter?," 2081.

[57] Susan Eileen Waltz, "Universalizing Human Rights: The Role of Small States in the Construction of the Universal Declaration of Human Rights," *Human Rights Quarterly*, 23, 1 (2001): 67.

[58] Issa Shivji, *The Concept of Human Rights in Africa* (London: Council for the Development of Economic and Social Research in Africa-Codesria, 1989), 1–2.

to focus on violations of human rights by African leaders while over-looking the deeper historical contexts and broader global socioeco-nomic forces that gave rise to these incidents. The fixation with individual-centered and state-centric rights reinforces this, producing a one-dimensional perspective of the African human rights experience. Shivji therefore calls for a historically situated discourse of human rights that legitimizes and mobilizes collective action and the struggles of the people.[59] Shivji is not alone. Other scholars have called for a broadening of the historical basis of the concept of human rights by seeing it as a specific manifestation of the shared experiences of all people seeking solutions to their sociopolitical challenges.[60] Along these lines, Mamhood Mamdani has argued for seeing modern human rights as the "present expression of a long history of struggles for social justice and resistance to oppression in all human societies."[61]

Indeed, the major foundational rights declarations that define human rights today emerged from political struggles and upheavals. The English Bill of Rights, the American Declaration of Independ-ence and Bill of Rights, and the French Declaration of the Rights of Man all arose from political revolutions. Similarly, many of the consti-tutional bills of rights adopted by African states at independence were put in place amid the ruptures of anti-colonialism and decolonization. The South African Bill of Rights was shaped by the country's history of racial segregation and anti-apartheid struggle. By seeing human rights as the product of long-standing histories of struggle for political inclusion, justice and resistance to oppression, we can better under-stand the contingent and dynamic nature of human rights.

Constructing human rights histories as histories of struggle is more likely to engender a sense of local "ownership" of universal human rights. It also allows us to transcend debates about ideological impulses of the human rights movement, to empirically investigate historical connections and continuities. Legal scholar Makau Mutua has drawn connections between the Christian-colonial conquest of Africa in the nineteenth century and the modern human rights move-ment. He uses the metaphor of *savages, victims* and *saviors* to describe

---

[59] Shivji, *The Concept of Human Rights in Africa*, 4.
[60] Abdullahi An-Na'im and Jeffery Hammond, "Cultural Transformation and Human Rights in African Societies," in *Cultural Transformation and Human Rights in Africa*, Abdullahi a. An-Na'im, ed. (New York: Zed Books, 2002), 19.
[61] Mahmood Mamdani, "The Social Basis of Constitutionalism in Africa," *The Journal of Modern African Studies*, 28, 3 (1990): 360.

the guiding framework of the human rights movement and the role of human rights organizations within it. The grand narrative of modern human rights, Mutua argues, contains a subtext that depicts an epochal contest pitting savages, on one hand, against saviors and victims, on the other. This framework reinforces a dual construct of Third World actors as either "savages" (despotic governments or traditional chiefly authorities implementing repressive customs) or hapless "victims" (ethnic minorities, women or other oppressed groups). Certain key players in the West position themselves as the gatekeepers of human rights, destined to save Third World victims from Third World savages. In this regard, the modern human rights "crusade" fits into the historical continuum of the violent Christian-colonial conquests in the South. Mutua argues that the same methods are at work and similar cultural dispossessions are taking place without dialogue or conversation.[62]

The historical connections between colonialism and human rights are more complicated than any single narrative of continuity allows. However, thinking of human rights in Africa in terms of historical struggles rather than just present-day violations addresses concerns about the homogenizing impulses of contemporary human rights discourse. Exploring human rights as struggle entails examining how people challenged the everyday oppressions and injustices they experienced – from antislavery through the anti-colonial and anti-apartheid movements, to pro-democracy movements and opposition to dictatorship and one-party rule in the era of independence. A "human rights as struggle" approach takes account of the real-world impact of rights ideas, policies and practices. It considers the practical dimensions of human rights violations and protections including restrictions on liberties and efforts to assert them. Constructing human rights as struggle also accounts for the mobilizing power of rights and the activities of modern human rights NGOs within the continuum of historical rights inclusion movements.

Conceived as discourse and struggle, the history of human rights becomes more than an account of codification and activism. It also becomes an account of moral and cultural norms that are at the foundation of human rights in principle and practice. Laws and institutions provide a means for instrumentalizing foundational moral and

[62] See Makau Mutua, *Human Rights: A Political and Cultural Critique* (Philadelphia: University of Pennsylvania Press, 2002), xi.

cultural rights norms, and the framework for enforcement. Because human rights are essentially protections against social and political abuses, the institutional framework for their protection is integral to their definition. For this reason, human rights histories must pay attention to codification and jurisprudence, as well as regulatory and policy frameworks for human rights protection. However, these do not stand in isolation. The moral discourse of rights and dignity provides the foundation for human rights law.[63] Legal codifications at domestic and international levels have typically followed rights discourses that galvanized social and political reform movements. In the African context, this trend is particularly evident in the histories of antislavery and anti-colonialism. The story of human rights presented here is therefore more than an account of canons and institutions. It is more broadly a story of struggle and empowerment, and the rights ideas that galvanized them.

★★★

Apart from the difficulties of conceptualizing human rights, constructing a continent-wide history of human rights poses other methodological challenges. Given that human rights experiences are best understood within specific spatial and temporal contexts, is a continental perspective a valid analytical approach for inquiry into the subject? How feasible is a single story of human rights in Africa? These questions call to mind long-standing skepticism of scholarship about Africa that tends toward homogenizing otherwise divergent stories about the continent. The question is relevant given the size of Africa and its cultural, linguistic, religious, national and regional diversity. Broad narratives of Africa risk producing overgeneralized and simplistic portraits of a complex continent. Apart from constituting a recognizable geographical space, "Africa," we are reminded, is not always an a priori meaningful category, and using it as such may invoke tropes about Africa as undifferentiated and timeless. The idea of Africa remains unsettled, and attempts at constructing continental histories must be attentive to the diversity and complexity of African experiences. Nonetheless, there is value in telling continent-wide stories in ways that help situate African experiences and perspectives in global histories.

---

[63] F. Hoffmann, "Foundations beyond Law," in *The Cambridge Companion to Human Rights Law*, C. Gearty and C. Douzinas, eds. (Cambridge: Cambridge University Press), 82.

On the topic of human rights, "Africa" constitutes a meaningful analytical category in the dual sense of geopolitical location, shared history and sociopolitical position in relation to the rest of the world. Given that human rights have come to be associated with notions of universality and globality, thinking of Africa and the African experience in global contexts is particularly meaningful. The subject of human rights also provides a fitting lens for scoping a continent-wide history because key events that have shaped rights conditions for many Africans, such as transatlantic slavery and colonialism, bear continental relevance.

Still, the danger of essentialism lurks behind any attempt at a wide-ranging history of Africa. The story of human rights in Africa is a complex one that can be told fully only through detailed particularistic studies attuned to the regional, national and societal diversities of the continent. The full picture will ideally take the form of a collage of many intricately painted vignettes. What I offer in this book is a broad-brush history that allows us to identify some of the commonalities and general patterns in the history of human rights in Africa. Human rights conditions are largely shaped by local political, social and cultural forces. Yet the present study proceeds from the premise that it is possible to map a broad outline of human rights as vision, discourse and struggle across the longue durée of African history. Ultimately, the historiography of human rights in Africa should account for the complex, multifaceted and culturally contingent nature of rights ideas and movements in the continent. This is why the present account can only be *a* history of human rights in Africa rather *the* history of human rights in Africa.

2

Elders and Sages

A person is a person through other people.

— South African proverb[1]

The essential elements of cultural continuity in African politics have been described in terms of four distinct indigenous traditions: the *elder* tradition, the *warrior* tradition, the *sage* tradition and the *monarchical* tradition. The elder tradition conveys the reverence for age and the wisdom that comes with it. It represents the sacredness of ancestry and the deference to ancestors. It signifies a predilection for stability and continuity rather than disruption and change. The warrior tradition is one of conflict and struggle. It includes conflict, not only in the sense of warfare but also in the sense of social and political disruption. The warrior tradition also conveys the discipline of consensus, the preference for obedience rather than reverence and the preference for enforced agreement rather than compromise. The sage tradition represents the intellectual traditions of the custodians of collective knowledge. It is the tradition of the community storyteller represented in the *griot* as historian, bard, poet and praise singer. The sage tradition conceptualizes leadership, not in the limited sense of political authority but in the sense of a mentor and teacher conveyed in the Swahili honorific, *Mwalimu*. The monarchical tradition is characterized by all three traditions. It is defined by the quest for aristocratic effect and the personalization of authority. It represents the recurrent

[1] This proverb provides the normative foundation of the ethical philosophy of ubuntu.

conditioning factor in the elder tradition, the warrior tradition and the sage tradition.[2] It is within all four of these traditions of cultural continuity in African politics and society that our substantive story of human rights in Africa begins. But the traditions of the elder and the sage bear the most relevance.

Interpretations of indigenous culture and moral traditions have figured prominently in human rights discourses in and about Africa. During the public hearings of the South African Truth and Reconciliation Commission (TRC) established to deal with human rights abuses under apartheid, heated debates ensued over indigenous notions of human rights and justice. Much of this discussion turned on Ubuntu as an expression of indigenous ethics and African moral tradition. At the TRC hearings, some witnesses attributed the human rights violations perpetrated under apartheid to the fact that the perpetrators did not possess traditional values associated with humanness. "They did not have Ubuntu," one witness explained.[3] A community guided by the principles of Ubuntu would have been more respectful of the dignity and human rights of all members of the community irrespective of their race, ethnicity or social status. In post-apartheid South Africa, Ubuntu became a way of asserting the relevance of indigenous African moral traditions and linking them with contemporary international human rights principles. Ubuntu was constructed as an indigenous expression of collective humanism and an affirmation of the principle of human dignity that stands at the core of modern human rights.

Ubuntu, as defined by its chief proponent Archbishop Desmond Tutu, who headed the TRC, encapsulates the notion of an interdependent humanity that is central to indigenous African cosmology. The essence of Ubuntu is captured in the famous phrase *Umuntu ngumuntu ngabantu* (A person is a person through other people). The humanness of the person who has Ubuntu comes from knowing that the fate of each person is inextricably intertwined with their relationship with others. Ubuntu, in Tutu's words, is to say: "My humanity is

---

[2] Ali Mazrui, "Ideology and African Political Culture," in *Explorations in African Political Thought: Identity, Community, Ethics*, Teodros Kiros, ed. (New York: Routledge, 2001), 99–106.

[3] South Africa Broadcasting Corporation, Truth Commission Special Report (SABC TRC) Hearings (1999); D. K. Koka, TRC Faith Community Hearings, East London, 17 November 1997. Available at http://sabctrc.saha.org.za/documents.htm. Accessed July 13, 2104.

caught up in your humanity, and when your humanity is enhanced – whether I like it or not – my humanity is enhanced. Likewise, when you are dehumanized, inexorably, I am dehumanized as well."[4] It is a distinctly African take on the golden rule or law of reciprocity, which is evident in many religions and cultures.

In the years following the collapse of apartheid and the establishment of democracy, Ubuntu became closely associated with the transitional justice and human rights project in South Africa. Beyond moral and ethical discourses, it was invoked in discussions about legal and constitutional human rights guarantees. Invocations of Ubuntu in the context of human rights often link indigenous moral traditions on human dignity with a sense of community. From the standpoint of Ubuntu, there can be no human rights without community. What makes Ubuntu as an African moral principle so significant for human rights is that it helps us see individuals not as isolated entities, but as linked in a web of social relationships founded on empathy and compassion.[5] Ubuntu scholars point out that the distinction is not simply between emphasis on the community (in African rights tradition) versus emphasis on the individual (in Western rights tradition). Rather, Ubuntu represents a unique paradigm for understanding and articulating the notion of human dignity. To its proponents, Ubuntu cannot be reduced to secular or religious conceptions of dignity or to a simple-minded communitarianism. To do so is to miss its contribution to giving shape and meaning to the very concept of dignity and human rights.[6]

The invocations of Ubuntu in South Africa's post-apartheid constitutional and human rights debates mirror earlier attempts by African leaders and intellectuals to link indigenous African moral traditions to modern political ideologies and ethical principles. In most cases, their goal was to legitimize political ideologies and statist agendas by drawing on what they presented as indigenous African moral philosophies. At independence in the 1960s, African leaders such as Julius Nyerere of Tanzania, Kenneth Kaunda of Zambia, Kwame Nkrumah of Ghana, Jomo Kenyatta of Kenya and Leopold Senghor of Senegal

---

[4] Desmond Tutu, *No Future Without Forgiveness* (New York: Doubleday, 2000), 31.

[5] Oche Onazi, *Human Rights from Community: A Rights-Based Approach to Development* (Edinburgh: Edinburgh University Press, 2013), 41.

[6] Drucilla Cornell and Nyoko Muvangua, eds., *Ubuntu and the Law: African Ideals and Post-Apartheid Jurisprudence* (New York: Fordham University Press), xi.

articulated socialist-leaning political ideologies that drew upon indigenous African moral traditions. In the case of Gamal Abdel Nasser of Egypt, the appeal was to socialist pan-Arabism. The core of these ideologies, from Nkrumah's *Consciencism* to Kaunda's *Humanism*, is a communitarian and interdependent worldview positioned in contrast with the isolating individualism of Western liberal thought.

Although few of these political philosophies explicitly articulated a rights agenda, they all conveyed the fundamental idea that indigenous moral principles on human dignity and freedom should serve as the ideological foundation of post-colonial political systems and international human rights. For example, Jomo Kenyatta claimed that traditional Kikuyu society practiced a "true democracy" that could provide a model for Kenya. A representative council of elders (kiama) guaranteed "universal tribal membership" and the freedom of the people to acquire and develop land under a system of family ownership as a means of ensuring the economic well-being of every member of the community.[7] Nyerere's notion of *Ujamaa* in Tanzania made the most explicit link between the indigenous African moral traditions and modern human rights principles. Ujamaa, a Kiswahili word for family-hood or fraternity encapsulated Nyerere's political philosophy and his brand of African socialism. As a nationalist political ideology, it rejected the capitalist colonial order and promised an indigenous communitarian path to Tanzania's national development. Ujamaa, Nyerere declared, is opposed to capitalism, which seeks to build its happy society on the exploitation of man by man. It is also opposed to doctrinaire socialism, which seeks to build its happy society based on the inevitable conflict between man and man.[8] Ujamaa represented a third way, a synthesis of what was considered best in indigenous African peasant society and the best of what the country had acquired from its more recent colonial experience.[9]

Ujamaa represented more than just a political ideology. It also expressed a communitarian humanism founded on notions of dignity, equality and interdependence. "The purpose of Ujamaa," Nyerere explained in 1968, is humanity and the practical acceptance of human

---

[7] Jomo Kenyatta, *Facing Mount Kenya: The Tribal Life of the Gikuyu* (New York: Vintage Books, 1965), 181.

[8] Julius Nyerere, *Ujamaa: Essays on Socialism* (Dar es Salaam: Oxford University Press, 1968), 170.

[9] Julius Nyerere, *Freedom and Unity/Uhuru na Umoja: A Selection from Writings and Speeches 1952–65* (London: Oxford University Press, 1967), 7.

equality, "[t]hat is to say, every man's equal right to a decent life before any individual has a surplus above his needs; his equal right to partici- pate in Government; and his equal responsibility to work to contribute to the society to the limit of his ability."[10] This idea is captured in the Swahili aphorism *Binadamu wote ni sawa* (All human beings are equal). The *Arusha Declaration*, a policy document issued in 1967 by the ruling Tanganyika National Union (TANU) made even more explicit links between Ujamaa as a political philosophy inspired by the "African way of life" and modern human rights. Referencing the Universal Declar- ation of Human Rights, the Arusha Declaration affirms the equality of all human beings and the inherent dignity all individuals.[11]

In North Africa and parts of West Africa, Islamic traditions have similarly been drawn upon to assert the indigeneity of human rights principles and as a counter to Western liberal rights traditions. In 1990 the Organization of the Islamic Conference, which includes several North African and West African countries, adopted the Cairo Declaration on Human Rights in Islam. A decade earlier, a group of Islamic scholars had produced "The Universal Islamic Declaration of Human Rights," which asserts that Islam has had its own tradition of human rights since its conception in the seventh century. In these documents Islamic traditions are interpreted in a progressive spirit that is broadly congruent with modern international human rights principles. The Cairo Declaration, for instance, asserts that funda- mental rights and freedoms according to Islam are an integral part of the Islamic religion. The Declaration emphasizes the centrality of the community and the Islamic *Ummah* to Islamic human rights trad- itions.[12] Like Ujamaa and Ubuntu, the Cairo Declaration can be read as attempts by ruling elites to draw on indigenous African norms to legitimize ideological and political agendas. But these invocations of indigenous cultural and religious traditions also represent efforts at synthesizing contemporary ideas of universal human rights with what is viewed as indigenous expressions of that idea.

To be sure, questions remain as to how well these interpretations of rights truly reflect indigenous ethics and moral traditions. Questions

---

[10] Nyerere, *Ujamaa: Essays on Socialism*, 103.
[11] Tanganyika African Union (TANU), *The Arusha Declaration and TANU's Policy on Socialism and Self-Reliance* (Dar es Salaam: TANU Publicity Section, 1967).
[12] Organisation of Islamic Conference, "Cairo Declaration on Human Rights in Islam," in Brownlie's Documents on Human Rights, Ian Brownlie and Guy Goodwin-Gill, eds. (Oxford: Oxford University Press, 2010), 1114–1117.

over cultural authenticity have spurned debates about the invention and reinvention of tradition.[13] In its socialist agenda and communitarian vision of human rights, Nyerere's Ujamaa seems closer to a post-colonial reinterpretation rather than a restoration of the traditions of a bygone pre-colonial era. Similar questions about cultural authenticity have been asked about Ubuntu. Critics argue that Ubuntu, as invoked by ruling elites in post-apartheid South Africa, represents a romanticized and ahistorical vision of traditional African society based on reciprocity, community cohesion and national solidarity. Ubuntu has also been interpreted as an instrument of post-conflict nation building that serves a statist agenda by mandating conformity and fostering a form of social cohesion that denies individual participatory difference.

While debates over the authenticity and political instrumentality of modern interpretations of indigenous moral traditions remain unresolved, what is clear is that these notions of indigenous ethics have become progressively linked with the idea of human rights in Africa. Invented or authentic, interpretations of secular and religious moral traditions have come to dominate intellectual and public debates about human rights in Africa. Invocations of African culture and moral traditions have also influenced official policies relating to human rights protection and promotion across the continent. This chapter is less concerned with the historicity or authenticity of these claims. Rather, the emphasis here is on examining the substance and salience of indigenous humanist traditions in contemporary human rights discourse.

Invocations of indigenous culture and moral traditions represent both an affirmation and a challenge to modern "universal" human rights. On one hand, cultural invocations assert the congruence between indigenous African ethics and modern human rights. The central argument here is that the core principles of modern human rights are also to be found in indigenous African social systems. On the other hand, however, invocations of indigenous culture also fundamentally question the universality of Western-inspired human rights ideas and their legitimacy in African contexts. The emphasis on communal solidarity and interdependence represents a corrective to the isolating individualism of Western liberal human rights

[13] Eric Hobsbawm and Terence Ranger, eds., *The Invention of Tradition* (Cambridge: Cambridge University Press, 1992), 249.

traditions. The key argument is that modern human rights being essentially a Western "invention" born out of the crises of nationalism in twentieth-century Europe is less relevant to the social and political realities of African and other non-Western societies. Questions about cultural legitimacy are central to assertions of congruence between indigenous ethics and modern human rights. These questions are also central to claims about the fundamental divergence between indigenous ethics and modern human rights.

The debate over the links between African moral traditions and modern human rights has centered on two main arguments: the *values* argument and the *legitimacy* argument. The values argument asserts that notions of human rights are rooted in African value systems and moral traditions. It makes the case for a uniquely African concept of human rights founded on indigenous moral principles and practices that are distinct from Western human rights traditions. The values argument therefore challenges the notion of universal human rights. The *legitimacy* argument, on the other hand, does not challenge the notion of universal human rights per se. Rather, it calls for legitimizing and reinforcing international or universal human rights through the moral values and normative practices of traditional African society.[14] This involves grounding the interpretation and observance of modern human rights in indigenous ethical and humanist principles. The assumption here is that all cultures recognize the inherent worth and dignity of the human person and postulate various norms for its pursuit. Universal human rights can therefore be validated in African societies by interpreting them through the lens of local culture and moral traditions.[15] Both the *values* and *legitimacy* arguments seek to establish historical and philosophical connections between indigenous moral traditions and modern human rights in different ways.

An African Concept of Human Rights?

The notion of an African concept of human rights is linked to long-standing philosophical debates about African conceptions of human nature. At the heart of this debate is the claim that communal African conceptions of human nature stand in contrast to Western liberal

---

[14] Abdulahi Ahmed An-Na'im and Francis M. Deng, eds., *Human Rights in Africa: Cross-Cultural Perspectives* (Brookings Institution Press, 1990), 9.

[15] Ahmed An-Na'im and Deng, eds., *Human Rights in Africa*, xiv.

conceptions, which foreground humans as an autonomous individual defined by their intrinsic worth. In the African conception of human nature, individual identity is grounded in social interaction and community life. The philosopher John Mbiti summed the African conception of human nature in the dictum "I am because we are, and since we are, therefore I am."[16] This is contrasted with Descartes's "I think, therefore I am." The discussion on African human rights values also partly proceeds from the debates about the origins and genealogy of human rights outlined in the preceding chapter. It relates to claims about the Western origins of human rights and questions about the universalist premise of the international human rights movement.

To be sure, references to "African culture" and "Western traditions" in these debates can be problematic. The notion of traditional Africa often evokes a unitary and static past that tends to overlook cultural diversity and dynamism, historical continuities and social complexities. Similarly, references to "Western traditions" present a picture of an undifferentiated and "Occidentalized West" that obscures the diversities of Western liberal thought and traditions. Like the Orientalized East, the Occidentalized West becomes more of an imagined entity, a constructed oppositional reference point against which the constructors seek to define and assert themselves. The debate over African values and human rights has largely been framed in these totalizing terms. I join the debate cognizant of the conceptual limitations of these framings.

The case for an African concept of human rights is essentially an argument for cultural relativism as a counter to the universalist claims of the modern human rights movement. The premise of this position is that culture shapes the articulation and fulfillment of human rights because of its formative influence on human thought and behavior. Human rights principles are therefore culturally relative to different contexts, and culture informs unique conceptions of human rights when grounded in African moral principles and cultural experiences. The culturally relativist argument for an African concept of human rights is not unique. Scholars and political leaders have made similar arguments for "Asian values" in conceptualizing human rights.[17]

---

[16] John Mbiti, *African Religions and Philosophy* (Oxford: Heinemann, 1990), 141.

[17] For a discussion of Asian values and human rights debate, see William Theodore De Bary, *Asian Values and Human Rights: A Confucian Communitarian Perspective* (Cambridge, MA: Cambridge University Press, 1998).

On the other hand, some proponents of African values in human rights interpretation premise their claim on an affirmation rather than a repudiation of the universalism of human rights. They contend that the core principles that underpin modern human rights are neither exclusive to Western liberal traditions nor alien to African cultural traditions. These are eternal and universal norms. There is nothing essentially Western or bourgeois about the fundamental rights to life, the right to personal and collective dignity or the right to a fair trial. These human rights principles have normative parallels in indigenous African moral principles and political and social practices. To argue otherwise has been rejected as paternalistic and ahistorical.[18]

The values argument posits that indigenous African societies developed norms that fostered individual and communal rights within social systems that were hierarchical but unified by common religious beliefs and ceremonial practices. This included deference to age, commitment to the family and the community and solidarity with other members of the community. These norms strengthened community ties and social cohesiveness, engendering a shared fate and a common destiny. The distinction between African conceptions and the Western notions of rights is most evident in the dynamic between individual and collective rights. Interpersonal and interdependent relationships between individuals within a given community are central to African moral philosophies and principles of social organization. In contrast to the unfettered individualism of Western liberal rights traditions, indigenous African societies were more likely to see individual rights in the context of group solidarity, with mutual support entailing rights and duties.[19] This interdependence is regarded as vital to the overall well-being, and therefore the fulfillment of rights, of both individuals and the community at large. Rather than seeking to address tensions between individual entitlements and group interests, the emphasis in this conception of human rights is balance and complementarity between individual rights and communal welfare.

This balance between individual rights and communal interests was essential in ethnically homogenous societies where the principal object

---

[18] Welshman Ncube, "Universality and Cultural Relativity of Human Rights," in *Human Rights Theories and Practices*, Lalaine Sadiwa, ed. (Bryanston: Mercuria, 1997), 8.

[19] Francis Deng, "Human Rights in the African Context," in *A Companion to African Philosophy*, Kwasi Wiredu, ed. (Malden: Blackwell Publishers, 2004), 502.

of law was to foster social order and group solidarity. In such societies, the dominant concept of human rights tended to be communal, fostering mutual respect and recognition of individual rights within the wider context of communal interests and obligations.[20] Rights entailments pertained not solely or even primarily to individuals but to the community, to which the individual related based on obligations and duties. Rights in this context included, but were not limited to, the right to social inclusion and political representation guaranteed by the family, the clan and the larger community.

Because individuals were not seen in isolation from the rest of the community, their rights are not abstracted from those of the community. In this communitarian vision of rights ascribed to traditional Africa, individual identities were inextricably tied to and defined by a process that recognized the interest of others. The sanctity of individuals was recognized and upheld in relation to those who shared similar human conditions in a matrix of entitlements and corresponding duties. However, there was also an implied understanding that personal human rights are subordinate to, and dependent on, communal interests and mutual well-being. There could therefore be no absolute individual rights because excessive individualism was considered antithetical to communal well-being. Under these conditions, human rights are also collective relational claims, not simply individual claims against authorial power.

Indigenous Humanism

The argument for an African concept of human rights based on indigenous humanist values centers mainly on conceptions of personhood, notions of human dignity and honor, and the value of community. Historian John Illife has noted that to understand African behaviors, in the past and the present, we must take account of the notions of honor. Until the coming of the world religions, honor was the chief ideological motivation for African behavior.[21] Rights claims and struggles in Africa have historically been tied to notions of dignity, honor and community. However, the concept of dignity in the context

---

[20] Keba M'Baye, "Organisation de L'Unite Africaine," in *Les Dimensions International de Droits de L'Homme* (Paris: UNESCO, 1987), 651.

[21] John Illife, *Honour in African History* (New York: Cambridge University Press, 2005), 1.

of universal human rights is notoriously problematic because notions of human dignity can be socially specific and culturally contingent. While many societies set minimum standards of respect for the life and basic liberties of social outsiders, the "humanity" of each individual was ultimately contingent on social and political belonging. Until the mid-twentieth century reframing of human rights as universal and inalienable, notions of human dignity were generally linked to individual identities measured along lines of race, caste, culture, gender, ethnicity, religion, nationality and social and economic status. It is useful to recognize these social and cultural specificities of pre-twentieth-century notions of human rights and human dignity.

Several historical, philosophical and anthropological studies of pre-colonial African social systems underscore the centrality of the relationship between notions of human dignity, individual rights and communal obligations. The philosopher Kwasi Wiredu has argued that human rights principles in Akan thought and the normative conception of a person centered on the three principles: the life principle (*okra*), the blood principle (*mogya*) and the personality principles (*sunsum*). "Through the possession of an okra, mogya and sunsum, a person is situated in a network of kinship relations generated through a system of rights and obligations."[22] By virtue of possessing the divine element of okra, every person has an intrinsic value. Associated with this value is the concept of human dignity, which implies that every human being is entitled in equal measure to basic respect. Other rights such as the right to political participation and the rights to a piece of lineage land are founded on the blood and personality principles. The political and social systems of the Akan people of Ghana guaranteed the right to political participation by making chiefs accountable to a council of elected lineage elders. In the administration of justice, the Akan systems ensured that no human being could be punished without trial, reflecting a core principle of modern human rights.[23]

As with the Akan, notions of human rights among the Dinka of present-day South Sudan are expressed in the value they place on life

---

[22] Kwasi Wiredu, "An Akan Perspective on Human Rights," in Human Rights in Africa: Cross-cultural Perspectives, Ahmed An-Na'im and Deng, eds. (Washington D.C: The Brookings Institution, 1990), 244. See also Kwame Gyekye, *An Essay on African Philosophical Thought: The Akan Conceptual Scheme* (Philadelphia: Temple University Press, 1995), 143.

[23] Wiredu, "An Akan Perspective on Human Rights," 244.

and human dignity, the ideals of relationships between peoples. The Dinka concepts of human relation known as *ceing* emphasizes dignity, integrity, honor, generosity, social harmony and respect for self and for others. Cieng also represents the sanctity of a good moral order that derives from God and the ancestors.[24] In making the case for a unique conception of human rights among the Dinka, Francis Deng has pointed out that Dinka cultural values and patterns of behavior have both positive and negative implications for modern human rights. On one hand, there would seem to be a high regard for the human being and human dignity in the moral code of the Dinka as defined by their value system. On the other hand, however, that value system stratified society and ascribed certain rights based on descent, age and gender. Moreover, Dinka human rights values weaken as one moves away from the structural center of Dinka community.[25]

A similar case has been made for an indigenous conception of human rights among the Yoruba of West Africa centered on a humanism that emphasized the interdependence between the individual and the community.[26] In this worldview, the scope of individual rights and liberties is linked with the purpose of communal social existence. The interdependence between individuals and the community requires the commitment of individuals to their community and the corresponding commitment of the community to the preservation of the life and well-being of all its members.[27] Human beings are conceived as the ultimate agents for the community's existence, and because of this, they are endowed with an inherent individual worth. These humanist traditions of Yoruba society are expressed in such concepts as *Omoluabi* (honorable person), *iteriba* (respect), *Inurere* (good mind) and *Iwa* (good character). Omoluabi connotes respect for self and others. It is expected that a person must be respectful toward other human beings within and beyond the community.

---

[24] For a fuller discussion of the concept of human rights among the Dinka, see Francis M. Deng, "A Cultural Approach to Human Rights among the Dinka," in *Human Rights in Africa: Cross-Cultural Perspectives*, Ahmed An-Na'im and Deng, eds. (Washington D.C: The Brookings Institution, 1990), 266–277.

[25] Ibid., 273, 280.

[26] See, for example, J. A. I. Bewaji, "Human Rights: A Philosophical Analysis of Yoruba Traditions," *Cambrian Law Review*, 37 (2006), 51; Moses Òkè, "An Indigenous Yoruba-African Philosophical Argument against Capital Punishment," *The Journal of Philosophy, Science & Law*, 7 (2007).

[27] Segun Gbadegesin, *African Philosophy: Traditional Yoruba Philosophy and Contemporary African Realities* (New York: Peter Lang, 1991), 58.

Significantly, such an expectation of respect implies recognizing the rights of others not only on the grounds of their age, social or political status but by the virtue of their simply being human.[28] This value placed on the intrinsic worth of human personhood has also been identified among the Igbo of West Africa. The Igbo concept of personhood, which centers on the community, is defined in terms of social relationships with the group as conditioned by reciprocal rights and obligations.[29]

What appears common to these interpretations of indigenous moral thought is a humanistic outlook that sees human dignity and honor as fundamental to individual and collective well-being. These interpretations suggest that the communitarian outlook of indigenous African social systems did not necessarily imply the absence or rejection of individual rights. If anything, the dynamic between individual rights and communal obligations is more complicated than is often presented. In many traditional African societies, individual identity was closely linked to collective identity, but the individual was not completely subsumed within the collective. This dynamic between individual and collective identities is best understood when located within the historical context of relatively homogenous family and clan-based subsistence agrarian societies where interdependence was key to survival.

More explicit references to human rights principles in indigenous humanism have been dated to thirteenth-century West African political thought. The Charter of Kouroukan Fouga (Manden Oath), proclaimed by the leaders of the Mandinka clans comprising the Mali Empire, has been described as Africa's declaration of the rights of man.[30] UNESCO describes the Manden Charter as one of the oldest constitutions in the world.[31] The Charter codifies customary law regulating social life and the values of traditional governance and conflict resolution, which had been part of the transmitted oral history

---

[28] A. K. Fayemi, "Human Personality and the Yoruba Worldview: An Ethico-Sociological Interpretation," *The Journal of Pan African Studies*, 2, 9 (2009), 169.

[29] See Joseph Thérèse Agbasiere, *Women in Igbo Life and Thought* (New York: Routledge, 2000).

[30] Souleymane Bachir Diagne, "Individual, Community, and Human Rights: A Lesson from Kwasi Wiredu's Philosophy of Personhood," *Transition*, 101 (2009), 12; "Africa Drafted Its Declaration on the Rights of Man in 1236," (translation), *Les Afriques Magazine*, July 24, 2008, 12.

[31] UNESCO, "Manden Charter, proclaimed in Kurukan Fuga." Available at www .unesco.org/culture/ich/index.php?lg=en&pg=00011&RL=00290. Accessed July 23, 2016.

of the Mandinka. Contemporary textual reconstruction of the edicts of the Charter show the parallels with modern human rights principles. The reconstructed Charter of Kouroukan Fouga contains edicts advocating social peace in diversity, the inviolability of the human life, the communal obligation to provide education, the integrity of the motherland, food security, the abolition of slave raiding, and affirmations of the freedom of expression and trade.[32] Also significant are the principles regulating social relationships between individuals and their communities. The Manden Charter mandates the principle of *sanankunya* (cordial relationship) and the *tanamannyonya* (blood pact), which prescribes peaceful relations between the constituent Mandinka clans and the amicable resolution of conflicts among the people. For proponents of African values in human rights, the Manden Charter is emblematic of the communitarian humanism that defines indigenous notions of human rights.

★★★

Humanist ideas in pre-colonial African theological thought have also been raised in the argument for African human rights values. The expansion of Islam to North Africa from the Arabian Peninsula from the eighth century and the interaction between Islamic and indigenous thought produced new social cultures and rights traditions. This is evident in the writings of Islamic thinkers such as the medieval Songhai jurist and theologian Ahmed Baba, who wrote in seventeenth-century Timbuktu. Ahmed Baba challenged the legal and theological arguments used at the time to justify the practices of enslavement. Unlike many of his contemporaries, he called for legal entitlements for slaves within the broader framework of the social regulation of slavery. Arguing that the enslavement of free black Muslims was unlawful, he stated that the burden of proof for rightful enslavement laid squarely on those who bought and sold slaves.[33] Although these early writings do not convey a normative questioning of the fundamental basis of

---

[32] Centre d'Etudes Linguistiques et Historiques par Tradition Orale (CELTHO) (Center for Linguistic and Historical Study of Oral Tradition), "La Charte de Kurukan Fuga: Aux sources d'une pensée politique en Afrique," *(The Mande Charter of 1340)* (Paris: L'Harmattan/SAEC, 2008); UNESCO, "Manden Charter Proclaimed in Kurukan Fuga." Available at www.unesco.org/culture/ich/index.php?lg=en&pg=00011&RL=00290. Accessed February 14, 2015.

[33] Chouki El Hamel, *Black Morocco: A History of Slavery, Race, and Islam* (New York: Cambridge University Press, 2013), 81.

slavery, they represent a humanist concern about the ethical limits of enslavement and a framework for regulatory intervention.

Such humanist concerns are also evident in the theological and philosophical traditions of Christian Ethiopia, which date back to the first century. One notable example of this is the writing of the seventeenth-century Ethiopian philosopher and theologian Zera Yacob, who is most renowned for his critique of divine law and theory on natural law. In *Hatata* (Discourse), his polemical treatise on rationalism and Christian theology, he asserted that human action should be judged essentially on whether it advances or degrades overall societal harmony. Yacob's ethics placed emphasis on human dignity, tolerance, non-violence and mutual responsibility. Two central themes in his work are the sanctity of life and individual freedom. The first assertion in the *Hatata* is that man is created a free being and "endowed with the power of reason and the light of intelligence."[34] In the *Hatata*, freedom is defined in relation to individual choice and initiative. Human freedom, like human intelligence, is a gift from God to "man" so that, through good choices, he may fulfill his destiny. Yacob's ethics in the *Hatata* also includes an affirmation of the communitarian duty of each person toward those individuals within the societies in which they live.

Although he drew on an eclectic mix of Christian, Muslim and indigenous thought, Yacob's ethics rejected many established Judeo-Christian and Islamic traditions of his time as oppressive and discriminatory. His point of departure was rationalism. Man is a creature of God, but he was created to be free and intelligent. On this ground, one Zera Yacob scholar has argued that Yacob's critique of discrimination against women marked, in the context of seventeenth-century Ethiopia, a radical defense of "human rights, equality and freedom."[35] Yacob also proffered a moral condemnation of the slave trade because, according to him, it was against God's will. He wrote: "It is stated in the text that buying and selling human beings like an animal is right ... this law does not come from the Creator of human beings, who created us equal as brothers, so that we call our creator our

---

[34] D. W. Kidane, *The Ethics of Zär'a Ya'eqob* (Rome: Gregorian & Biblical Press, 2012), 320. See also Teodros Kiros, *Zara Yacob: Rationality of the Human Heart* (Asmara: Red Sea Press, 2005), 81.

[35] Kidane, *The Ethics of Zär'a Ya'eqob*, 326.

Father."[36] For proponents of African human rights values, the humanist ideas in these theological and philosophical writings provide the normative foundations for a conception of human rights founded in African history and culture.

Rights and Duties

A defining attribute of the notion African human rights values is the contingent relationship between rights and duties. This is the idea that rights entitlements enjoyed by individuals and groups do not stand in isolation but are tied to obligations. For every right to which a member of society was entitled, there was a corresponding duty to the community. Such communal obligations include deference to age, commitment to the extended family or clan and solidarity with other members of the community. These ideals strengthen community ties and social cohesiveness, engendering a shared fate and a common destiny. The relationship between rights and duties has been emphasized in several historical and contemporary interpretations of indigenous African political and social systems. In these interpretations, the individual in traditional pre-colonial African societies was valued both as a member of the community and for his or her intrinsic worth. While certain rights attached to the individuals by virtue of birth and membership of the community, others were contingent on corresponding duties. This approach to rights that links rights entitlements to duties and obligations fostered communal solidarity and sustained the kinship system.

This interpretation of the reciprocal relationship between rights and duties in traditional African societies informs contemporary human rights laws and policies. The African Charter on Human and People's Rights (also known as the Banjul Charter) adopted by African countries under the auspices of the Organization of African Unity in 1979 stresses the link between human rights and duties. Like all international human rights documents, the African Charter affirms individual human rights, but unlike most international instruments it also makes provisions for duties and the collective human rights of peoples. Linking rights and duties, the Charter emphasizes individual rights alongside obligations

---

[36] Zara Yacob, *Hatata* [English translation] in Kidane, *The Ethics of Zär'a Ya'eqob*, 399.

to the family and community. It states that every individual shall have duties toward his family, society and the state, and that the "rights and freedoms of each individual shall be exercised with due regard to the rights of others, collective security, morality and common interest."[37] The individual is also duty bound to "preserve the harmonious development of the family and to work for the cohesion and respect of the family; to respect his parents at all times, to maintain them in case of need."[38] The duties spelled out in the Charter have been interpreted as a recreation of the bonds among individuals in pre-colonial Africa and a reflection of the nuanced nature of societal obligations.[39] I return to the issue of individual duties and communal rights as expressed in the African Charter later in this book.[40]

Similar linkages between human rights and duties can be found in the Cairo Declaration on Human Rights in Islam, which stresses Islamic traditions of human rights alongside individual duties. The Declaration proclaims that it is the *duty* of individuals, societies and states to safeguard the right to life, which is guaranteed to every human being.[41] This expression of Islamic notions of human rights combines a system of rights and obligations, which gives the community cohesion and viability. In this conception of rights, the individual is a moral being endowed with rights but also bounded by duties arising from his interdependent relationship with others in the community. While some human rights scholars interpret this dynamic between individual rights and duties as providing a cross-cultural perspective that enriches human rights, others argue that making human rights contingent on duties undermines the very essence of human rights as unfettered entitlements owed to human beings simply because they are human beings.

As noted in Chapter 1, pre-modern ethics and moral principles in Africa or elsewhere in the world are not entirely congruent with modern human rights principles. Certain aspects of indigenous cultural practices clearly stand in conflict with modern international

---

[37] African Charter on Human and Peoples Rights, preamble.   [38] Ibid., Article 29.
[39] Makau Mutua, "The Banjul Charter: The Case for the African Cultural Fingerprint," in *Cultural Transformation and Human Rights in Africa*, Abdullahi An-Na'im, ed. (New York: Zed Books, 2002), 86.
[40] See the discussion of the Organization of African Unity and the African Charter on Human and Peoples' Rights in Chapter 6.
[41] Cairo Declaration on Human Rights in Islam, Article 2.

human rights norms. It can be argued that indigenous secular and religious humanism lacked the key attributes of inalienability and universality that have come to define modern universal human rights. The distinctions between indigenous African notions of human rights in contemporary political ideologies and the modern international human rights regime relates primarily to the scope of rights. Contemporary international human rights doctrine is unique in its vision of universal rights that are inherent to one's humanity. Prior articulations of human dignity, rights and liberties whether within indigenous humanism or Enlightenment liberalism were much more limited in scope. Such rights entitlements were rarely framed as universal or absolute. Rather, they were intricately linked with the security of being an insider or group member and the deprivations of being an outsider or foreigner.

In Enlightenment liberalism, for example, the much vaunted "rights of man" centered not so much on universalist inclusion but on particularistic entitlements for privileged groups – often propertied men defined by race, religion and class – to the exclusion of the rest of the population. In their progressive vision of rights, Enlightenment liberal philosophers still bought into some conservative and exclusionary ideas of their age. The rights declared to be universal and self-evident by eighteenth-century Euro-American thinkers and revolutionaries were never really intended to be all-inclusive. Slaves, women, foreigners and religious minorities were largely excluded from this vision of "universal" rights.

The same can be said of indigenous African notions of human rights. The scope of individual and collective rights was often limited to community members and restricted by ethnicity, caste, gender, power and status. Prioritizing communal solidarity over individual liberties often implied the exclusion of those considered outsiders, minorities and non-conforming members of the community. The emphasis on communal well-being and the contingent relationship between individual rights and duties also meant that rights were ultimately not conferred based on the intrinsic value of each human being but, rather, based on community membership, and social status and obligations. The scope of rights that a person enjoyed within a given society was determined by factors such as lineage, place of birth and membership in political, social and cultural groups. One who had lost his membership in the social unit or one who did not belong – an outcast or a stranger – lived outside the range of rights protection by the social unit.[42] It is safe to say therefore that indigenous rights-based perspectives of morality were premised on ascribed status. This departs from the foundational premise of modern human rights as inalienable entitlements that pertain to humans qua humans.

In drawing the links between historical and modern notions of rights, certain defining questions arise. When natural and positive rights are constructed upon a foundation of correlative duties, can inalienability be sustained? What then makes human rights different from any other conditional legal or normative entitlement? In addressing these questions, it is, I think, possible to draw correlative normative links between rights and duties. Ultimately, human rights are concerned with how individuals and groups interact with one another within society. This implies that the most fundamental unit of social life is neither solely the individual nor solely the group but, rather, the association between the two. Individuals cannot exist apart from the group, and the group cannot persist without its individual members. This relationship between the individual and society manifests in terms of both rights and duties.[43]

Although the correlation between rights and duties has not been traditionally emphasized in international human rights documents, it is evident in human rights laws that increasingly refer to individual and collective rights and duties. Apart from the detailed provisions for duties in the African Charter on Human and People's Rights, the American Convention on Human Rights (Pact of San José) includes sections on "Personal Responsibilities" that outline the relationship between duties and rights.[44] Similarly, the UN International Covenant on Civil and Political Rights and the International Covenants on Economic, Social and Cultural Rights include references to individual duties. The UN Declaration on the Right to Development, adopted in 1986 with the strong support of countries of the Global South, affirms the responsibility of all human beings for development, individually and collectively, as well as "their duties to the community, which alone can ensure the free and complete fulfilment of the human being."[45]

---

[42] Chris Mojekwu, "International Human Rights: The African Perspective," in *International Human Rights: Contemporary Issues*, Jack Nelson and Vera Green, eds. (Stanfordville, NY: Human Rights Publishing Group, 1980), 86.

[43] Christopher Roberts, *The Contentious History of the International Bill of Human Rights* (Cambridge: Cambridge University Press, 2015), 230.

[44] See Article 32, American Convention on Human Rights.

[45] Declaration on the Right to Development. Adopted by General Assembly resolution 41/128 of 4 December 1986, Article 2(2).

African Human Rights: Limits and Possibilities

Critics contend that the notion of African human rights values is fundamentally at odds with the universalist premise of modern human rights. Given the emphasis on community and social obligations in the African values position, some scholars have questioned its normative congruence with individual-centered universal human rights. Central to this critique is the conceptual debate concerning the relevance and suitability of the concept of human rights in analyzing pre-twentieth-century rights struggles. It has been reasoned, for example, that the African concept of human rights, as articulated by proponents, is really a concept of human dignity that defines the moral worth of the human person and their proper relationship with society. Human dignity and human rights are not equivalent concepts. The notion of human rights normally implies an affirmation of human dignity, but human dignity does not in itself imply recognition of the full spectrum of intrinsic liberties conveyed in the notion of human rights. Moreover, human dignity can be protected in a society that is not based on rights. As one writer puts it: "There is no specifically African concept of human rights. The argument for such a concept is based on a philosophical confusion of human dignity with human rights, and on an inadequate understanding of structural organization and social change in African society."[46] Debates about Akan and Dinka perspectives on human rights, for example, have therefore been characterized as discussions of African "ethics of human dignity and social justice" rather than human rights.[47]

Traditional African societies developed political and social systems that conveyed respect for human dignity. However, the ways in which human dignity was understood and protected were evidently different from the ways we have come to interpret it within modern human rights. All human societies, including those in Africa, have gone through a peasant or agrarian stage of development when the communal organization of a relatively homogenous society was necessary for individual and collective subsistence. This communal social structure

---

[46] Rhoda Howard, *Human Rights in Commonwealth Africa* (Totowa, NJ: Rowman & Littlefield, 1986), 23.

[47] Rhoda Howard, "Group versus Individual Identity in African Debate on Human Rights," in *Human Rights in Africa: Cross-Cultural Perspectives*, Ahmed An-Na'im and Deng, eds. (Washington D.C: The Brookings Institution, 1990), 166.

allowed for the development of humanistic ideals that upheld human dignity in a restricted sense but did not share the key visions of universality and inalienability that define modern human rights. However, generalized representations of indigenous African rights traditions as inherently communal rather than individualistic are open to question. These representations have been critiqued for promoting a "myth of communalism" founded on an idealized image of a non-stratified, consensual pre-colonial African society. Such interpretations of indigenous Africa tend to overlook aspects of African social systems that do not fit neatly into this collectivist and communitarian ideal. It is perhaps no coincidence that the case for African human rights values has focused more on centralized societies such as the Akan and Yoruba of West Africa and the Zulu of South Africa than on politically decentralized and acephalous societies such as the Igbo of West Africa and the Akamba of East Africa.

Even if we accept the interpretation of indigenous African social and political systems as being essentially communal, the relevance of these systems to human rights in modern Africa is uncertain. Invocations of African human rights values have often been framed in terms of their contemporary relevance. But rather than the persistence of traditional cultural values in the face of modernity, the reality in contemporary Africa, as in much of the developing world, is the erosion of traditional societies amid disruptive Westernization, globalization and cultural hybridization. The ideals of an indigenous communitarian humanism used to justify calls for a uniquely African human rights order often no longer exist.

Questions about contemporary relevance also arise from concerns that ruling elites appeal to African cultural values as a means of restricting rather than expanding human rights. Arguments against international human rights norms on the grounds of culture, religion and indigeneity have mostly come from dominant groups and ruling elites, not those in need of human rights protection. Such culture-based arguments become cover for elite privilege and for pretexts by authoritarian rulers to consolidate power and justify repression. In Malawi, for example, President Hastings Banda invoked indigenous morality and utilized "traditional courts" less to promote human rights and more to suppress political opposition outside the regular legal system. In Zaire, President Mobutu introduced the practice of *salongo*, a form of compulsory labor that supposedly marked a return to the values of communalism and solidarity rights inherent in traditional society. In fact, salongo had more in common with the French colonial practice of corvée labor or Belgian colonial labor obligations than indigenous labor practices. These contradictory aspects of the politics of cultural appropriation and human rights in African states are taken up in detail in subsequent chapters of this book. Here, it suffices to stress that conceptual and philosophical debates about indigenous human rights values are not simply academic. They hold wide-ranging implications for human rights principles, policies and practices.

Beyond elite invocations of African cultural values, we must also consider the broader social and political salience of these ideas. The accent on culture and indigeneity in the human rights discourse in Africa cannot be entirely reduced to the demagogic posturing of ruling elites. Every assertion of African culture in human rights discourses cannot be dismissed as masking a defense of privilege and inequality at the expense of individual rights.[48] Ideas about African human rights values also resonate among subaltern non-elite groups such as women and ethnic minority groups who find the language of culture and indigeneity useful in expressing rights claims. Human rights struggles in Africa, from anti-colonial movements to pro-democracy campaigns, have drawn on both individual-centered rights espoused in international human rights documents and indigenous ethical norms. Women's advocacy groups appeal to cultural and religious traditions to promote women's rights even as they critique discriminatory customary practices. Those involved in women's rights struggles in the continent consider cultural norms relating to individual rights and duties, communal solidarity and collective obligations all relevant to the gender equality agenda.[49]

The salience of culture in the human rights discourse is also evident with Ubuntu in South Africa. Despite the debate over its authenticity and historicity, Ubuntu as an indigenous African concept of human rights and justice served to legitimize the work of the South African TRC, especially among Africans. Ubuntu was invoked not only by

---

[48] Mahmood Mamdani, ed., *Beyond Rights Talk and Culture Talk: Comparative Essays on the Politics of Rights and Culture* (New York: St. Martin's Press, 2000), 3.

[49] See, for example, Florence Butegwa, "Mediating Culture and Human Rights in Favour of Land Rights for Women in Africa: A Framework for Community Level Action," and Hussaina J. Abdullah, "Religious Revivalism, Human Rights Activism and the Struggle for Women's Rights in Nigeria," in *Cultural Transformation and Human Rights in Africa*, An-Na'im, ed. (London: Zed Books, 2002), 108–125, 151–191.

ruling elites invested in the TRC project, but also by ordinary South Africans who saw it as a means of coming to terms with the human rights violations under apartheid. Many black Africans thought that the TRC amnesty process matched traditional African concepts of justice, humanity, reconciliation and communal solidarity.[50] Ubuntu was therefore useful to the extent that it allowed for the legitimation of a forward-looking national human rights regime and national reconciliation process.

Seen from this utilitarian perspective, the debate about an African concept of human rights is not a futile academic exercise. It holds relevance in terms of legitimizing and fulfilling modern human rights through indigenous moral principles. Here, the African values argument and the cultural legitimacy argument converge in what may be expressed as the vernacularization of universal human rights. The notion of vernacularizing human rights describes the process by which universal human rights norms are grounded in local communities. It requires seeing human rights in specific situations rather than as the application of abstract principles. Vernacularizing human rights is therefore a constructive process that grounds and expands the scope of human rights in different cultural contexts. It is a process whereby global impulses intersect with indigenous ideas to produce new human rights norms and practices that are relevant to local situations. The process of vernacularization connotes critical local engagement with international human rights norms with the goal of investing them with local meaning that can potentially strengthen recognition and enforcement. I return to the debate over vernacularizing human rights in Africa in the concluding chapter of this book.

★★★

We can draw certain normative parallels between modern human rights and indigenous humanist traditions relating to human dignity and communal solidarity. However, there are also substantive distinctions between pre-modern notions of human dignity and the modern idea of human rights as inherent human entitlements enforceable against authority. A more compelling case can be made for interpreting and legitimizing universal human rights through the lens of

---

[50] Gunner Theissen, "Object of Trust and Hatred: Public Attitudes toward the TRC," in *Truth and Reconciliation in South Africa: Did the TRC Deliver?*, Hugo Van der Merwe and Audrey R. Chapman, eds. (Philadelphia: University of Pennsylvania Press, 2008, 207).

African cultural traditions. Such invocation of cultural norms and indigenous rights traditions must be recognized as a selective process. There is much in indigenous African social systems relating to human dignity and communal solidarity that affirms modern human rights principles. But indigenous systems also include beliefs and practices that reinforce exclusion based on ascribed status, in ways that contradict the universally inclusive premise of human rights.

The proposition to vernacularize universal human rights through African culture and moral principles expands a historiography long centered on the invention of human rights within European liberalism. Vernacularization allows us to go beyond the Eurocentric genealogy of human rights centered on a familiar course that runs from Enlightenment liberalism through the European and American revolutions of the eighteenth centuries to the post–World War II universal human rights movement. Exploring the ways in which indigenous African moral principles have shaped rights movements in the continent offers an alternative narrative of the global history of human rights. Although it is useful to distinguish between abstract ideals of human dignity and the more formal legal principles of modern human rights, we must not overlook the normative connections between these sets of concepts and the ways they reinforce each other.[51] Indigenous notions of human dignity and justice provide a basis for understanding local engagement with modern international human rights, which gives us a fuller picture of the history of human rights in Africa. Indigenous humanist traditions and notions of human dignity can, in this sense, be considered part of the *pre-history* of human rights in Africa.

Another way of interpreting the normative connections between indigenous cultures and modern human rights is to think in terms of human rights *affirming* and human rights *constricting* traditions. While certain African traditions promoted human dignity, the sanctity of life and collective well-being, other traditions placed restrictions on the scope of individual freedoms and collective liberties. Thinking of the relationship between indigenous systems and modern human rights in terms of affirmation and constriction allows us to see how human rights affirming aspects of indigenous social and cultural systems have been used to legitimize international human rights at local levels. It also shows allows us to see how, in other situations, the human rights

---

[51] Ahmed An-Na'im and Deng, eds., *Human Rights in Africa*, 3.

constricting attributes of culture and tradition have been used to limit the scope of rights and justify human rights violations. Ultimately, the analytical framework of rights *affirmation* and *constriction* allows us to transcend a linear and progressivist narrative to explore the paradoxes of nineteenth- and twentieth-century human rights struggles. This framework guides the discussion in the next chapter, which examines discourses of rights and liberty within abolitionism and antislavery struggles.

3

Humanitarians and Abolitionists

Each day the traders are kidnapping our people – children of this country, sons of our nobles and vassals, even people of our own family. This corruption and depravity are so widespread that our land is entirely depopulated. We need in this kingdom only priests and schoolteachers, and no merchandise, unless it is wine and flour for Mass. It is our wish that this Kingdom not be a place for the trade or transport of slaves.
    – King Afonso of Kongo (Letter to King João III of Portugal, 1526)[1]

Antislavery and abolitionism resonate deeply in historical and contemporary public debates about human rights. The growing enterprise of memorializing historical atrocities and struggles as human rights events has brought renewed attention to the age of abolitionism as a defining moment in the human rights story.[2] At a transnational level, antislavery continues to resonate within international human rights law, which places slavery and the slave trade firmly within a rights

---

[1] "Afonso of Kongo: The Evils of the Slave Trade," in Constance B. Hilliard, *Intellectual Traditions of Pre-colonial Africa* (Boston: McGraw-Hill, 1998), 357.

[2] For example, an official plaque erected to the memory of the victims of the trans-Atlantic slave trade in Paris states: "By their struggles, with their undying desire for freedom and dignity, the slaves of the French colonies have contributed to the universality of human rights and to the ideal of Liberty, Equality, Fraternity that founds the Republic. France pays tribute to them." Francoise Verges, "The Slave Trade, Slavery, and Abolitionism: The Unfinished Debate in France," in *A Global History of Anti-Slavery Politics in the Nineteenth Century*, William Mulligan and Maurice Bric, eds. (Hampshire: Palgrave Macmillan, 2013), 210.

framework recognizing them as crimes against humanity.[3] Antislavery also echoes in present day human rights and neo-abolitionist campaigns against so-called modern slavery and human trafficking. Given that Africa is historically central to Atlantic slavery and the abolitionist response to it, it is fitting that the quest for connections between antislavery and human rights begin with Africa.

The literature on antislavery and abolitionism is expansive and continues to grow. Engaging the rich historiography of transnational antislavery, this chapter offers an Africa-centered narrative of antislavery rights discourse. My goal here is not simply to reinterpret abolitionism in Africa through a human rights lens or to fit antislavery neatly into a genealogy of human rights. Rather, the task here is to explore the place of antislavery as both discourse and struggle in the development of human rights ideas in and about Africa. I examine the links between antislavery and human rights in the context of the emergence of a globally organized abolitionist movement, the international process of abolition and the role of Africans in emancipation. I also examine the long-standing debate about the relative significance of European legal abolitionism, economic transformations and slave resistance in compelling abolition. While early scholarship on African abolitionism suggested a smooth transition from slavery to freedom, later studies have made the case that abolitionism occasioned a radical restructuring of socioeconomic and governance relations that reflected transformations in African societies. To this old debate, I propose to add new questions: To what extent were the social transformations occasioned by abolition driven by a discourse of rights? How did abolition and emancipation transform notions of individual and collective rights, and conditions of personal liberties?

My discussion of antislavery comes with important caveats. The processes of abolition and emancipation varied widely across Africa. In some parts of the continent, the decline of slavery and the slave trade was dramatic and transformative, while in other parts it was less so. Multiple internal and external factors shaped the uneven process of abolition across the continent – local socioeconomic conditions and demographics of slavery, divergent colonial policies and varied African responses. Like slavery, abolition and emancipation also affected men, women and children in different ways. Female slaves faced difficulties similar to those of men on the road to emancipation, but their options were usually more

---

[3] The Universal Declaration of Human Rights and other UN human rights documents affirm the prohibition of slavery and the slave trade in all their forms.

limited because of the general subordination of women to men in most societies. International pressures for reforms that varied across colonies and territories also shaped the course of antislavery. Given these intricacies, my discussion of rights within antislavery can only offer a snapshot of a complex and multifaceted topic.

The discussion here is not limited to eighteenth- and nineteenth-century antislavery. I also explore earlier indigenous perspectives on the ethics of enslavement, framing them as normative historical antecedents of antislavery. Nineteenth-century abolitionism was unique in its fundamental and universal rejection of slavery and the slave trade. However, long before the age of abolition, indigenous and foreign notions about the ethical boundaries of enslavement practices opened up limited possibilities for emancipation and manumission for those enslaved. I argue that these earlier debates concerning the ethics of enslavement and the qualified rights of social insiders constitute an integral part of the longue durée pre-history of human rights in Africa.

Linking Human Rights and Antislavery

Among the defining historical moments that have shaped the course of human rights, antislavery had the most significant direct impact and affected the greatest number of people. Nineteenth-century abolitionism broadened the scope of individual rights and provided new international legal frameworks for their protection. Several histories of human rights present the antislavery movement as a story of human rights struggle led by transnational activists who took on the powerful interests of state, church and big commerce. With organization, enthusiasm and imaginative campaigning that foreshadowed the work of present-day human rights activists, abolitionists mobilized public opinion in opposition to slavery and forced governments to uphold the rights and humanity of enslaved people. This wave of global antislavery activism marked a defining moment in the development of the modern human rights idea. It was, as one writer argues, "the first time in history that a large number of people became outraged, and stayed outraged for many years over someone else's rights."[4] Like the modern human rights movement, the antislavery campaigns of the nineteenth century were broad-based social

---

[4] Adam Hochschild, *Bury the Chains: Prophets and Rebels in the Fight to Free an Empire's Slaves* (Boston: Houghton Mifflin, 2005), 5.

movements founded on public support. Abolitionist leaders set up transnational coalitions and organized public campaigns appealing to the empathy in their audiences in ways that mirror modern human rights NGO advocacy techniques.[5]

Nonetheless, the historical links between antislavery and human rights remain contested. Essentialist human rights scholars reject any connection between antislavery and modern human rights, and insist that antislavery campaigns were not framed as rights issues. While they acknowledge the possible merit of viewing the transnational cooperation of antislavery movements as a bridge toward later human rights activism, they reject claims of continuity between notions of rights and human dignity expressed within antislavery and modern human rights. Rights claims, they argue, figured only marginally in antislavery. This makes nineteenth-century antislavery and twentieth-century human rights two distinct stories of empowerment struggle. For this reason, essentialist human rights scholars argue that nineteenth-century abolitionism is not the proper place to understand rights.[6] A related argument against reading antislavery into the human rights story is the view that antislavery did not extend to what historian Samuel Moyn describes as the "scaled space of global politics" that the human rights movement assumed in the mid- to late twentieth century.[7] In other words, nineteenth-century antislavery lacked the distinctly universalist legal and political character of twentieth-century human rights.

Other scholars have made similar distinctions between human rights and the humanitarian impulse of antislavery. While human rights rely on a discourse of *rights*, humanitarianism is predicated on a discourse of *needs*. Human rights are thus based on a legal code, while humanitarianism is based on a moral code.[8] Those who subscribe to these hard distinctions locate the emergence of abolitionism in the eighteenth century as the origins of the history of

---

[5] William Mulligan, "Introduction: The Global Reach of Abolitionism in the Nineteenth Century," in *A Global History of Anti-Slavery Politics in the Nineteenth Century*, Mulligan and Bric, eds. (Hampshire: Palgrave Macmillan, 2013), 13.

[6] Samuel Moyn, "Substance, Scale, and Salience: The Recent Historiography of Human Rights," *Annual Review of Law and Social Science*, 8 (2012): 130. See also Samuel Moyn, *The Last Utopia: Human Rights in History* (Cambridge, MA: Harvard University Press), 2010, 1–43.

[7] Moyn, "Substance, Scale, and Salience," 131.

[8] William Mulligan, "Introduction: The Global Reach of Abolitionism in the Nineteenth Century," in *A Global History of Anti-Slavery Politics in the Nineteenth Century*, Mulligan and Bric, eds. (Hampshire: Palgrave Macmillan, 2013), 6.

humanitarianism, but not necessarily of human rights.[9] Antislavery, they insist, was not a human rights movement and abolitionists were humanitarians, rather than rights activists. Indeed, abolitionists who passionately fought against the transatlantic slave trade and demanded military intervention against this violation of common sense humanity did, at the same time, endorse the paternalistic colonial rationality of a mission to civilize Africans without granting them equal rights. Campaigns for a "common humanity" within antislavery movements did not necessarily extend to the granting of equality or the full spectrum of civil and political rights associated with the rights of man.[10]

At their core, these arguments for delinking antislavery from human rights hinge on the notion that the conceptual architecture of human rights in the eighteenth and nineteenth century differs fundamentally from the one in the late twentieth century.[11] It is one with which I disagree. True, antislavery was not primarily predicated on a discourse of rights. However, the claim that rights discourses featured only *marginally* within antislavery remains open to debate. The declared objective of the British and Foreign Antislavery Society, a key organization in the antislavery movement, was the universal abolition of slavery and commitment to "watching over the *rights* of all persons captured as slaves."[12] Abolitionists were pioneers in developing the modern concept of human rights. From 1835 to 1839 the American Anti-Slavery Society published a monthly journal entitled *Human Rights*. This marked the first time that the term "human rights" was used extensively in public discourse. "Slavery," the journal announced in its inaugural issue, is "the greatest possible violation of human rights."[13] Moreover, the complex interconnections

---

[9] Michael Barnett, *Empire of Humanity: A History of Humanitarianism* (Ithaca, NY, 2011), 16–17, 32–64.

[10] See, for example, Fabian Klose, "The Emergence of Humanitarian Intervention: Three Centuries of 'Enforcing Humanity,'" in *The Emergence of Humanitarian Intervention: Ideas and Practice from the Nineteenth Century to the Present*, Fabian Klose, ed. (Cambridge: Cambridge University Press, 2015), 18, and Mulligan, "The Global Reach of Abolitionism in the Nineteenth Century," 6.

[11] For a discussion of this conceptual debate, see Peter De Bolla, *The Architecture of Concepts: The Historical Formation of Human Rights* (New York: Fordham University Press, 2013).

[12] Joseph Alexander, *Sixty Years against Slavery: A Brief Record of the Work and Aims of the British and Foreign Anti-Slavery Society* (London: The Anti-Slavery and Aborigines Protection Society, 1900), 3.

[13] Manisha Sinha, *The Slave's Cause: A History of Abolition* (New Haven: Yale University Press, 2016), 249.

between the long history of transnational humanitarianism within antislavery and twentieth-century human rights defy rigid dichotomies. For instance, nineteenth-century antislavery treaties influenced the Antislavery Convention enacted under the League of Nations, which in turn shaped the prohibition of slavery within the framework of the UN and the Universal Declaration of Human Rights. In addition, the strategies of petitioning and economic boycotts used by nineteenth-century antislavery campaigners have influenced the activist work of contemporary neo-abolitionists and human rights activists.

To be sure, nineteenth-century antislavery differs from twentieth-century human rights in certain important respects. For one, antislavery campaigns were predominately framed in terms of religious and moral imperatives that did not necessarily challenge ascribed status or entrenched social hierarchies and inequities. There are also the more obvious distinctions of scope and scale. Antislavery centered on the abolition of the slave trade and slavery, and the emancipation of the enslaved. Modern human rights encompasses a broader agenda of political, economic and social inclusion. However, if we think about the history of human rights as a story of the tensions between rights inclusion and exclusion, it is easier to see the normative link between antislavery and human rights. The human rights story then consists not only of accounts of struggles to expand rights and enhance inclusion, but also of accounts of counter-movements to restrict rights and maintain exclusion.

With specific regard to African history, it is unfeasible to completely separate antislavery from the human rights story given the intersections between antislavery, colonialism and anti-colonialism. The discussion in this chapter proceeds from the premise that it is both possible and necessary to map normative and historical connections between antislavery and human rights. It is also useful to explore the similarities and contrasts between the philosophical impulses of nineteenth-century antislavery campaigns and those that have animated twentieth-century human rights movements. The notion of a shared humanity provided broad moral foundation for the antislavery campaigns and the later human rights movement. Both movements represented grassroots efforts at broadening social inclusivity and expanding the boundaries of rights. They further aimed to change the past by reasserting inherent human dignity and to create new liberal futures. Just as modern day human rights activists declare "war" on state atrocities and impunity, coalitions of antislavery organizations created a humanitarian emergency and declared "war on slavery."[14]

Beyond their normative parallels, historical antislavery resonates in contemporary campaigns against "modern day slavery" and human trafficking. Present day human rights campaigners frame as slavery the trafficking of vulnerable people through violence, coercion and deceit. They make explicit connections between "historical" and "modern" slavery. One organization at the forefront of the modern "antislavery" campaign claims that "slavery did not end with abolition in the 19th century" and that the practice continues in one form or another in every country in the world.[15] By studying slavery in its historical forms, we can better understand and address such claims about its twenty-first-century manifestations. In addition, examining the normative impulses of antislavery can help us better understand the moral and ideological foundations of human rights.

Abolitionism and Emancipation

In making the connection between antislavery and human rights, it is also necessary to make the distinction between *abolition* – the immediate process of ending slavery – and *emancipation* – the longer process by which those enslaved become formally free. While the act of abolition was largely state-sponsored, often through legislative enactments arising from activist campaigns and public pressure, the process of emancipation involved a combination of social, political, economic and cultural forces. Africans in the continent and abroad were involved in both processes.

Attempts to locate antislavery within a broader human rights story have centered on mapping a genealogy that links nineteenth-century international antislavery legislation with contemporary international human rights law. Spurred by religious beliefs and Enlightenment conceptions of natural rights, abolitionists in Europe pushed their governments to make the suppression of the slave trade a focus of diplomacy and treaty making. The result, in the early nineteenth

---

[14] Amalia Ribi Forclaz, *Humanitarian Imperialism: The Politics of Anti-Slavery Activism, 1880–1940* (Oxford: Oxford University Press, 2015), 139

[15] Anti-Slavery International, "What Is Modern Slavery?" Available at www.antislavery .org/english/slavery_today/what_is_modern_slavery.aspx. Accessed October 20, 2015.

century, was the emergence of a novel network of international treaties prohibiting the slave trade and mandating slave emancipation. These treaties resulted in the establishment of the world's first international "human rights" courts – the Admiralty Tribunals and the Courts of Mixed Commission – empowered to confiscate ships engaged in the illegal slave trade and liberate Africans found onboard.

Legal scholar Jenny Martinez portrays the Mixed Commission Courts as "the first international human rights courts."[16] She traces the origins of international human rights law back to nineteenth-century antislavery campaigns, arguing that the slave trade provided the first instance in which international law protected non-citizens abroad. The conceptualization of the slave trade as a crime against humanity and of slave traders as *hostis humani generis* (enemies of humankind) helped lay the foundation for twentieth-century international human rights law. Legal action against the slave trade introduced into modern international legal discourse the idea that violations of human rights were offenses of concern to humankind generally, not just between people and their sovereign. This, Martinez argues, is the key conceptual step that separates the contemporary world of international human rights law from the idea of natural rights that arose during the Enlightenment and took national legal form in documents such as the US Declaration of Independence or the French Declaration of the Rights of Man.[17]

Other scholars have gone beyond law to make broader normative connections between antislavery and human rights. The role of antislavery in shaping transnational debates on ethics and morality in the nineteenth century was far-reaching. With the emergence of the antislavery campaign, something new and permanent developed that represented a significant break with the old political morality. Antislavery did not guarantee freedom for everyone, and sometimes even created new orthodoxies that took on elements of older oppressive structures. However, the success of antislavery as "anti-structure" is that it provided new opportunities to former slaves and captives, or those most at risk, to escape from old structural constraints. It was the ethics of a second chance for such former slaves and the simultaneous emphasis on individual responsibility and a common humanity that gave

---

[16] Jenny Martinez, *The Slave Trade and the Origins of International Human Rights Law* (New York: Oxford University Press, 2012), 6.
[17] Ibid., 149.

antislavery its anti-structural force and transformative power.[18] This radically anti-structural impulse is what the antislavery movement shares with human rights.

Secular humanitarians and evangelicals at the forefront of the transnational antislavery movement promoted universal humanism in both thought and activism. Within this humanist framework, antislavery became a universal movement of rights, representing a new social radicalism that challenged the structure of profit, domination and advantage that sustained slavery. Abolitionists in Europe and across the Atlantic employed a language of ethics and rights to articulate their opposition to slavery, which is most evident in missionary literature. For example, in its journal, *The Anti-Slavery Examiner*, the American Antislavery Society challenged slavery, not only in terms of Christian ethics but also as an affront to human rights and dignity.[19] An 1839 issue of the journal titled "The Bible against Slavery: An Inquiry into the Patriarchal and Mosaic Systems on the Subjugation of Human Rights," has been described as one of the strongest contemporary intellectual statements that we possess on the human rights character of antislavery.[20]

Although the antislavery campaigns were not always explicitly framed in terms of rights, notions of human dignity, common humanity and individual liberties featured prominently in antislavery discourse. Abolitionists articulated antislavery through the language of Christian morality and the inherent rights and dignity of the enslaved. In his autobiographical narrative published in furtherance of the cause of antislavery, Olaudah Equiano recalled the brutality of slaveholders responsible for his capture and enslavement, characterizing them as "sable destroyers of human rights."[21] Writing in 1850, Theodore Dwight Weld, one of the architects of the American abolitionist movement, criticized the hypocrisy of so-called benevolent slaveholders by drawing a distinction between the moral and rights-based rationales of antislavery. "Slaveholders talk of treating men well," he wrote, "and yet

---

[18] Lamin Sanneh, *Abolitionists Abroad: American Blacks and the Making of Modern West Africa* (Cambridge, MA: Harvard University Press, 1999), 10.

[19] Theodore Dwight Weld, "The Bible against Slavery: An Inquiry into the Patriarchal and Mosaic Systems on the Subject of Human Rights," *Anti-slavery Examiner*, 6 (1838).

[20] Sanneh, *Abolitionists Abroad*, 278.

[21] Olaudah Equiano, *The Interesting Narrative of the Life of Olaudah Equiano* (Radford, VA: Wilder Publications, [1793], reprint 2008), 18.

not only rob them of all they get, and as fast as they get it, but rob them of themselves also . . . their bodies and minds, their time and liberty and earnings, their free speech and rights of conscience, their right to acquire knowledge, and property, and reputation – and yet they, who plunder them of all these, would fain, make us believe that their soft hearts ooze out so lovingly toward their slaves."[22]

We cannot fully comprehend the transformative influence of antislavery without considering the established forces and structural orthodoxies that resisted the accomplishment of its aim. The story of antislavery, considered as part of the longue durée history of human rights, was certainly not a steady process of progressive rights expansion. Rather, it was a complex and uneven course of rights inclusion and exclusion, defined by tentative shifts toward extending freedom to those enslaved, amid counter-movements committed to maintaining a repressive status quo. Abolitionists had to respond constantly to forthright defenders of slavery who upheld the institution on the grounds of economic efficiency, social convention, custom and race. Opposition to abolition came from slaveholders and from political and mercantile elites concerned about economic losses and disruptions to the existing social and political order. Contradictions between the interests of individuals, families, social orders and communities also played a part in prolonging the trade even as people fought against it.[23] Yet, by the early twentieth century, slavery had been formally abolished in most parts of the African continent and the struggle for emancipation was well under way. The process of abolition and the struggles for emancipation would be complex, prolonged and contested. My account centers on the discourse of rights and liberty within antislavery from four related perspectives: slave resistance, the ethics of enslavement, legal abolitionism and emancipation struggles.

Slave Resistance

All slave systems dehumanize enslaved victims and deny them of the rights and liberties enjoyed by other members of society. From Greco-Roman slavery to indigenous forms of slavery in Africa, all slave systems are sustained by alienation and exclusion. However, the Atlantic slave

[22] Theodore D. Weld, "Slavery, a System of Inherent Cruelty," in *Slavery as It Is*, reprinted in *Slave Narratives*, William Andrews and Henry Louis Gates, eds. (New York: Penguin, 2000), 663.

[23] Sylviane Diouf, *Fighting the Slave Trade: West African Strategies* (Athens: Ohio University Press, 2003), ix.

trade and chattel slavery in the Americas was exceptional in terms of the extent of brutalization and dehumanization to which captives were subjected.[24] The torturous conditions that African captives endured during their journey through the middle passage and upon arrival in the New World provided the impetus for antislavery. Apart from the psychological trauma inflicted during the process of capture and sale, many captives died because of the conditions in overcrowded slave ships through diseases, physical injuries and suicides. In the famous Zong slave massacre of 1781, British slave traders threw 133 enslaved Africans overboard from a stranded ship for the purpose of claiming insurance money against their loss. Upon arrival in the Americas, enslaved Africans were subject to a life of servitude and "social death." The uniquely racialized character of the Atlantic slave trade and slavery in the Americas imposed strict barriers on social integration, making race an inflexible marker of status, exclusion and inequality. In short, every stage of the slave trade process was characterized by what today would be termed gross and systematic violations of human rights.[25]

Scholars have explained the end of slavery in Africa in terms of three main social and economic transformations. First was the structural changes in the political economy that affected slave capture and holding. The second was the abolitionist policies of colonial governments. The third was the changes in regional and international commodity markets as well as changes in local economic and demographic conditions that affected the demand for labor and opened new options to free slaves.[26] Alongside the political and economic impetus for abolition, we must add the humanist and egalitarian impulse within indigenous ethics, Christian morality and modernist liberalism that sustained the work of African and transnational abolitionists. Abolitionism legitimized its existence on a form of faith-based humanitarianism and evangelical social activism. It also drew on the radical philosophies of the

---

[24] Although scholars continue to debate the connections between indigenous forms of slavery and the Atlantic slave trade, there is agreement on the point that indigenous slavery had broader social significance. Indigenous forms of slavery often did not share the rigid chattel character of New World slavery. Slaves were more socially integrated and valued as political supporters, soldiers and consorts.

[25] Philip Alston, "Does the Past Matter? On the Origins of Human Rights: An Analysis of Competing Histories of the Origins of International Human Rights Law," *Harvard Law Review*, 126 (2013): 2046.

[26] Suzanne Miers and Richard Roberts, eds., *The End of Slavery in Africa* (Madison: University of Wisconsin Press, 1988); 17; Toyin Falola, "Pawnship in Colonial Southwestern Nigeria," in *Pawnship in Africa*, Toyin Falola and Paul Lovejoy, eds. (Boulder: Westview Press, 1994), 245–266.

eighteenth-century "age of reason" and Enlightenment, the natural rights of man and the inherent values of liberty in society. Other related themes converged in the antislavery movement, such as the belief in the power of law to change the character of man, slave agitation and self-understanding, the undoing of customs and other established social structures and the moral transformation of African society. Where does the discourse of rights and liberties fit in with these themes?

The historiography on antislavery has until recently concentrated on European and New World abolitionism, highlighting the role of middle-class men and women in eighteenth- and nineteenth-century Britain and America who, driven by religious and moral considerations, challenged their governments to abolish the slave trade and emancipate slaves worldwide.[27] Recent studies have offered more balanced accounts of antislavery by exploring the various strategies devised by African populations against the slave trade.[28] We now recognize that the story of antislavery must begin with the struggles of those enslaved. It is only natural that those who experienced first-hand the brutality and indignities of slavery would be most invested in ending it. Long before European humanitarians and abolitionists took up the cause of antislavery, enslaved Africans, acting individually and collectively, opposed and resisted their enslavement. Resistance to capture and deportation was an integral part of indigenous antislavery. Resistance mechanisms took the form of slave flight and rebellion, to attacks on slave ships and sabotage of slave-holding forts. Such resistance to enslavement and exploitation in Africa and the Americas challenged the institutional foundation of slavery and was crucial to the system's demise.

Although surviving records are sparse and filtered, we know that Africans organized and participated in militias and secret societies to protect and defend their communities from slave raiders. Contemporary observers noted the instinctive and reflexive resistance of African captives to their sudden loss of freedom. One account tells of a 1798 revolt led by a captive African chief on board a slave ship bound

---

[27] AmaliaRibi Forclaz, *Humanitarian Imperialism: The Politics of Anti-Slavery Activism, 1880–1940* (Oxford: Oxford University Press, 2015), 2

[28] See, for example, Sylviane Diouf, ed., *Fighting the Slave Trade: West African Strategies* (Athens: Ohio University Press, 2003); Bronwen Everill, *Abolition and Empire in Sierra Leone and Liberia* (Houndmills: Palgrave Macmillan, 2013); Paul Lovejoy and Suzanne Schwarz, *Slavery, Abolition and the Transition to Colonialism in Sierra Leone* (Trenton, NJ: Africa World Press, 2015).

for the Americas. Upon suppressing the captives' revolt, the ship's captain inquired about the ringleader. According to contemporary records, "the Chief came out boldly and avowed that he was the man; that he wished to *give liberty* to all slaves on board; that he regretted his defeat on their account – but that he was [satisfied] with the prospects of immediately obtaining what he termed his own liberty." He was hanged soon afterward.[29]

Resistance was not limited to the middle passage. In the Upper Guinea Coast, enslaved Africans defended their freedom by outright rejection and opposition to servitude. From the mid- to late eighteenth century, many revolts broke out in this region as enslaved Africans fought against African and European slave traders and holders. In 1756, the enslaved population of Futa Jallon rose against the slave-owning class, declared themselves free, and migrated northward where they founded new communities. Two other well-studied rebellions in the region – the Mandingo Rebellion in the eighteenth century and the Bilali Rebellion in the nineteenth century – attest to the tenacity of the enslaved in resisting slavery and in struggling for their freedom.[30]

It is difficult to ascertain precisely the ideas and forms of social consciousness that motivated slave resistance, especially since most of the historical evidence is refracted through the lens of European travelers, abolitionists and colonial administrators with their own agendas. We cannot be sure about the extent to which these acts of resistance were driven by a natural instinct toward self-preservation or deeper philosophical rejection of slavery and the slave trade. However, the testimonies of lettered African and European interlocutors give us some insights into the African antislavery consciousness. From these limited records, we can infer that Africans who opposed and resisted slavery were driven by multiple motivations and considerations. These records point to the opposition to enslavement by Africans that manifested in rebellious actions, the existence of free communities and, in some cases, the appropriations and creative (re)interpretations of hegemonic ideas.[31]

---

[29] Carl Bernhard Wadström, *An Essay on Colonization, Particularly Applied to the Western Coast of Africa* (New York: A. M. Kelley, [1794], reprint 1968). My emphasis.

[30] Ismail Rashid, "'A Devotion to the Idea of Liberty at Any Price': Rebellion and Antislavery in the Upper Guinea Coast in the Eighteenth and Nineteenth Centuries," in *Fighting the Slave Trade*, Diouf, ed. (Athens: Ohio University Press, 2006), 133.

[31] Rashid, "A Devotion to the Idea of Liberty at Any Price," 133

Africans who resisted slavery in the continent and the New World justified resistance by making political and social claims to dignity, freedom and rights, which other people recognized. These rights-based claims provided nodes for cooperation and alliance. The rise of transnational abolitionism gave African captives new opportunities to articulate longstanding struggles for freedom and social inclusion. Rights rhetoric underpinned the legitimacy of slaves' resistance, whether in the forms of collective military action, individual flight or sabotage. The rebellions and the free communities created by those who resisted slavery became focal points for combating servile oppression and for nurturing the normative and legal impulses of antislavery.

The Ethics of Enslavement

Even before the age of abolition, Africans leaders and elites were involved in debates about ethical limits on enslavement and the slave trade. As John Thornton has argued, the fact that African leaders participated in the slave trade does not mean that they did so without recognizing the ethical problems that the trade presented. This is evident in the written records of sixteenth- and seventeenth-century African rulers such as King Afonso I and Garcia II of Kongo and Queen Njinga Mbande of Matamba. These records show that these monarchs led societies that accepted the legal possibility that an individual could have a bundle of rights over another person that surpassed those of any other in the community or the sovereign. This provided the social and legal framework for indigenous slavery but also set the boundaries of enslavement. Recognizing that slavery was legally permissible did not mean that the slave trade did not pose ethical problems for these African leaders.[32] These African leaders expressed strongly that there were legal limits to who could be enslaved, when and under which conditions. In some cases, they felt that European slave traders violated these ethical and legal limits of enslavement.

As the Atlantic slave trade decimated his kingdom in the sixteenth century, the growth of the trade became a matter of personal concern

---

[32] John Thornton "African Political Ethics and the Slave Trade," in *Abolitionism and Imperialism in Britain, Africa and the Atlantic*, D. R. Peterson, ed. (Oxford: Ohio University Press, 2009), 39.

for King Afonso. In 1526, he appointed a commission of three chiefs to ascertain whether the slaves bought were really captives of war or his own subjects, and appealed to the Portuguese king to impose some restraint on Portuguese subjects involved in the trade.[33] Writing to King João III to stop the slave trade, he stated, "Each day the traders are kidnapping our people – children of this country, sons of our nobles and vassals, even people of our own family." He added that the "corruption and depravity are so widespread that our land is entirely depopulated ... It is our wish that this kingdom is not to be a place for the trade or transport of slaves."[34] He proposed to King João that he send no more merchants or merchandise to Kongo, but only priests to support the Church, emphasizing, "Our will is that there be no trade in slaves in our kingdoms."[35]

Writing to the Rector of the Jesuit Order in 1643, Afonso's successor, King Garcia II made similar denunciations of the slave trade. He stated that "there can never be peace with this Kingdom [Angola] ... because in place of gold, silver and other things which serve as money in other places, the trade and money are pieces [slaves], which are not gold nor cloth, but creatures."[36] He demanded in a proposed treaty with Portugal the appointment of impartial judges to examine those captured for export to determine if they were "free or stolen or are truly slaves." Queen Njinga's correspondence with the king of Portugal in the seventeenth century also suggests that although slavery and slave capturing were licit under her country's laws, there were definite legal limits and rules about who could and could not be enslaved. She asked that the Portuguese return her subjects who had been captured and enslaved illegally. Queen Njinga may not have had a philosophical difficulty with holding slaves or selling them, but she clearly had a desire to regulate the market and set limits to the exploitation of these forms of labor.[37]

Recent studies on the ethics of slavery in the Yoruba societies of West Africa suggest that that they too developed ethical rules that limited opportunities for enslavement. A series of laws demarcated the

---

[33] Quoted in René Lemarchand, *Political Awakening in the Belgian Congo* (Berkeley: University of California Press, 1964), 75.

[34] Reproduced in Constance B. Hilliard, *Intellectual Traditions of Pre-colonial Africa* (Boston: McGraw-Hill, 1998), 357.

[35] Anne Hilton, *The Kingdom of Kongo* (New York: Oxford University Press, 1985), 58.

[36] Quoted in Thornton, "African Political Ethics and the Slave Trade," 52.

[37] Ibid., 49.

"other" and defined the legal boundaries of the enslavable social outsiders or non-kin and protected kin or insiders. The enslavement of a social insider was considered illegal, a crime and an abomination that attracted stiff sanctions. Those who could be justifiably enslaved differed from their enslavers through cultural and physiological symbols such as tattoos, names, faith and ethno-political idiosyncrasies. Yoruba laws also regulated the treatment of captives by prescribing the rights and obligations of captors and their victims.[38]

Under the stress of overseas demands, indigenous African slavery changed from a system with social and legal boundaries to a more exploitative one aimed at foreign commerce. The rise of the Atlantic slave trade and the transformation of indigenous slavery narrowed the scope of social and political protection against enslavement. In Kongo, for example, the protection from enslavement enjoyed by women and freeborn Kongos dissipated during the course of the seventeenth and eighteenth centuries as internal strife led competing factions to enslave partisans or rivals. The distinctions between foreign-born slaves and freeborn Kongos quickly disappeared, making every Kongo a potential slave.[39] This breakdown in the ethics of slaving reduced the scope of protection from enslavement hitherto enjoyed by large sections of Kongo's population. If we interpret the longue durée history of human rights in Africa in terms of rights expansion and contraction at different historical moments, rather than a saga of unrelenting progress, the rise of the Atlantic slave trade clearly marked an era of rights contraction in Kongo.

It would be misleading, however, to characterize the opposition of rulers such as King Afonso and Queen Njinga as *antislavery* in the abolitionist sense of the word. Rather, their positions on the ethics of enslavement fit better into a tradition of legal, moral and conscientious objections that we can find throughout the history of slavery. Such objections were sometimes premised on the fair and humane treatment of slaves, or on opposition to the enslavement of the "wrong" types of people.[40] King Afonso and Queen Njinga's objections were not against the institution of slavery itself, but against

---

[38] Olatunji Ojo, "The Atlantic Slave Trade and Local Ethics of Slavery in Yorubaland," *African Economic History*, 41 (2013): 89.

[39] Linda M. Heywood, "Slavery and Its Transformation in the Kingdom of Kongo 1491–1800," *The Journal of African History*, 50, 1 (2009): 22.

[40] Joel Quirk, *Unfinished Business: A Comparative Survey of Historical and Contemporary Slavery* (Paris: UNESCO, 2009), 74.

violations of the established proper order of enslavement. Specifically, they objected to the expansion of the slave trade to *untarnished social insiders* within their communities who were hitherto free from enslavement. In contemporary parlance, these social insiders enjoyed exclusive rights to the freedom from enslavement. However, to the extent that this "right" to freedom from enslavement did not extend to all members of the community, they were not human rights in the modern sense of the term. Nonetheless, the anxieties expressed by these African rulers suggest that the freedom from enslavement constituted a right in the limited sense of a legal and ethical principle of freedom owed to certain members of their communities. African anxieties concerning the legal limits of enslavement also point to indigenous systems of ethics that foregrounded abolitionism and later emancipation struggles.

Transnational Abolitionism

A more coherent discourse of rights by Africans within antislavery is evident in the works of lettered Africans in the diaspora, especially Afro-British abolitionists such as Olaudah Equiano and Ottobah Cugoano. Drawing on their personal experiences of enslavement, these African abolitionists allied with British antislavery campaigners such as Granville Sharp, Thomas Clarkson and William Wilberforce to convey crucial information about slavery and the slave trade to public audiences. They built coalitions to raise political and public awareness about the indignities of slavery and the imperative of legal abolition. In the nineteenth century, much of this work was undertaken under the auspices of humanitarian organizations such as the British and Foreign Anti-Slavery Society (BF-ASS), which merged with the Aborigines Protection Society (APS) in 1909 to form the Anti-Slavery and Aborigines Protection Society (AS-APS). The organization's publications, the *Anti-Slavery Reporter* and *Aborigines' Friend*, were effective instruments for promoting the antislavery cause. The Anti-Slavery Society framed its opposition to slavery in terms of a common humanity invoking empathy, public morality and Christian ethics. The central premise of its campaigns was the notion that slavery is morally abhorrent and that those enslaved were entitled to certain fundamental rights and liberties. The seal of the Anti-Slavery Society, which symbolized the humanistic framing of antislavery, was an image of a supplicant slave in chains along with the words, "Am I not a man and a brother?" Antislavery groups deployed advocacy techniques such as petition campaigns, economic boycotts and lobbying political leaders for change. They also built networks around advocacy forums such as the 1840 World Anti-Slavery Convention, which provided the legal and activist framework for abolitionism.

By recounting their experiences of capture and enslavement in their writings and public speeches, Cugoano and Equiano became symbols of the transnational abolitionist movement. Cugoano's book, published in 1787, was the first published African critique of the transatlantic slave trade. In this and other works, he demanded the total abolition of the slave trade and the freeing of enslaved Africans. Invoking Enlightenment notions of natural rights, he argued that Africans had the moral right to resist slavery. He condemned the taking away of their "natural rights and liberties" and called for the restoration to black people of "the common rights of nature."[41] The first-hand accounts of African abolitionists brought credibility and legitimacy to the antislavery movement at a time when some in Europe were wary of passive abolitionists who offered only rhetorical support for the antislavery cause. Within their black solidarity, Cugoano and Equiano drew a distinction between passive sympathizing and active abolitionism in which trust and alliance were of key importance.[42]

As antislavery ideals and activism took hold in the late nineteenth and early twentieth centuries, Africans in the continent became more directly involved in local and transnational antislavery campaigns with the establishment of local branches of antislavery organizations. The Aborigines' Rights Protection Society (ARPS) was founded in the Cape Coast (Ghana) in 1897, and in 1911 the Lagos (Nigeria) Auxiliary of the Anti-Slavery and Aborigines Protection Society was formed with the support of the parent body in Britain. The Cape Coast ARPS and Lagos AS-APS were composed mainly of Western-educated African elites who were active in the antislavery movement and sought to stamp out practices of slavery that persisted in the continent after formal abolition.

---

[41] Ottobah Cugoano, *Thoughts and Sentiments on the Evil and Wicked Traffic of the Slavery and Commerce of the Human Species* (London: n.p., 1787), 2, 77.

[42] Thomas Clarkson and Ottobah Cugoano, *Essays on the Slavery and Commerce of the Human Species* (Peterborough: Broadview Press, 2010), 27.

African Christian missionary converts also played important roles in the antislavery campaign. Like their counterparts in the diaspora, they engaged public sympathies by bringing firsthand accounts of the horrors of slavery and their condemnations of the slave trade to African and global audiences. The Yoruba Anglican Bishop Samuel Ajayi Crowder and the Egba clergyman Joseph Wright were former slaves who became prominent missionary educators and passionate advocates for emancipation in West Africa. Contemporary accounts of Crowder's missionary activities in the 1860s describe him as a dogged fighter against the slave trade and a passionate advocate for the freedom of African slaves.[43] Captured in 1821 and sold to Portuguese slave traders, Crowder and other enslaved Africans were rescued on the high seas by British naval squadron vessels and taken to Sierra Leone. He joined the British Church Missionary Society (CMS), rising through its ranks to become the first African Anglican bishop of West Africa in 1864. Spurred by his experience of the brutality of the slave trade, Crowder became a persistent advocate against slavery and the slave trade. He also condemned other forms of servitude such as debt-bondage and pawnship, urging local kings and chiefs to abandon these practices.[44]

Crowder anchored his condemnation of slavery and slavery-like practices on Christian morality and the idea of "God-given rights." He wrote, for example, that women imprisoned and enslaved in harems deserved better treatment because "they are reasonable beings in whom God has planted certain rights and feelings in common with other people." He criticized "selfish oppressors" who took these rights away from them and cruelly suppressed their God-given liberties.[45] Crowther's moral commitment to antislavery has been described as a demonstration of the fact that Africans were no exception to "the rule of righteousness" that opposed any compromise with slavery and its supporting structures.[46]

[43] Duke Akamisoko, *Samuel Ajayi Crowther: His Missionary Work in the Lokoja Area* (Ibadan: Sefer, 2002), 83.

[44] "Narratives of Samuel Ajayi Crowder," in Philip Curtin, *Africa Remembered: Narratives by West Africans from the Era of the Slave Trade* (Madison: University of Wisconsin Press, 1967), 289–316.

[45] Samuel Crowder, *A Charge Delivered on the Banks of the River Niger in West Africa* (London: Seeley, Jackson & Halliday, 1866), 31.

[46] Lamin Sanneh, *Abolitionists Abroad: Black Americans and the Making of Modern West Africa* (London: Harvard University Press, 1999), 156.

In the Gold Coast, African missionaries such as Reverend David Asante and Theophilus Opoku of the Basel mission were prime proponents of emancipation. Asante was particularly uncompromising in his condemnation of slavery and insisted on the reform of indigenous institutions and practices that he believed condoned and perpetuated servitude. This brought him and other missionaries into conflict with the influential *Okyenhene* (king) of Akyem Abuakwa, who forbade Christian proselytization in his domain. In their commitment to emancipation, Asante and his supporters defied the Okyenhene's authority and continued their antislavery activities. When 200 royal slaves threw off the king's authority and proclaimed their freedom in 1877 based on emancipation laws, the king blamed the undermining of his power on the work of Reverend Asante and his mission.[47]

The work of African antislavery campaigners such as Crowder and Asante underscores the links between legal abolition and emancipation. The mid-nineteenth-century abolition of slavery and the slave trade did not immediately translate into the emancipation of those enslaved. For many African captives, freedom remained elusive until the early twentieth century. Before antislavery manifested in law and official policies, it manifested as political discourse and in social struggles. After legal abolition, slave emancipation also took the form of activist social and political struggles. These activist struggles were critical to actualizing legal abolitionism.

Legal Abolitionism

The legal abolition of slavery represented a break with thousands of years of historical precedent. In the nineteenth century, slavery, long considered a morally acceptable and often highly profitable institution, was formally abolished across the globe.[48] Yet abolition also represented a broader historical continuity. The global movement to abolish slavery and the slave trade drew from a long tradition of moral and legal objections to slavery. We have seen, for example, the attempts by African rulers such as King Afonso of Kongo to

---

[47] Raymond Dumett and Marion Johnson, "Britain and the Suppression of Slavery in the Gold Coast Colony, Ashanti, and the Northern Territories," in *The End of Slavery in Africa*, Miers and Roberts, eds. (Madison: University of Wisconsin Press, 1988), 87.

[48] Quirk, *Unfinished Business*, 74.

place normative limits on enslavement. Such legal and conscientious objections to enslavement were evident elsewhere. In his famous judgment in the Somerset case in 1772, Lord Mansfield held that chattel slavery was unsupported by the common law in England even though the position elsewhere in the British Empire remained ambiguous. The Somerset case affirmed the premise that certain legal rights are available to all, even enslaved Africans. By setting free Somerset, the runaway slave, Lord Mansfield affirmed Somerset's identity as a human being and not chattel to be owned and moved without his consent.

We can point to other important legal continuities between abolitionism and the emergence of international human rights in the mid-twentieth century. Beginning from the early nineteenth century, a network of bilateral and multilateral agreements and treaties laid the legal groundwork for the eventual abolition of slavery and the suppression of the slave trade. At the Vienna Congress of 1814–1815, eight European powers signed a Declaration on the "Universal Abolition of the Slave Trade." The Declaration proclaimed the slave trade to be "repugnant to the principles of humanity and universal morality" and pledged the signatories to work toward its abolition. This was the first of several major multinational treaties aimed at eliminating the slave trade. Others include the Treaty of London of 1841, which committed a number of European powers to the suppression of the slave trade. Later twentieth-century international agreements, such as the League of Nations Antislavery Convention of 1926, make explicit reference to these nineteenth-century antislavery treaties. The Antislavery Convention, which became the international legal foundation for the prevention and suppression of the slave trade, provided an enduring definition of slavery, servitude and forced labor. Later international human rights laws prohibiting slavery, such as the 1956 Supplementary Convention on the Abolition of Slavery, were founded on the 1926 Antislavery Convention. Thus, the nineteenth-century antislavery movement provided the ongoing momentum for establishing antislavery within modern international human rights law.

A key factor that facilitated legal abolition was the easing in the defense of state sovereignty in international law, particularly with regard to the law of the sea. The Westphalian concept of state sovereignty, and the rights associated with it, hitherto ensured that during peacetime no state had the right to intercept and search the ship of another state without an explicit agreement. This legal position posed a major hindrance to the eradication of the transatlantic slave trade. However, by the late nineteenth century, notions of state sovereignty in relation to maritime commerce had eased, allowing for extraterritorial jurisdiction in the enforcement of antislavery legislation.[49] Here, we see one of the most direct links between nineteenth-century legal abolitionism and modern human rights. Legal abolition was premised on a new multilateral internationalism and the weakening notion of state sovereignty for the purpose of bringing liberty to those enslaved. Similarly, the need to limit state power over individual liberties and to assert the protective obligations of the international community was a driving consideration in the emergence of universal human rights in the mid-twentieth century.

The historical connection between legal abolitionism and modern human rights is also evident in the nature of the judicial institutions that emerged to enforce abolition and suppress the slave trade. Britain's abolition of the West African slave trade in 1807 provided a legal mechanism for searching and seizing slave ships in territorial waters and on the high seas. It also provided the legal authority to prosecute apprehended slave dealers in the Vice-Admiralty Courts established to adjudicate cases involving slave ship seizures. Empowered by domestic and bilateral treaties, British naval authorities policed the high seas and disrupted slave routes by seizing vessels involved in slave trading, emancipating their cargo of captives and bringing the slave traders to the Mixed Commission Courts. By 1820, the Mixed Commission Courts established under various treaties operated in a number of locations, including Rio de Janeiro in Brazil, Havana in Cuba, Surinam and Freetown in Sierra Leone. These courts were, in many respects, the precursors of present-day international human rights tribunals.

As European colonial influence in Africa grew in the mid- to late nineteenth century, legal abolition was proclaimed across Africa, initially in areas of British influence and later extended to areas of French and Portuguese influence. Anxieties about the loss of political authority and socioeconomic disruptions led some African kings and chiefs to resist European incursions and the extension of antislavery laws to their domains. In such cases, legal abolition was often forcefully imposed. Britain annexed Lagos in 1861 ostensibly to end slavery

---

[49] Andrea Nicholson, "Transformations in the Law Concerning Slavery: Legacies of the Nineteenth Century Anti-Slavery Movement," in *A Global History of Anti-Slavery Politics in the Nineteenth Century,* Mulligan and Bric, eds. (Hampshire: Palgrave Macmillan, 2013), 215.

there and in 1873 pressured Zanzibar to ban the slave trade. Antislavery also provided the justification for French wars against Samory Touré and Amadou Bamba in West Africa in the 1880s.

In Liberia and Sierra Leone, colonies created as settlements for freed slaves established by British and American antislavery organizations, discourses on antislavery, political rights and liberties were all interlinked. Both settlements played crucial roles in the development of antislavery ideology in metropolitan and African contexts. The African repatriates who settled these colonies were inspired by ideas of civilizing Africa via the end of the slave trade, the spread of Christianity and the introduction of "legitimate commerce."[50] In Liberia, antislavery featured prominently in discussions of political and civil rights. The American antislavery movement, which provided the impetus for the abolition of slavery in the United States in 1865 under the Thirteenth Amendment to the Constitution, also influenced antislavery in Liberia after the country formally severed itself from the American Colonization Society. The Liberian Declaration of Independence of 1847 draws much of its rhetoric about individual rights and liberties from the US Declaration of Independence. It affirms that "all men" are entitled to "certain inalienable rights; among these are life, liberty, and the right to acquire, possess, enjoy, and defend property." The Declaration also specifically repudiates the slave trade in words that echo the Christian and humanist impulse of antislavery. It states: "The native African bowing down with us before the altar of the living God, declares that from us, feeble as we are, the light of Christianity has gone forth, while upon that curse of curses, the slave trade, a deadly blight has fallen, as far as our influence extends."[51]

Emancipation

Across Africa, legal abolitionism was a tentative process that unfolded as European powers extended their influence in the continent. Despite the rhetoric of antislavery, it sometimes suited the interests of the early colonial authorities to tolerate slavery. Although most colonial states

[50] Everill, *Abolition and Empire in Sierra Leone and Liberia*, 13.
[51] Liberian Declaration of Independence, 1847. Reprinted in Henry Wilson, ed., *Origins of West African Nationalism* (London: Macmillan, 1969), 60.

including self-governing Ethiopia and Liberia passed laws against
slavery, enthusiasm for complete abolition waned in the face of
responses to freedom of both former slaves and slave owners. European colonial officials generally favored a cautious approach to the
enforcement of antislavery laws and emancipation policies. Some
officials were reluctant to interfere with African customs of servitude
and "traditional" forms of unfree labor that they felt bound to respect
in principle. Others feared that abrupt and blanket abolition would
provoke backlash, disrupt local economies and trigger social upheavals. This was indeed the case in the British Cape Colony where
Afrikaner slave owners opposed the Emancipation Act and resisted
emancipation policies. This became one of the grievances that led
many Afrikaners to leave the colony in the Great Trek into the South
African hinterland to establish their own homeland, independent of
British rule.

Colonial officials defended their ambivalence toward the persistence of slavery by arguing that it was enough to limit abolition to
ending enslavement rather than mandating immediate emancipation
of those enslaved. Even metropolitan abolitionists accepted the idea
that some indigenous forms of slavery were more benign and were
willing to see the attack on slavery concentrated on the elimination of
what they considered the cruelest forms of chattel slavery.[52] The
British colonial administrator Frederick Lugard prohibited enslavement and the trade in slaves in northern Nigeria but worried that full
emancipation would lead to social and economic chaos. He was
cautious not to alienate influential slave-holding emirs on whom
Britain's indirect rule system relied. One compromise was to require
slaves to purchase their freedom. In other British colonies such as the
Sudan, colonial officials did little beyond the official proclamation of
legal abolition to stop enslavement and even tolerated a clandestine
slave trade.[53] The French also adopted a gradual approach toward
abolition, enacting a series of laws prohibiting slavery that were not
always well enforced. The situation was no different in independent
Ethiopia where slavery persisted even after Emperor Haile Selassie
(then Ras Teferi) issued a proclamation in 1923 outlawing the slave
trade on pain of death and granted freedom to those enslaved. Despite

[52] Miers and Roberts, *The End of Slavery in Africa*, 48
[53] Martin Klein, ed., *Breaking the Chains: Slavery, Bondage, and Emancipation in Modern Africa and Asia* (Madison: University of Wisconsin Press, 1993), 24.

the weak enforcement of abolition and emancipation laws, however, legal changes had a salutary effect on slavery across Africa. By with-holding state support for slavery and outlawing new enslavement and slave dealing, abolition created the conditions that enabled the slaves to seize the initiative to free themselves.[54] Many of these acts of slave self-emancipation have been well documented and studied. In the early twentieth century, slave revolts broke out in Senegambia, for example, interrupting the slave trade in that region of West Africa for several years.[55]

It is important to stress, however, that self-emancipation was not always premised on legal suppression. Slave struggles for emancipation sometimes occurred without legal abolition. In German East Africa, for example, colonial officials pursued a deliberate policy of non-abolition. German colonial authorities believed that abolition should be avoided at all costs since it would undermine the power and prosperity of the local slave-owning elite, whose effective collaboration was thought to be indispensable to the functioning of colonial rule. Although ostensibly committed to the antislavery course, the government allowed slavery to persist under official supervision. In the end, the slaves themselves ended the dehumanizing institution. As Jan-Georg Deutsch has argued, the decline of slavery in German East Africa is not a history of European knights in shining armor eradicating the evils of slavery, as claimed by the government and missionaries. On the contrary, the decline of slavery in Tanganyika came about as a result of the prolonged struggle between owners and slaves, in which slaves tried to make the best of the limited choices and opportunities available to them.[56] Self-emancipation was not always achieved through heroic struggles, however. Sometimes they took the form of flight and indirect subversion against servile relationships.

One of the great paradoxes of antislavery is that the lexicon of rights deployed within abolitionism was also often simultaneously used as

---

[54] Richard Roberts, "The End of Slavery in French Soudan 1905–1914," in *The End of Slavery in Africa*, Miers and Roberts, eds. (Madison: University of Wisconsin Press, 1988), 302.

[55] For example, thousands of Banamba slaves in French West Africa left their masters and endured many hardships in the attempt to return to their places of origin or to establish new communities. The Banamba exodus ultimately served to destroy slavery as a labor system in large swards of West Africa. Martin Klein, *Slavery and Colonial Rule in French West Africa* (Cambridge: Cambridge University Press, 1998), 159.

[56] Jan-Georg Deutsch, *Emancipation Without Abolition in German East Africa 1884–1914* (Athens: Ohio University Press, 2006), 242.

justification for maintaining slavery. This is to be expected because at the heart of all institutions of slavery and servitude is the notion of "rights-in-persons as property" – the rights that one person or group exercises over another as possession.[57] The defense of transatlantic slavery rested partly on property rights and the view that emancipation without adequate compensation infringed on the ownership rights of slave owners. Abolitionists countered these claims by arguing the primacy of the dignity and liberties of those enslaved over the property rights of the slaveholding elites. Writing in 1830, one British abolitionist pondered this question thus: "When the right to property is pleaded, is the property of the Slaveholder alone to be considered? The Slaves too are men, and have they no right to the free enjoyment of the property in their person?"[58]

This tension between the rights of captives to personal liberty and the property rights of slaveholders was evident throughout the abolitionist movement. In early nineteenth-century discussions about abolition in the Cape Colony, for example, British officials and Dutch elites stressed the need to respect the ownership rights of slaveholders and to ensure that the "property rights in the slave were left undisturbed."[59] In French West Africa, colonial officials worried that the 1848 Emancipation Decree, which abolished slavery in all French colonies, did not adequately protect the property interests of slaveholders. Seeking to placate disaffected slaveholding elites who opposed the Emancipation Decree, Auguste Baudin, the French colonial governor in Senegal, stated: "I agree that the principle which declares all slaves who touch French soil are free is just, but in certain local conditions and needs, like those found in place in Senegal, the rigorous application is difficult and appears contrary to *human rights*."[60] In these debates over African labor, colonial

---

[57] Igor Kopytoff and Suzanne Miers, "'African Slavery' as an Institution of Marginality," in *Slavery in Africa: Historical and Anthropological Perspectives*, Suzanne Miers and Igor Kopytoff, eds. (Madison: University of Wisconsin Press, 1977), 7.

[58] H. V., "West Indian Slavery," *The Monthly Repository of Theology and General Literature* 4 (1840): 739.

[59] Per Chief Justice Truter Wayne [1825]. Quoted in Wayne Dooling, *Slavery, Emancipation and Colonial Rule in South Africa* (Athens: Ohio University Press, 2008), 87.

[60] Governor Auguste Baudin to Minister Arago, Feb. 12, 1849, St. Louis, Archives Nationales, Section Outre-Mer (ANSOM), Senegal. I/35. Cited in Trevor R. Getz, *Slavery and Reform in West Africa: Toward Emancipation in Nineteenth-Century Senegal and the Gold Coast* (Athens: Ohio University Press, 2004), 82. My emphasis.

administrators invoked rights more in terms of property claims than the personal liberties of those enslaved.

The tension between emancipation and property rights continued well into the post-abolition period as colonial officials sought to balance what they saw as conflicting rights claims. To prevent slaves from abruptly withholding their labor and endangering the economy, the abolition decree enacted by the British in Zanzibar in 1897 made emancipated slaves liable to tax, corvée labor and vagrancy laws. Those who wished to leave their masters had to go to court where they were pressured into remaining on the plantations as contract laborers.[61] The situation was similar in French Sudan where officials reclassified many slaves as "domestic servants" and required them to buy their freedom and receive a "certificate of liberty."[62] French officials would later abandon this practice, mainly due to pressure from abolitionist groups.

★★★

In Ottoman North Africa, legal abolition and resistance took a slightly different turn. The suppression and eventual abolition of the slave trade from Africa into the Ottoman Empire was not predicated upon popularized antislavery ideological currents. Unlike European leaders, Ottoman viziers and provincial governors who ruled in North Africa did not face mobilized public opinion and pressure to end the slave trade. In general, elite public opinion rejected Western abolitionist rhetoric and the notion that Ottoman enslavement was wrong, inhuman or immoral. In addition to religious and legal justifications put forward by Ottoman leaders, the resistance to abolition by political elites in Ottoman North African societies may be explained in terms of their vested socioeconomic interests.[63] Conservative Muslim thinkers of the period defended enslavement in their societies by contrasting the institution of slavery in Islamic societies with Atlantic slavery. They emphasized domestic household slavery and practices of slave

---

[61] Frederick Cooper, *From Slaves to Squatters: Plantation Labor and Agriculture in Zanzibar and Coastal Kenya, 1890–192* (New Haven: Yale University Press, 1980), 72.

[62] Paul Lovejoy, *Transformations in Slavery: A History of Slavery in Africa* (Cambridge: Cambridge University Press, 1983), 260.

[63] Ehud R. Toledano, *As If Silent and Absent: Bonds of Enslavement in the Islamic Middle East* (New Haven, CT, and London: Yale University Press, 2007), 108–152. For detailed discussion of abolitionism in North Africa, see Ehud Toledano, *Slavery and Abolition in the Ottoman Middle East* (Seattle: University of Washington Press, 1998).

concubinage, which they depicted as a more benign mode of servitude. This portrayal was effective in initially deflecting foreign abolitionist pressures on Muslim North African societies. It stifled antislavery discourses and initially prevented the emergence of a homegrown abolitionist movement in Ottoman North Africa. There were, of course, notable exceptions. Ahmed Bey, the Ottoman Bey of Constantine, abolished slavery in 1846, several years before abolition under French protectorate rule in Algeria and Tunisia. Generally, however, the traffic in slaves was sustained in many parts of North Africa throughout the nineteenth century.

Although organized antislavery movements did not take hold in North Africa as they did elsewhere in the continent, it would be wrong to assume that antislavery ideas were completely absent in North Africa. Recent studies have highlighted the role of key antislavery reformers in North Africa and antislavery discourses among North African Muslim thinkers and theologians. These thinkers drew on Islamic texts to make their arguments against slavery, even if their efforts ultimately failed to affect prevailing social attitudes in these societies.[64] The ethics of slavery was a topic of vigorous debates between North African Muslim modernists and the traditionalist conservative thinkers at the turn of the nineteenth century. Modernists and reformers such as the Egyptian thinkers Muhammad Abduh and Rashid Rida tried to change social attitudes on slavery and servitude through innovative reinterpretation of Islamic law and scripture.[65] For example, the prominent nineteenth-century Muslim reformist in Egypt, Abd al-Rahman al-Kawakibi, condemned the Ottoman government for its noncommittal approach to the suppression of the slave trade and urged European powers to increase pressure on the Ottomans to stop what remained of the traffic.[66]

The push for the formal abolition of slavery that began with individuals and organized group campaigns eventually involved bilateral government negotiations, diplomatic pressures and the rise of antislavery in foreign policy. Beginning from the 1840s, the British government engaged in wide-ranging consultations with Ottoman

---

[64] Amal N. Ghazal, "Debating Slavery and Abolition in the Arab Middle East," in *Slavery, Islam and Diaspora*, Behnaz A. Mirzai, Ismael Musah Montana and Paul E. Lovejoy, eds. (Trenton, NJ: Africa World Press, 2009), 139–154.

[65] William Gervase Clarence-Smith, *Islam and the Abolition of Slavery* (Oxford: Oxford University Press, 2006), 205 and 218.

[66] Ghazal, "Debating Slavery and Abolition in the Arab Middle East," 146–148.

leaders to set up treaties to prohibit the slave trade from Africa and the Caucasus. In this task, British consuls were aided by an active international abolitionist community that consisted of organizations such as the British and Foreign Antislavery Society that reported on violations of the prohibition by Ottoman subjects. Abolitionist campaigners documented cases in their diaries and published stories in British and other European newspapers.[67] These efforts did not always end slavery or bring freedom for those already enslaved. The trade in slaves across the Indian Ocean continued well into the late nineteenth century, while struggles for emancipation and the suppression of practices of slavery and unfree labor within Africa continued into the early twentieth century. In most cases, abolition meant only the emancipation of particular classes of enslaved Africans. Many other forms of slavery and unfree labor practices such as indentured servitude and pawnage continued to be tolerated. Legal abolition also did not mandate the social integration of former slaves, many of whom continued to live on the margins of society with limited rights and opportunities.

Antislavery and Colonialism

Antislavery intersects in several ways with the imposition of colonial rule in Africa. Antislavery provided an important legitimizing rationale for colonialism and became part of the "inter-imperial repertoire of idiom and imaginaries of colonial rule."[68] Eradicating the slave trade and granting freedom to those enslaved was a declared motivation of many early European adventurers, missionaries and colonists. Atlantic slavery and the movement to abolish it marked the beginning of Europe's conquest and colonization of Africa, provoking what became known as the scramble for Africa and one of the most pernicious land grabs in human history. Here we confront another paradox of rights discourse within antislavery. Nineteenth-century missionary and humanitarian activism that rallied public support against slavery also provided moral justification for colonization, which ultimately denied

---

[67] Ehud Toledano, "Abolition and Anti-Slavery in the Ottoman Empire: A Case to Answer?," in *A Global History of Anti-Slavery Politics in the Nineteenth Century*, Mulligan and Bric, eds. (Hampshire: Palgrave Macmillan, 2013), 119.

[68] Amalia Ribi Forclaz, *Humanitarian Imperialism: The Politics of Anti-Slavery Activism, 1880–1940* (Oxford: Oxford University Press, 2015), 1.

millions of Africans their right to self-determination. Abolition
featured prominently in the rhetoric of European colonial powers
during the partitioning of the continent. The clearest expression of
this is the antislavery resolution contained in the General Act signed
by European powers at the Berlin Conference of 1884–1885. At the
conference, which formalized the scramble for Africa, European states
committed themselves to ending slavery and to the international prohibition of the slave trade throughout their respective spheres. European powers reiterated the antislavery commitments at the Brussels
Conference of 1889–1890, resulting in the Brussels Act, which was the
first far-reaching international agreement against the slave trade on
land and sea. The Act bound the contracting states to suppressing
slave trading and repatriating freed slaves.

The Berlin and Brussels Acts provided an international legal foundation for humanitarian action to suppress the slave trade. Although
the primary goal of these treaties was to promote the political and
economic interests of the contracting European powers, they also
outlined the humanitarian obligations of colonizing states under international law. In this sense, antislavery went hand in hand with the
notion of the "civilizing mission" in providing the legitimizing foundation for colonial rule. This connection between antislavery and the
civilizing mission of Empires is also evident in the General Act of the
Berlin Conference, which bound the contracting European powers to
the suppression of slavery while simultaneously "instructing the
natives and bringing home to them the blessings of *civilization.*"[69]

The suppression of slavery provided the main justification for King
Leopold's claim to the territory of the Congo, over which he gained
unfettered personal control with the creation of the Congo Free State
in 1884. King Leopold positioned himself as both an agent for the
abolition of the slave trade and the harbinger of civilization to the
Congo. By presenting himself as a philanthropist striving to abolish
the "Arab slave trade in Africa," Leopold successfully campaigned
to get other world powers to recognize his territorial claim to the
Congo. Leopold's rule turned out to be one of the most brutal colonial
regimes in Africa. His rule instituted a coercive labor scheme that
contemporary critics widely denounced as slavery. In the quest
to maximize economic benefits accruing from rubber production,

---

[69] General Act of the Berlin Conference, Article 6.

Leopold's agents perpetrated grave atrocities against the people of the Congo. His regime ruthlessly enforced a quota system for rubber production that involved widespread killing, torture and mutilations. Eyewitness reports tell of massacres and accounts of soldiers ordered to collect human body parts to serve as proof of disciplinary punishment and executions. Leopold held the view that his humanitarian desire excused the conduct of his agents, describing Belgians who had lost their loved ones colonizing the Congo as martyrs.

As with the earlier Atlantic antislavery campaigns, the accounts of missionaries and conscientious individuals eventually brought the atrocities of Leopold's rule to world attention. Visitors to the Congo such as the African American historian and journalist George Washington Williams exposed the violence and exploitation of Leopold's rule in the Congo.[70] The most prominent figure in the efforts to bring global attention to the atrocities of King Leopold's rule in the Congo was E. D. Morel, a British journalist who co-founded the Congo Reform Association (CRA) in 1904. Morel's declared goal was to stir the conscience of the world to confront the atrocities of Leopold's rule in the Congo. Along with his colleagues in the CRA, he mounted a global campaign against Leopold's regime by drawing attention to its exceptional brutality. Morel publicized these atrocities through newspaper articles, books and pamphlets that included graphic photographs of mutilated African bodies.

Morel deployed the language of rights quite extensively in his campaign against the atrocities in the Congo. One of his campaign publications was titled *A Memorial on Native Rights in the Land and Its Fruits in the Congo Territories Annexed by Belgium*. In it, Morel asserted that the "rights of the natives to their land and produce of their own soil has been taken away from them and vested in aliens living thousands of miles away."[71] Sustained campaigns, combined with the resulting public outrage, ultimately pressured governments in Europe and the United States to intervene to end King Leopold's unfettered rule in the Congo. In some respect, Morel and the CRA pioneered the advocacy techniques of "naming and shaming" oppressive regimes

[70] John Hope Franklin, *George Washington Williams: A Biography* (Durham: Duke University Press, 1998), 206.
[71] Edmund Dene Morel, *A Memorial on Native Rights in the Land and Its Fruits in the Congo Territories Annexed by Belgium* (London: Edward Hughes, 1908), 8.

and mobilizing global public opinion against them – a technique that later human rights activists would adopt.

***

The use of antislavery as an alibi for the imposition of colonial rule and exploitation at the turn of the nineteenth century was not unique to the Congo. The suppression of the slave trade in Africa was central to legitimizing British, French and German colonial conquest and expansion. In German East Africa, rhetoric against the slave trade brought various interest groups together, forging a powerful pro-expansionist collaboration between the government, commercial interests and Christian churches.[72] The abolition of slavery also set the stage for the imposition of colonial rule in Algeria and much of West Africa where French abolitionism became linked with Republican colonialism and assimilationist policies. In Algeria, the 1848 French law that prescribed financial compensation for slave owners as an incentive for abolition was quickly followed by another law integrating Algeria into a wider imperial community of French departments. In British East Africa, antislavery went hand in hand with a colonizing agenda, starting with Zanzibar where the sultan came under British pressure to stop the slave trade. This followed an 1822 treaty that abolished the Omani slave trade and gave British antislavery naval squadrons the right to patrol the Indian Ocean and secure trade. This treaty provided Britain with a military and political foothold for colonial expansionism into East Africa. Stopping the slave trade was also central to missionary and colonial incursion into Buganda.

The discourse of antislavery persisted well into the colonial period. Humanitarians, activists and emancipated slaves used abolitionist language to draw attention to the continued social exclusion of former slaves and the enduring stigma of slave origins. Africans also invoked abolitionist language to tackle the starkly unequal power relations of colonial governments and to transform partisan political interests into a moral problem that demanded attention.[73] This prompted renewed post-abolition international antislavery campaigns. Following reports of slave raiding along the Ethiopian borderlands, antislavery

---

[72] Jan-Georg Deutsch, *Emancipation Without Abolition in German East Africa 1884–1914* (Athens: Ohio University Press, 2006), 244–245.

[73] Derek Peterson, "Introduction: Abolitionism and Political Thought in Britain and East Africa," in *Abolitionism and Imperialism in Britain, Africa, and the Atlantic*, Derek Peterson, ed. (Athens: Ohio University Press, 2010), 1.

campaigners under the auspices of the Antislavery Society pressed for the League of Nations to investigate the allegations. The League subsequently established a Slavery Commission in 1924.

Antislavery within the League of Nations and post–World War I internationalism is analogous to what human rights became within the UN and the post–World War II international order. When the League's Slavery Commission commenced its work, countries made strenuous efforts to deny the existence of slavery in their territories and publicly denounced the existence of slavery elsewhere. Like human rights in the post–World War II era, antislavery in the 1920s was a measure of national respectability and the legitimacy of humanitarian intervention. All the members of the Slavery Commission played the "antislavery card" to further their national geopolitical interests. The French and the Italians demanded that the Commission endorse their military campaigns against the Tuaregs in the Sahara on the grounds that they were attacking slave raiders, while Britain demanded recognition of its efforts to repatriate fugitive slaves.[74] The work of the Slavery Commission led to the adoption of the Slavery Convention of 1926, which bound signatory states to the suppression of slavery in all its forms.

Apart from international antislavery pressures, colonial officials also faced domestic agitation demanding the full social inclusion of former slaves. Although legal abolition provided opportunities for those enslaved to escape servitude, it did not protect them from discrimination or mandate their equal treatment. In many communities, former slaves and their descendants continued to be treated as social outcasts and second-class citizens. Under such circumstances, former slaves took it upon themselves to mount concerted campaigns to redress the prejudice and social stigmatization that they continued to suffer in spite of legal abolition. In 1922, settlements of former slaves in eastern Nigeria, locally called *Ohu*, launched an insurrection to force the freeborn community to permit them to participate in the social and political life of the community.[75] These struggles continued over several decades. In court cases and petitions to the colonial officials,

[74] Suzanne Miers, "Slavery and the Slave Trade as International Issues," in *Slavery and Colonial Rule in Africa*, Martin Klein and Suzanne Miers, eds. (Portland: Frank Cass, 1999), 27.

[75] Carolyn Brown, "Testing the Boundaries of Marginality: Twentieth-Century Slavery and Emancipation Struggles in Nkanu, Northern Igboland 1920–29," *Journal of African History* (1996): 37.

activist campaigners demanded that the government go beyond the legal abolition of slavery to enforce non-discrimination and equal rights for former slaves and their descendants. Between 1935 and 1945, a group of Igbo former slaves organized themselves under the name Idumuashaba Family Union to demand full social integration. In protracted court cases, petitions and public protests, they drew public attention to the prejudices and discrimination against them within the larger community. They demanded the government's intervention to restore their "rights of full citizenship."[76] In one petition, they stated: "We are treated most disdainfully as outcasts, and even that condition is aggravated by our exclusion from the exercise of civic rights as well as the enjoyment of our native privileges and social equality." They pressured the government to secure and establish their "freedom and rights as free people unencumbered by limitations."[77]

The standard response of colonial governments to these demands for equal rights was that, having already abolished slavery, the state could not go further to decree social equality. As historian Don Ohadike has noted, the post–World War II problem of slavery in this part of Africa was not one of emancipation but of incomplete assimilation. The government's position was that there was nothing it could do for those who were legally free to leave the communities that kept them in social bondage but who, in practice, could not or would not do so. No law or state policy could free them from their social marginalization or make them enjoy all the rights and privileges of other sections of society.[78] In some parts of Africa the struggle to achieve full social inclusion of citizens with slave ancestry would continue well into the era of independence, constitutional democracy and universal human rights.

★★★

The political and socioeconomic transformations ushered in by anti-slavery and colonial conquest in late nineteenth-century Africa

---

[76] Nigeria National Archives, Ibadan (hereinafter NNAI), Ben. Prof. 203/ 252. Petition by Nicholas Nwaukpele and others on behalf of the Idumuashaba Family Union to the Senior Resident of Benin Province, March 3, 1937. For a detailed discussion of these petitions and court cases, see Bonny Ibhawoh, *Imperialism and Human Rights: Colonial Discourses of Rights and Liberties in African History* (Albany: State University of New York Press, 2007), 128–132.

[77] NNAI, Ben. Prof. 203/ 252. Petition by Nicholas Nwaukpele and others.

[78] Don Ohadike, "The Decline of Slavery among the Igbo People," in *The End of Slavery in Africa*, Miers and Roberts, eds. (Madison: University of Wisconsin Press, 1988), 454.

marked a period of simultaneous expansion and contraction of individual and collective rights and liberties. Abolition and emancipation allowed for more inclusive societies, extending in principle, if not always in practice, certain basic rights and personal liberties to those enslaved. With antislavery, the freedom from enslavement, a right previously restricted to rulers, powerful elites and untarnished insiders, expanded to include millions of enslaved and vulnerable people. In this sense, antislavery was a defining movement toward rights inclusion in Africa. However, as we have seen, antislavery also marked a period of transition defined by the loss of African autonomy following colonial conquest and expansion. In many African communities, this meant the erosion of the collective right to self-determination as European authorities ousted or marginalized indigenous ruling elites through conquest, intimidation or deception. In the name of antislavery, many African leaders were killed, deposed or exiled. Using present-day human rights standards, such political usurpations may be justified as acts of humanitarian intervention to restrain sovereign powers in defense of individual rights. However, in some cases, as in King Leopold's Congo, antislavery was merely an excuse for colonial subjugation and economic exploitation.

The history of antislavery in Africa thus illustrates the complexities and paradoxes of the human rights story. As a rights movement, antislavery had the greatest impact on expanding individual liberties and extending personal freedoms to the greatest number of people. However, it also provided a powerful and compelling alibi for conquest, repression and subjugation. This restricted collective rights and liberties. As I show in the next chapter, colonialism and the loss of indigenous autonomy had wide-ranging implications for the political, social and economic rights of most Africans in the twentieth century.

4

—

Natives and Colonists

Equal rights for all *civilized men* south of the Zambezi.
— Slogan of Cecil Rhodes's British South African League[1]

Among the world's problems today is the appeal which goes from the heart of the African to be accorded certain rights which are common to humanity.

— Casley Hayford, 1923[2]

Colonialism shaped the history of human rights in Africa in definitive ways. The human rights dimensions of Africa's colonial experience manifest across multiple registers, from the legitimizing rights discourses of colonial rulers to the oppositional rights struggles of colonized subjects. The nexus between colonialism and rights relates not only to the scope of imperial power and its transformative impact on rights, but also to political and social struggles that reflect indigenous agency and reveal the limits of imperial power. We can imagine the connection between colonialism and human rights on at least three levels. The first centers on the origins and rationale of European colonialism, including notions of the "civilizing mission" and "the white man's burden" that fundamentally shaped ideas and conditions

---

[1] This was a revised version of the nineteenth-century slogan of the League, "Equal rights for every white man south of the Zambezi."

[2] Casley Hayford, "Presidential Address to the National Congress of British West Africa, January 1923," in *African Aims and Attitudes: Selected Documents*, Martin Minogue and Judith Molloy, eds. (London: Cambridge University Press, 1979), 17.

of "native" rights and liberties. This was the view, genuinely believed by some and used as an alibi by others, that colonizers had a responsibility to spread the "benefits" of European civilization to indigenous peoples under their control. These benefits included European Christianity as well as European liberal traditions of personal liberty and the "rights of man." The extension of certain liberal rights to colonized peoples was a key justification for European colonialism and became a measure of modernist progress.

As we have seen in the preceding chapter, European colonial interventions were often justified on the basis of antislavery, the emancipation of those enslaved and the promotion of legitimate trade. The language of freedom, free enterprise, liberty and civilization characterized many of the treaty agreements signed between the European colonial powers and African chiefs in the early colonial period. European authorities saw their role in terms of promoting the liberties of colonized people under their influence through active intervention in local politics. They rationalized military conquest and violent "pacification" campaigns against indigenous rulers partly on the grounds of protecting the liberties of European and indigenous subjects living within their colonial domains. Political and social interventions were sometimes framed in terms of protecting "native rights" and the welfare of indigenous peoples.

The second link between colonialism and human rights is the record of wide-ranging human rights violations by colonial governments. Colonial rule was founded on inequality between colonizers and colonized, creating regimes of domination and exclusion that restricted the rights and liberties of colonial subjects.[3] Ultimately, colonial rule meant the loss of indigenous self-government as well as the loss of socioeconomic autonomy. In particular, colonial labor policies curtailed the economic freedoms and social liberties of indigenous people. Thousands of Africans were coercively expelled from their lands to allow for European settlements, while African labor was tightly controlled to serve overarching metropolitan economic interests. Nevertheless, colonial subjects were entitled to certain rights

---

[3] James Silk, "Traditional Culture and the Prospects of Human Rights in Africa," in *Human Rights in Africa: Cross-Cultural Perspectives*, Abdulahi Ahmed An-Na'im and Francis M. Deng, eds. (Washington, DC: The Brookings Institution, 1990), 292–293, and Francis M. Deng, "A Cultural Approach to Human Rights among the Dinka," in ibid., 280–281.

mandated by the underlying liberal promise of the civilizing mission. These rights were constrained by the limitations of colonial socio-economic and political apparatuses. However, in some cases, colonial legal regimes and judicial processes expanded rights for previously marginalized groups such as women and ethnic minorities. For example, women took advantage of the right to divorce enshrined in colonial marriage laws to escape patriarchal control and forced marriages and to promote their social and economic interests. Colonial law also provided the framework for constitutional bill of rights and other legal rights protections introduced as part of late colonial political reforms.

The third link between colonialism and human rights centers on the demise of colonialism. Twentieth-century anti-colonial movements drew on an emergent lexicon of universal human rights to strengthen longstanding demands for independence and self-determination. In contrast to the discourse of limited "native rights" deployed within colonial officialdom, anti-colonial rights discourse laid claim to universality and inalienability. The language of universal human rights that gained prominence in the post–World War II era was deployed extensively by anti-colonial activists to challenge colonial rule. The central premise was that colonized peoples were entitled to the full range of universal human rights and not just to certain limited rights suited to their subordinate status. Anti-colonial activists in Africa took advantage of the new emphasis on the right to self-determination espoused in international documents such as the Atlantic Charter, the United Nations Charter and the Universal Declaration of Human Rights to demand independence. In response to anti-colonial pressures, colonial authorities introduced tentative legal and policy reforms aimed at protecting human rights in their colonies.

Some scholars have sought to explain contemporary human rights conditions in Africa in terms of the legacies of colonial repression and authoritarianism. In law making and the administration of justice, the primary consideration of colonial authorities was not the protection of the rights and liberties of the colonized, but the maintenance of social order on a scale conducive to colonial interests. Thus, several political and legal constraints on the exercise of human rights that characterize the post-colonial African state were inherited from colonial rule.[4]

---

[4] Issa Shivji, *The Concept of Human Rights in Africa* (London: Council for the Development of Economic and Social Research in Africa-Codesria, 1989), 102.

Critics have compared the human rights movement to colonial projects. Contemporary international human rights doctrine is said to have an inherently colonial dimension since it involves challenges to the practices, and sometimes even sovereignty, of particular regions in the name of universal standards deriving from, and largely enforced by, the West. In the case of Africa, such asymmetrical moral discourse has its roots in the literal history of colonialism.[5]

How do we address these complex intersections between colonialism and human rights? For one, the story of human rights under colonial rule is not a linear narrative of liberal progress and rights expansion, or simply a narrative of imperial subjugation and rights violations. It also cannot be understood as a homogeneous African story. Rights discourses and struggles varied widely across the continent, and were largely dependent on the nature of local encounters with colonial policies and practices. As with other aspects of the imperial enterprise, colonial discourses of rights reflected a tension over the making of the modern African subject. This played out in two antithetical registers: the register of *modernist individualism* and the register of *customary collectivism*.[6] The former had to do with the construction by European colonists of the "civilized" African subject and his or her equivocal status as a citizen with guaranteed citizenship rights. The latter, which defined people by virtue of their membership in "customary" political communities, concerned the attribution of limited collective rights to colonial subjects. The ascription of primordiality and primitivism to certain groups of Africans justified the restrictions imposed on their rights and liberties. The coexistence of these two registers of rights laid a practical basis for the material and political subordination of Africans under colonial rule. While promising to incorporate and enfranchise indigenous people, it afforded colonizers a means to legitimate and naturalize their command over colonized peoples. Paradoxically, colonialism also created the "rights

[5] Makau Mutua, *Human Rights: A Political and Cultural Critique* (Philadelphia: University of Pennsylvania Press, 2002), 3.

[6] Others have made similar distinctions. John Comaroff and Jean Comaroff refer to *radical individualism and primal sovereignty*, while Mahmood Mamdani refers to *Citizen and Subject*. John L. Comaroff and Jean Comaroff, *Of Revelation and Revolution: The Dialectics of Modernity on a South African Frontier*, vol. 2 (Chicago: University of Chicago Press, 1997), 369–370; Mahmood Mamdani, *Citizen and Subject: Contemporary Africa and the Legacy of Late Colonialism* (Princeton: Princeton University Press), 1996.

spaces" in which colonized peoples could refigure themselves, mobilize and articulate their struggles.[7] Using the analytical framework of modernist individualism and customary collectivism, this chapter offers a wide-ranging exploration of human rights in the colonial state, from discourses of native rights within colonial officialdom to the impact of colonial rule on objective human rights conditions. This chapter also examines how colonialism transformed understandings of rights at a discursive level and, at a practical level, restricted or expanded the scope of rights enjoyed by individuals and groups within the colonial state.

The Civilizing Mission and Native Rights

European colonists claimed a rights agenda that was inherent in the notions of the "civilizing mission" and the "white man's burden." This was the view that colonizers had a responsibility and obligation to spread the benefits of European civilization to colonized peoples. These "benefits" included the doctrines of Christianity alongside enlightened liberal political institutions and social values. The argument for extending European liberal rights traditions to colonized people proved to be a powerful justification for Empire. In many parts of Africa, colonial rule was founded on the redemptive goals of anti-slavery and the broader agenda of promoting the welfare of native subjects. The discourse of the civilizing mission and imperial trustee-ship was tied to the discourse of rights and liberties. The British colonial administrator Frederick Lugard outlined the correlation between trusteeship and rights in terms of the dual mandate of British rule in Africa. "The British empire," he stated, had a dual mission for "*liberty* and self-development." These could best be "secured to the native population by leaving them free to manage their own affairs through their own rulers, proportionally to their degree of advancement, under the guidance of the staff, and subject to the law and policy of the administration."[8]

Inherent in this notion of the civilizing mission was a cosmopolitan universality that was constantly in tension with the racialized otherness

[7] Comaroff, *Of Revelation and Revolution*, vol. 2, 370.
[8] F. D. Lugard, *The Dual Mandate in British Tropical Africa* (Edinburgh: Blackwood, 1922), 94.

of those colonized. The self-justifying moral principles of the civilizing mission would constantly be questioned by the harsh realities of Africans' subordinate status as subjects of empire. The idea of the civilizing mission gestured toward imperial inclusivity. The liberal promise of Britain's civilizing mission, or the republican ideas behind France's *mission civilisatrice*, depended as much on visions of a shared humanity as on a discourse of racial difference. These notions captured the essence of what may be termed the "colonial contract." The metropole's claim to ownership of colonial land, resources and labor was predicated on the corresponding duty to uphold "native rights" and to promote the welfare and development of colonial inhabitants.

The paternalistic impulse of colonial civilizing mission is evident in the General Act of the Berlin Conference of 1884 by which European powers negotiated the political partitioning of West Africa. The Act referred to the "development of trade and civilization" in Africa, and declared the goal of civilizing African natives. In the age of the scramble for Africa, European colonial powers did not think of Africans as sovereign peoples with inherent rights of self-determination. The Berlin Act rooted sovereignty not just in ethnicity or nationality but in race and the domination of Africans by colonists dispatched from European metropoles. The logic of the civilizing mission implied that at some point in the distant future, Africans would become developed enough to exercise sovereignty, with the result that the political map of Africa would resemble that of Europe.[9]

To this end, the Berlin Act outlined the obligations of signatory European powers to Africans within their acquired territories. All the powers exercising sovereign influence in Africa committed themselves "to watch over the preservation of the native tribes, and to care for the improvement of the conditions of their moral and material well-being." They were obligated to "protect and favor all religious, scientific or charitable institutions which aim at instructing the natives and bringing home to them the blessings of civilization."[10] These goals of the civilizing mission were affirmed decades later in the 1919 Covenant of the League of Nations, which declared as a "sacred trust of

---

[9] Eric Weitz, "From the Vienna to the Paris System: International Politics and the Entangled Histories of Human Rights, Forced Deportations, and Civilizing Missions," *The American Historical Review*, 113, 5 (2008): 1321.

[10] General Act of the Berlin Conference 1884, Article 6 in E. Hartslet, *The Map of Africa by Treaty* (New York: Routledge, 2012), 473.

civilization" the well-being and development of peoples "not yet able to stand by themselves under the strenuous conditions of the modern world."[11]

The rhetoric of civilization and humanitarianism also featured prominently in official colonial discourse. As I showed in Chapter 3, the notion of the civilizing mission was featured alongside the language of humanitarianism within antislavery and the early European colonial incursion into Africa. Antislavery humanitarianism rested partly on the view that colonial rule was the only way of effectively protecting the populations of Africa from the scourge of Atlantic and indigenous slavery. Antislavery treaties such as the Brussels Act of 1890, which also provided the legal framework for Africa's colonization, were precursors of the international community's efforts to deploy its collective strength to protect both individual and group rights.[12] International treaties regularizing African colonization offer the closest indication of what may be considered the international legal obligations of colonializing European powers to protecting the rights and liberties of colonized Africans. Indeed, humanitarian activists of the period interpreted these provisions as imposing both moral and legal obligations on colonizing powers even if the signatories did not.

In their campaigns against the atrocities of King Leopold's rule in the Congo and colonial abuses against indigenous people elsewhere in the continent, individuals such as Edmund Morel and humanitarian organizations such as the Aborigines Protection Society (APS) often appealed to the legal obligations of the Great Powers under international treaties. Under the leadership of Fox Bourne, the APS actively promoted aboriginal rights and welfare. Morel's criticisms of the Congo Free State, for example, stressed the rights of Africans living under colonial rule. His campaign against King Leopold's rule in the Congo centered not only on the regime's brutality but also on violations of the Belgian monarch's obligations under international law to protect the rights and welfare to the natives under his rule. He wrote in 1908:

---

[11] League of Nations, "Covenant of the League of Nations, 1919." Available at www
.unhcr.org/refworld/docid/3dd8b9854.html. Accessed June 28, 2016.

[12] Mairi MacDonald, "Lord Vivian's Tears: The Moral Hazards of Humanitarian Intervention," in *The Emergence of Humanitarian Intervention: Ideas and Practice from the Nineteenth Century to the Present*, Fabian Klose, ed. (Cambridge: Cambridge University Press, 2015), 112.

The appropriation by the governing authorities of the Congo of the land's natural wealth, on the plea that the land possesses no native owners, stands out as a violation of native law, of *native rights*, of international law, and of elementary morality, without precedent in contemporary history, and the Great powers, I submit, cannot allow that policy to be perpetuated by the Belgian Government.[13]

★★★

To be sure, the goal of the civilizing mission was not necessarily to remake Africans in the image of the Europeans but to make "perfected natives." The perfected native required by the colonizing project was a willing, grateful and thoroughly domesticated worker imbued with egalitarian values and a limited scope of rights and liberties suited to his station.[14] Herein lays the great paradox of the colonial project. The mandate to civilize the native required the extension of certain rights to the colonies. In this sense, the civilizing mission suggested the extension of certain rights and liberties to the colonized. But this had to be done in a way that did not fundamentally disrupt the indigenous customary order since a notion of universal rights would have unsettled the rigidly hierarchical social foundations of the colonial order from the very beginning. It meant that Africans could not be availed of the same range of rights and liberties as their European colonizers. What was required for "native rights" was a supple, yet hegemonic notion of the universal, one that would require constant tinkering and reinterpretation. If the language of civilization and modernity represented a universalist fulcrum of Empire and rights inclusivity, the language of race, tribe and custom framed the exclusion of Africans from certain rights regimes that was essential to maintaining imperial hierarchies of rule and difference.[15]

The mandate of the civilizing mission also meant wide variation in the scope of rights and liberties Africans enjoyed, depending on the level of civilization that colonial officials ascribed to them as individuals and communities. For example, in 1919 the highest court of appeal in

[13] Edmund Dene Morel, *A Memorial on Native Rights in the Land and its Fruits in the Congo Territories Annexed by Belgium* (London: Edward Hughes, 1908), 12. My emphasis.

[14] Ann Laura Stoler, *Along the Archival Grain: Epistemic Anxieties and Colonial Common Sense* (Princeton: Princeton University Press, 2009), 105.

[15] Bonny Ibhawoh, "Confronting Colonial Otherness: The Judicial Committee of the Privy Council and the Limits of Imperial Legal Universalism," in *Colonial Exchanges: Political Theory and the Agency of the Colonized*, Burke A. Hendrix and Deborah Baumgold, eds. (Manchester: Manchester University Press, 2017).

the British Empire, the Privy Council, held in a Southern Rhodesian case that indigenous land rights were contingent on the relative level of civilization of each African tribe. The case dealt with the legal status of African claims to land occupied by the British South African Company. "Some tribes are so low in the scale of social organization," the English Lords of the Privy Council held, "that their usages and conceptions of rights and duties are not to be reconciled with the institutions or the legal ideas of civilized society ... It would be idle to impute to such people some shadow of the rights known to our law and then to transmute it into the substance of transferable rights of property as we know them." The Court recognized, however, that there were other African communities whose legal conceptions, though differently developed, are hardly less precise than British conceptions. Once these native legal conceptions are studied and understood, they are "no less foreseeable than rights arising under English law."[16]

This ruling by the Privy Council pertaining to native land title offers insights into how colonial authorities (in this case, British judicial officers) approached questions of native rights. It shows that even within imperial officialdom, there was no singular approach dealing with the rights of indigenous people. Since all natives were not considered equally uncivilized, the scope of individual and collective rights they could claim within the colonial state varied accordingly. This reinforces my point that the story of human rights in colonial Africa cannot be a monolithic narrative. Human rights discourses under colonial rule were ultimately contingent on a variety of factors, perhaps the most significant of which were colonial attitudes on indigenous laws and customs. Rights struggles under colonial rule also varied widely, reflecting the tumult of political transitions and the dynamics of social and economic change.

Imperial Obligations

What legal and moral rights obligations did colonizers have toward colonized subjects? Apart from the mandate of the civilizing mission, colonial rights obligations were founded on treaty provisions, which defined the terms of European political and economic control over African territories. Many nineteenth-century peace and friendship

---

[16] *Re Southern Rhodesia* [1919] Appeal Cases 211 at 233–234, per Lord Summer.

treaties between European colonists and African rulers centered on the abolition of the slave trade, freedom of trade and the propagation of Christianity. By the 1880s when the scramble among European powers for African territories had reached a fever pitch, these treaties began to demand exclusive European access to economic resources and greater European political control. These treaties outlined the political and social obligations of European colonizers toward indigenous people. The language of freedom, free trade, liberty and civilization characterized many of the treaty agreements. British and French colonial officials, for example, saw their role partly in terms of promoting the liberties of Africans under their influence through active intervention in local politics. Building on nineteenth-century abolitionist rhetoric, they justified their military campaigns against uncooperative communities and the overthrow of indigenous rulers partly on the grounds of protecting the freedoms and liberties of Europeans and natives living within their acquired colonial territories.

Britain spelled out its social obligations to its African subjects to include the protection of their liberties in the "free enjoyment of their possessions." These obligations were made clear in several official documents emanating from both the Colonial Office in London and the various colonial governments. Late nineteenth-century letters patents and royal instructions to colonial governors outlined the function of the government toward indigenous people in newly acquired territories. The British Foreign Jurisdiction Act of 1890, which was reproduced in many colonial constitutions in Africa, gave colonial officials the mandate to protect "natives in their persons and in the free enjoyment of their possession and by all lawful means prevent and restrain all violence and injustice which may in any manner be practiced against them."[17] There were also declared commitments to uphold the dignity of the native as well as to promote equality and fairness in dealings with native subjects. These colonial laws and policy declarations gave officials wide powers to intervene in various aspects of the political and social life of colonial subjects. But they also placed limits on the extent of state restrictions to the basic rights and liberties of indigenous people.[18]

---

[17] Article 11 of the Foreign Jurisdiction Act 1890. Reprinted in *Instructions to the Governor, Northern Rhodesia. Government Gazette, No. 211*, 1924, 12.

[18] Bonny Ibhawoh, *Imperialism and Human Rights: Colonial Discourses of Rights and Liberties in African History* (Albany: State University of New York Press, 2007), 56.

To be sure, the notion of "native rights" differed in scope and content from human rights as we understand them today. References to native rights in early colonial discourse had specific meanings that are reflected in writings of the nineteenth-century British ethnologist Mary Kingsley. This is the notion that Africans were entitled to certain basic rights and liberties that they could exercise within their "racial" limits.[19] Though unsuited to European ways, the African had qualities worth preserving and the innate ability to improve his own condition with minimal interference from missionaries, merchants and colonial trustees. Europeans were superior and rightly placed as colonial overlords, but not justified in denying Africans of their culture or humanity.[20] This thinking produced a specific moral and legal discourse of native rights.

French colonialism exposed a similar discourse of native rights. In theory, the French administrative policy of assimilation was aimed at incorporating colonized people into French culture as part of the broader *mission civilisatrice*. At a time of ascendant liberalism in France, Republican elites maintained that colonized peoples in Africa and Asia should be freed from the material and moral want that had once oppressed the French nation. As early as 1792, a revolutionary decree proclaimed: "all men, without distinction of color, living in the French colonies are French citizens and enjoy all the rights assured in the constitution." This informed a prevalent view within French officialdom that France had an obligation to extend its republican principles of liberty, equality and fraternity to its overseas territories. The assumption was that colonized peoples were still to evolve within their own cultures, but they were to do so in a way that respected the *universal rights* of all individuals. This thinking, which influenced French policy in realms as different as education and labor, convinced committed French democrats and republicans that colonialism was advancing the cause of human rights and liberty.

Assimilation had some meaning in the old colonies in Africa, the Four Communes, but most administrators did not believe in it and were not influenced by it. In education and labor, universal rights ideals became important only after World War II. Assimilation policy

---

[19] John Flint, "Mary Kingsley: A Reassessment," *Journal of African History*, 4 (1963): 99–104.
[20] Philip Serge Zachernuk, *Colonial Subjects: An African Intelligentsia and Atlantic Ideas* (Charlottesville: University Press of Virginia, 2000), 63.

was premised on the selective assimilation of an elite group of Africans who had learned French, demonstrated loyalty to the French administration and submitted themselves to the precepts of French law and the Civil Code. Assimilated Africans, official discourse promised, would be included in the French family of citizens with a full complement of rights regardless of race or ethnicity. Conversely, those who failed to meet these criteria would remain *sujets*, with "duties instead of rights."[21] Rights, in this sense, were clearly not considered inherent and inalienable humanistic entitlements but, rather, entitlements to be earned through civic obligations and duties.

Violence and Pacification

In recounting episodes of colonial violence and atrocities, some historians have been cautioned that their task is to provide accounts of empirical source material and historical context. The presumption is that there is little analytical purpose or scholarly value in trying to measure the levels of cruelty of imperial powers by counting the dead from colonial wars, repression and other forms of violence. Although we need to know who such victims were, and how many there were, a comparative history of colonial violence should not become some polemical league table of barbarity.[22] Rather, the focus should be on trying to explain why recourse to extreme violence seemed not only logical, but defensible, even ethically imperative, to those who authorized or performed it.[23] Seeing colonial violence through the lens of human rights requires that we pay as much attention to the suffering of victims as to the motivations of perpetrators.

Colonial rule clearly did not live up to the liberal and republican ideals put forward by colonial officials. In realms as diverse as education, labor and trade, colonial policies often fell short of the rights ideals set out by European colonizers. Colonial governments promised native rights, but these were often undermined from the beginning by official policies and actions. The violence and brutality that characterized colonial conquest provides a fitting starting point

---

[21] Alice Conklin, *A Mission to Civilize: The Republican Idea of Empire in France and West Africa, 1895–1930* (Stanford: Stanford University Press, 1997), 166.

[22] Anderson, *Histories of the Hanged*, 6.

[23] Martin Thomas, *Fight or Flight, Britain, France, and the Roads from Empire* (Oxford: Oxford University Press, 2014), 7.

for examining human rights under colonial rule. In many parts of Africa, colonial rule was imposed through violence and coercion that restricted the rights and liberties that indigenous people enjoyed. Such colonial violence included the use of force to maintain orderly governance and economic control.[24] Violence was deployed to dominate, to resist domination and to create conditions for compromise.

Some of the most egregious cases of colonial violence and atrocities occurred under the rule of the Belgian King Leopold in the Congo and under German rule in South West Africa. The German military campaign of racial extermination and collective punishment against the Herero of South West Africa resulted in the death of an estimated 60,000 Herero and 10,000 Nama people between 1904 and 1908. Legal scholar Jeremy Sarkin has argued that the brutal German suppression of indigenous resistance amounted to genocide as legally defined at the time, making it the first genocide of the twentieth century.[25] The German colonial *Schutztruppe* (protection force) responsible for the genocide came armed not only with guns and bullets but also with a formal ideology of race. To Lieutenant General Lothar von Trotha, the commander of the German troops in South West Africa, the suppression of native revolt was part of an epic struggle between the races, a position he articulated in his writings with references to social Darwinist notions of the survival of the fittest.[26]

Other European powers also used military force to impose colonial rule. In 1858 Portuguese colonial authorities in Angola embarked on expansionist campaigns financed by hut taxes levied on the local population. Resentment toward this and other repressive policies led Africans to resist through sporadic rebellions, which were brutally suppressed in a cyclic pattern of violence that persisted in Portuguese colonies until the era of decolonization. The dictatorship that controlled Portugal for part of its imperial history had few scruples

---

[24] Toyin Falola, *Colonialism and Violence in Nigeria* (Bloomington: Indiana University Press, 2009), x.

[25] Jeremy Sarkin argues that although the term "genocide" entered usage in the 1940s, the concept of the crime was an internationally accepted violation at the turn of the twentieth century. Jeremy Sarkin-Hughes, *Colonial Genocide and Reparations Claims in the 21st Century: The Socio-Legal Context of Claims under International Law by the Herero against Germany for Genocide in Namibia, 1904–1908* (Westport: Praeger, 2009), 5. See also Jeremy Sarkin-Hughes, *Germany's Genocide of the Herero: Kaiser Wilhelm II, His General, His Settlers, His Soldiers* (Rochester: James Currey, 2011).

[26] Weitz, "From the Vienna to the Paris System," 1323.

about unleashing violence against indigenous people in the course of conquest and consolidation. This pattern of violent conquest and repression, perhaps most evident with German and Portuguese colonialism, also characterized colonial rule elsewhere in the continent.

This scale of colonial violence and what would be termed "gross human rights violations" today was not confined to nineteenth-century imperialism. The atrocities perpetrated in the British campaigns against the Mau Mau in Kenya and in the French war against the Algerian National Liberation Front (FLN) marked some of the most egregious human rights violations of the twentieth century. These conflicts were characterized by war crimes, repression policies, relocation measures and the use of torture and detention camps.[27] By operating within the framework of a state of emergency, British and French officials in each conflict created legal conditions for the unregulated use of force and violence that severely curtailed fundamental rights codified under domestic and international human rights regimes.[28] In Algeria, the French military command ruthlessly applied collective punishment to villages suspected of sheltering or supporting FLN guerrillas. Villagers in the Algerian countryside endured indiscriminate aerial bombardment in contravention of the Geneva Convention's provisions on the humane rules of war. French authorities also expanded the use of torture, which had been a feature of the colonial penal system. In a bid to curtail the influence of the FLN rebels in the rural areas, French officials initiated a program of concentrating large segments of the population, including whole villages, in camps under military supervision. Between 1957 and 1960, more than 2 million Algerians were removed from their villages in so-called regroupment programs. Algerians confined in these camps suffered deplorable living conditions and were denied their most basic liberties.

---

[27] For Kenya, see Caroline Elkins, *Imperial Reckoning: The Untold Story of Britain's Gulag in Kenya* (New York: Henry Holt, 2005); David Anderson, *Histories of the Hanged: The Dirty War in Kenya and the End of Empire* (New York: W. W. Norton, 2005); Wunyabari Maloba, *Mau Mau and Kenya: An Analysis of a Peasant Revolt* (Bloomington: Indiana University Press; 1998). For Algeria, see Alistair Horne, *A Savage War of Peace: Algeria 1954–1962* (London: Macmillan, 1977); Martin Evans, *Algeria: France's Undeclared War* (Oxford: Oxford University Press, 2012). For both conflicts, see Fabian Klose, *Human Rights in the Shadow of Colonial Violence: The Wars of Independence in Kenya and Algeria* (Philadelphia: University of Pennsylvania Press, 2013).

[28] Klose, *Human Rights in the Shadow of Colonial Violence*, 8.

It is estimated that the eight-year Algerian war of decolonization produced up to a million casualties.[29]

British campaigns against the Mau Mau in Kenya followed similar patterns. The crux of the eight-year insurgency was Kikuyu resistance against increasing economic marginalization amid white settler expansion, which deprived them of their traditional land holdings. British authorities responded to the rebellion with two parallel campaigns that included the use of emergency legislation, arbitrary detentions, torture and capital punishment. The first campaign was in the remote mountain forest of Kenya where security forces engaged in a long offensive against guerrilla insurgents. In the second campaign directed at a larger civilian enemy, the British and their African loyalists targeted many Kikuyu believed to be Mau Mau supporters or sympathizers (see Figure 4.1). Many native Kenyans spent several years in notorious barbed-wire enclosures and detention camps that have been described as the "British gulag."[30] Security forces used beatings, sexual assaults and other forms of torture during so-called screenings to extract information about the Mau Mau threat or to force detainees to renounce their allegiance to the insurgency. Historian Caroline Elkins has described these measures as part of a "murderous campaign to eliminate the Kikuyu people, a campaign that left tens of thousands, perhaps hundreds of thousands dead."[31] In 2012, a British court granted some surviving elderly victims the right to sue the government of the United Kingdom for the abuses they suffered during the conflict. The British government ultimately opted to settle the case and issued a formal apology, agreeing to pay nearly £20 million in damages to Kenyan claimants.

In these conflicts, the colonial state did not have a monopoly of violence. Atrocities were committed on all sides in the guerrilla warfare campaigns that brought colonial rule to a close. The most brutal of these conflicts – the Algerian and Kenyan insurgencies and the wars of liberation in the Portuguese colonies of Mozambique and Angola – were characterized by indiscriminate violence perpetrated by all sides. To make this claim is not to assert moral equivalence. Indeed, anti-colonial violence was often a reaction to institutional oppression and violence of the colonial state. Colonial conflicts such as the Algerian revolutionary war and the Mau Mau rebellion had

---

[29] Horne, *A Savage War of Peace*, 538.   [30] Anderson, *Histories of the Hanged*, 7.
[31] Elkins, *Imperial Reckoning*, xvi.

FIGURE 4.1 British army operations against the Mau Mau
Credit: Imperial War Museum

far-reaching consequences for international human rights. Both conflicts decisively influenced international debates about decolonization and the right to self-determination. The discourse of rights within the specific contexts of these decolonization struggles and the link with the post–World War II universal human rights movement is taken up in detail in the next chapter.

Land and Labor

Colonial land and labor policies had perhaps the most far-reaching social and economic impacts on the everyday lives of Africans. Some of the earliest rights struggles in colonial Africa concerned the ownership and control of land. Colonial rule often vested control of land and other resources in European authorities. At the core of these transformations were differing concepts held by rulers and the ruled on human relations with land. European and African conceptions of the relationship between people and land were fundamentally different. Colonial regimes pushed the notion of land as something that could be measured, plotted and delineated into units that became property to be subjected to rights assigned to holders. To be sure, comparable views of individual propertied land tenure and rights existed in some pre-colonial African communities such as the Kikuyu, who had a long-established system of private land holding. However, in most pre-colonial African societies, people were linked to land though membership in communities. The emphasis was on land *use* rights rather than absolute *ownership* rights.[32]

Although various colonial governments recognized indigenous codes of land tenure, most colonial legal regimes vested ultimate control of land in the state. Intent on rapid economic development through European enterprise, colonial governments tended to define African land rights as narrowly as possible and to recognize only land being used. This left large tracts of free land for European companies and settlers. Across Africa, new land tenure laws declared all lands to be public lands at the disposal of colonial administrators. In British and French colonies, the governor was empowered to grant land for a specified period. Given the importance of land as the subsistence base of indigenous economies, these changes in land ownership and control had broad social and political implications, engendering multifaceted contestations over land rights and ownership between colonial officials and Africans, between competing groups of European colonists and settlers, and among various groups of Africans. Competition over land was most intense in the settler colonies of eastern and southern Africa where there was more pressure on land for permanent occupation by Europeans. Under these circumstances, it was inevitable that colonial governments would impinge on the traditional land rights of natives even where they accepted an obligation to preserve existing rights and to recognize local custom.

In resisting unfavorable colonial land policies, Africans and their metropolitan allies drew on a language of rights anchored in the social

---

[32] Elizabeth Colson, "The Impact of the Colonial Period on the Definition of Land Rights," in *Colonialism in Africa 1870–1960*, vol. 3: *Profiles of Change: African Society and Colonial Rule*, Victor Turner, ed. (Cambridge: Cambridge University Press, 1971), 188.

and political obligations of colonizers to their subjects. The struggle against colonial land policies in the Gold Coast provides a typical example. With the rise of the gold-mining industry in the Gold Coast in the late nineteenth century, British authorities sought to control the pace and scale of land acquisition by European mining interests. To this end, the government proposed a law in 1894 to check acquisition of land by the Europeans. The proposed Crown Land bill, which vested forest lands and minerals in the British Crown, was vigorously opposed by traditional chiefs and a new class of Western-educated African leaders who interpreted it as an attempt to deny African control of their lands. The leaders mobilized popular opposition against the bill. In alliance with European merchants, who also opposed the law, they organized mass meetings and penned newspaper editorials that conveyed their collective opposition to the law. As part of the well-orchestrated protest against the bill, the Aborigines' Rights Protection Society in Cape Coast sent a delegation to London in 1898 to persuade the Colonial Office to drop the bill on the grounds that there were no vacant lands in the Gold Coast and that every piece of land was owned by one extended family or another. In the face of stiff resistance to the lands bill, the Secretary of State for the Colonies, Joseph Chamberlain, oversaw the redrafting of the bill in London. The new land bill was framed to give the Crown rights of administration but not of ownership. The attempt to vest vacant and forest land in the British Crown was also abandoned. Instead, the government held that fallow public lands would be administered by the Crown for the general good of the community. Chiefs were allowed all reasonable authority, but Britain, as the "paramount protecting power," would ensure that private rights were not improvidently created over public lands. Although the revised bill gave the British courts some supervision over the validity of concessions, it also made quite clear that the Africans retained possession of their land.[33]

In the neighboring colony of Nigeria, the same drama played out over native land rights. A similar land bill was also blocked by the local branch of the Aborigines' Rights Protection Society, founded by traditional and Western-educated leaders. The group took a legal appeal to the Privy Council in London, which ruled that ownership of land was the undisputed right of the community. As a result of these

[33] Tapan Biswal, *Ghana: Political and Constitutional Developments* (New Delhi: Indian Council of Social Science Research, 1992), 23.

victories, the British abandoned the policy of direct control of land even if in theory all lands in the conquered areas of British West Africa or lands ceded to the British Crown were considered owned by the Crown, while lands in the Protectorates were assumed to be held in trust by the Crown for the people.

French authorities asserted similar control over land, perhaps nowhere more forcefully than in Algeria. There, colonialization was particularly structured to serve colonial interests in ways that exacerbated the exploitation of the labor and land resources of indigenous people. Colonialism in Algeria was spurred by a policy of populating Algeria with Europeans. The large number of European settlers, a belief in the French civilizing mission and clear advantages that were enshrined in law and enforced militarily firmly established the repressive dominance of the colonials and the colonial regime.[34] Settler interests put additional pressure on land, which the colonial state appropriated with impunity as political power shifted and social systems were torn apart. The result was large-scale dispossession of indigenous populations' access to and control over land. This would be the fate of many indigenous people in settler colonies across Africa.

★★★

Colonial labor policies and practices also generated debates over native rights. As we have seen in Chapter 3, despite official antislavery rhetoric, colonial authorities were mostly ambivalent about the persistence of unfree labor practices and relied on various forms of forced labor. Several studies have drawn attention to the brutal and exploitative conditions under which Africans were forced into contract labor by colonial officials.[35] From the cotton plantation concessions of Portuguese Angola to the gold mines of the British Gold Coast, colonial regimes used forced labor in public, agricultural and mining enterprises, particularly before World War II. But even with seemingly more benign colonial rule after 1945, the use of coercion to extract African labor persisted. Compulsory labor was believed important to imbue the native with a European work ethic. As one Portuguese

---

[34] Susan Waltz, *Human Rights and Reform: Changing the Face of North African Politics* (Berkeley: University of California Press, 1995), 79.

[35] For example, Opolot Okia, *Communal Labor in Colonial Kenya: The Legitimization of Coercion, 1912–1930* (New York: Palgrave Macmillan, 2012), and Thaddeus Sunseri, *Vilimani: Labor Migration and Rural Change in Early Colonial Tanzania* (Portsmouth: Heinemann, 2002).

colonial administrator argued, the colonial state had a duty as "sovereign of semi-barbarous populations" to "force them to work in order for [them] to improve themselves, to acquire a happier kind of existence."[36] To this end, colonial authorities devised coercive strategies to extract African labor. One of these was through the imposition of taxes that had to be paid by physical labor for several days each year. In some cases, local chiefs were compelled to make their subjects available for compulsory collective labor, and harsh penalties were prescribed for failure to meet labor quotas. Such corvée labor was used extensively in French West Africa, the Belgian and Portuguese colonies and Spanish Guinea.

An 1899 Portuguese law called "Regulations for Native Labor" formalized forced labor in Portugal's African colonies. This legitimized the conscription of thousands of Africans to work on the Portuguese plantations of Cape Verde and the mines of Angola. By the 1940s, Portuguese polices had impoverished the Ovimbundu people who inhabited the area and driven much of the adult population into forced labor. Similarly, French authorities enforced a brutal system of forced labor in West Africa known as the *indigénat*, while in British West Africa, colonial rulers facing a decline of coercible labor turned to what has been termed "political labor."[37] This was labor that was supplied not by the market but by administrators who ordered local chiefs to send in the required number of workers for compulsory labor. In South Africa and Rhodesia, African labor was regulated and controlled using restrictive "pass laws," which ensured the availability of African labor for the white minority population when required but otherwise confined Africans to segregated reserves.

Colonial forced labor practices drew not only the attention of antislavery activists but also, from the 1920s, the international worker's rights movement as the International Labor Organization (ILO) became increasingly involved in Africa. Antislavery campaigners condemned practices in colonies such as Kenya where the abolition of slavery was accompanied by the implementation of vagrancy laws that compelled freed ex-slaves to continue working on settler plantations. The adoption of the Forced Labor Convention by the

[36] Quoted in Jeremy Ball, *Angola's Colossal Lie: Forced Labor on a Sugar Plantation, 1913–1977* (Leiden: Brill, 2015), 29.

[37] Suzanne Miers and Richard Roberts, eds., *The End of Slavery in Africa* (Madison: University of Wisconsin Press, 1988), 45.

ILO in 1930 brought into international focus the question of workers' rights in the colonies. Colonial regimes faced pressures from European and African activists who demanded international supervision of colonial labor policies. These campaigners draw attention to labor practices that fell short of the international standards advocated by the ILO. The institutional networks that developed around the ILO's activity in the colonial world created new opportunities for challenges to colonial rule by actors within and beyond Africa.[38]

Scholars and activists published evidence of forced labor in colonial Africa. One such publication, which triggered an international campaign against forced labor in Angola and the islands of Sao Tomé and Principe, was the 1906 book titled *A Modern Slavery* by the British journalist Henry Nevinson. Nevinson chronicled the use of slave labor and forced labor in the Portuguese colonies, noting that that in his travels in Africa, he encountered few Portuguese who recognized the natives as fellow-men with rights of their own.[39] He concluded that the problem of slave labor had not been solved by legal abolition but had continued in new forms under colonial rule. "We need not think that the problem of slavery has been settled by a century's noble enthusiasms about the Rights of Man and equality in the sight of God," Nevinson wrote.[40] This view was echoed a decade later in a 1925 report submitted to the Temporary Slavery Commission of the League of Nations by the American sociologist E. A. Ross. Following interviews with African workers in Angola and Mozambique, Ross described the system of labor recruitment in Portuguese Africa as "state serfdom."[41] Similar reports on the colonial labor systems in French Equatorial Africa and the Belgian Congo described widespread forced labor and corporal punishments meted out by administrators to villages that refused to participate in the rubber harvest for concessionary companies.[42]

The issue of forced labor was not limited to European-colonized Africa. Concerns about the use of slave and forced labor by the settler

---

[38] For a discussion of the internationalization of labor politics in colonial Africa, see Nick Bernard, "The Internationalization of Labour Politics in Africa," *Critical African Studies*, 7, 1 (2015): 15.

[39] Henry Nevinson, *A Modern Slavery* (London: Harper & Brothers, 1906), 118.

[40] Ibid., 12.

[41] E. A. Ross, *Report on the Employment of Native Labor in Portuguese Africa* (New York: Abbott Press, 1925), 9.

[42] André Gide, *Voyage au Congo: carnets de route* (Paris: Gallimard, 1927).

Americo-Liberian ruling elites in Liberia prompted the League of Nations to send a fact-finding mission to the country in the 1930s. The mission reported that while no form of organized slave trading existed, labor was wastefully and forcibly recruited for public works, for private use and for export with the collaboration of the Liberian Frontier Force and high government officials.[43]

For many Africans, the use of forced labor came to represent the fundamentally exploitative nature of colonial rule. Anti-colonial resistance therefore coalesced around issues of labor and workers' rights. By the 1930s, resistance from Africans and pressure from international activists and organizations such as the Aborigines' Protection Society, the League against Imperialism, and the ILO forced colonial regimes to introduce policies to curtail the use of forced labor, particularly by private companies. In Portuguese territories, the Native Labor Code, introduced in 1928, prohibited the use of forced or compulsory labor for public purposes such as building roads or for private purposes. Regulations introduced in 1930 also formally abolished the "legal obligation" to work. However, the "moral obligation" was maintained, and informally, the standard patterns of forced labor recruitment continued almost unaltered.[44]

In French West Africa, colonial commandants were hesitant about implementing metropolitan directives to suppress domestic slavery and other forms of forced labor practices. Official discourses of rights centered more on property rights than on workers' rights. In early colonial debates about legal abolition, some French officials seemed more concerned about the injustice of depriving masters of their property than upholding the rights of those enslaved or subjected to forced labor. Presiding over a case involving the rights of natives working under servile conditions in Guinea in 1903, one French colonial judge addressing the aggrieved workers stated: "If you wish your rights to be respected, should you not respect the rights of your masters, if those rights are not suppressed by mistreatment, by refusal of food or clothing or some other cause ... there is one way to obtain

---

[43] M. B. Akpan, "Liberia and Ethiopia, 1880–1914: The Survival of Two African States," in *General History of Africa*, vol. 7: *Africa under Colonial Domination 1880–1935*, A. Adu Boahen, ed. (Berkeley: University of California Press, 1985), 310.

[44] Corrado Tornimbeni, "Land and Labour Contestation in Manica, Mozambique: Historical Issues in Contemporary Dynamics," in *State, Land and Democracy in Southern Africa*, Arrigo Pallotti and Corrado Tornimbeni, eds. (Farnham: Ashgate, 2015), 88.

liberty. It is to pay for it."[45] For French officials concerned about the supply of African labor and wary of social upheavals arising from the transitioning labor economies of early colonialism, *property rights* clearly trumped *human rights*.

Colonial labor policies and workers' rights would become key issues in post–World World II anti-colonial struggles as Africans resisted colonial coercive labor measures. The war affected labor conditions in the colonies owing to heightened economic exploitation and strategic use of the colonies as a source of Allied war provisions. The high demand for labor for the war effort and colonial agricultural and mining enterprises was filled by the indigenous population partly through conscription and, in some cases, a resurgence in the use of forced labor. African workers resisted these exploitative working conditions through desertion, public protests and workers' strikes. Dissatisfaction with colonial labor policies led to general strikes in Nigeria in 1945; Dakar in 1946; Dar es Salaam, Mombasa, Sudan and Tunisia in 1947 and Zanzibar in 1948. Railway strikes took place in French West Africa sporadically throughout the late 1940s and in Ghana and Southern Rhodesia in 1947. Widespread worker-led urban protests also took place in Douala (Cameroon) in 1945 and in Accra (Ghana) in 1948. Labor issues and workers' protests became increasingly linked with the broader anti-colonial political struggle. The rhetoric of self-determination and freedom that underpinned Allied war propaganda became a rallying cry for African workers and nationalists, who demanded that the same rights ideals espoused by allied leaders be extended to Africans.

Law and Liberties

Modern human rights are founded on law. Legal positivists for whom the validity of law rests on formal enactment by authority define human rights by their legal foundation and judicial enforceability. Rights claims can be considered legitimate human rights entitlements only to the extent that they are premised on specific laws and can be enforced in courts or other judicial institutions. Obviously, this is a narrow and rather restricted definition of human rights that fails

---

[45] Quoted in Martin Klein, *Slavery and Colonial Rule in French West Africa* (Cambridge: Cambridge University Press, 1998), 235.

to consider the broader normative and moral foundations of rights claims. Such definitions of human rights also tend to discount human rights discourses and struggles that occur beyond legal systems in the form of popular activism and civic advocacy. However, human rights struggles have played out most prominently within legal and judicial spaces. This was particularly true of colonial law and legal systems.

While coercion played a crucial role in the imposition of colonial rule in Africa, law proved to be a more enduring means of administrative control. Force could weaken the will of conquered peoples, but it could not make colonial rule endure. Establishing the "rule of law" was the touchstone of colonial modernizing agendas. However, the imperatives of maintaining the supremacy of the colonial state and protecting metropolitan political and economic interests repeatedly ran counter to the principles of the rule of law. Colonial imperatives meant that despite the rhetoric of judicial liberalism, the rule of law could not, in practice, be blind and fully impartial. Colonial legality was premised on judicial oversight of executive power and subordination to well-defined and established laws. But it was also founded on the assumption that the boundaries of racial, ethnic and cultural difference in the colonial state had to be recognized and maintained.

The unequal application of law and enforcement of justice meant that colonial legal regimes often fell short of their own liberal rights agendas. The constraints imposed on individual and group rights by colonial legal systems is most evident in what has been described as the despotism of the rule of law.[46] This refers to the selective and shifting ways in which the colonial state defined and selectively prosecuted crime to accentuate offenses that challenged its economic interests or threatened its political authority. By defining challenges to state authority as criminal, the colonial state made political activism a crime.

In British Africa, law in the form of ordinances and proclamations administered through British-style colonial courts was crucial to promoting British colonial hegemony at the expense of indigenous rights and liberties. In the hands of colonial governments, law was a tool of conquest and control, stronger in many ways than military force. Typical of the repressive laws introduced to further British

---

[46] Elizabeth Kolsky, *Colonial Justice in British India: White Violence and the Rule of Law* (Cambridge: Cambridge University Press, 2009), and Radhika Singha, *A Despotism of Law: Crime and Justice in Early Colonial India* (New York: Oxford University Press, 1998).

administrative control were the deportation laws and collective punishment laws enacted in West Africa in the early colonial period. Under collective punishment laws, certain crimes were treated as crimes of the entire community when individual offenders could not be identified. The practice of punishing whole villages for the isolated offenses of individuals acting alone, and the outright denial of any form of legal redress against such punishments, clearly contradicted the English common law principle of individual responsibility for criminal liability – a principle assumed to be applicable in the colonies by virtue of the extension of the English legal system to the colonies. However, colonial officials justified collective punishment laws on the grounds that collective rights and communal obligations are integral to African customary law and social practices.

Colonial authorities used Deposition and Deportation laws to suppress African resistance to colonial rule, as in the case of Jaja of Opobo in the Niger delta, Urabi Pasha of Egypt and Samori Toure of the Madinka. The invasion of Ashanti by a British military force in 1896 was followed by the overthrow of the Ashanti King Prempeh and his replacement with a British official as the new political authority in the territory. A similar scenario played out in Nigeria where, upon conquering the Ijebu, British authorities deposed several local leaders on the grounds that the Ijebu had too many chiefs and kings. Preferring to deal with a single African king rather than several chiefs, British officials proceeded to impose a king on traditionally disparate Ijebu communities.[47]

The practice of deposing and deporting African rulers continued into the late colonial period when the Governor of Uganda deposed the *Kabaka* (king) of Buganda and ordered his exile to London to forestall Buganda's demands for independence. In Morocco, colonial authorities seeking to undermine the monarchy and establish France's supremacy handpicked a new sultan in 1927. When the selected sultan, Mohammed V, stood up against French rule and endorsed the cause of political independence two decades later, French authorities promptly deposed him. Deposition and exile did not diminish the power and influence of the sultan among the

---

[47] Tunde Oduwobi, "Deposed Rulers under the Colonial Regime: The Careers of *Akarigbo* Oyebajo and *Awujale* Adenuga," *Cahiers d"Etudes Africaines*, 43, 3 (2003): 553.

people, however. He would later return to negotiate Moroccan independence from French rule.

★★★

In other contexts, colonial law provided new opportunities for reframing rights at both discursive and practical levels. In this sense, law and the discourse of rights associated with it was a double-edged sword. On one hand, it was a devastating weapon of conquest like no other. On the other hand, colonial law provided the dispossessed with a means that could be used for self-protection, even if not always successfully. As an example, the British dual legal system that allowed English common law rights and liberties to exist alongside African customary law regimes opened opportunities for redefining the scope of individual and collective rights within colonial social and political spaces. The rhetorical emphasis on extending the republican ideals of the French Revolution – liberty, equality and fraternity – to colonial subjects also provided some opportunities for some Africans to assert their rights within the legal system.

Colonial law ushered new regimes of private rights and a liberal egalitarianism founded on individual freedom of action, which provided openings for marginalized groups to challenge and escape traditional institutions of patriarchy, servitude and oppression. In colonial courts where European-style laws prevailed, African women could assert new rights by challenging indigenous customary practices on marriage, divorce and property inheritance. In this sense, colonial laws expanded individual rights and liberties for certain groups of Africans. The most far-reaching social interventions occurred in British colonies. British authorities outlawed customary practices such as trial by ordeal, forced marriages, child betrothals and caste systems considered contrary to civilization and "repugnant to natural justice, equity and good conscience."[48] These progressive legal reforms marked an expansion of certain personal legal rights.

British colonial courts were expected to enforce a curious blend of English Common Law principles, colonial statute law and local African customary law within a framework of supposedly universal notions of morality and natural justice. While indigenous customary laws were tolerated, even accommodated within colonial legal systems, the goal

---

[48] Bonny Ibhawoh, *Imperial Justice: Africans in Empire's Court* (Oxford: Oxford University Press, 2013), 56.

was to create some legal and judicial standards across the Empire that represented British ideals. One of the first statues that introduced English law to Africa, the Gold Coast Supreme Court Ordinance of 1867, stipulated the enforcement of the Common Law, the Doctrines of Equity and the laws of England in the colonies. Similarly, the Judicature Act, which introduced English Law to East Africa in the late nineteenth century, obligated local courts to apply "English Common Law, the Doctrines of Equity and the Statutes of General Application in force in England as at 12th August 1897" when English law officially took effect in the colony.[49] The doctrine of *justice, equity and good conscience* gave colonial courts wide discretionary powers in the administration of justice. Invoking this doctrine, colonial courts could bypass local statues and draw instead from a variety of legal traditions including English law, Roman law, laws of continental European countries and even natural law. Whenever they came across a situation to which no local custom was applicable or where local customs were considered repugnant, colonial judges resorted to deciding cases according to "natural justice, equity and good conscience."

Forced marriages and child marriages provide the clearest examples of a rights-related social transformation brought about by colonial law.[50] In traditionally patriarchal African societies where family ties and communal solidarity were paramount, girls and women typically had limited freedom in their choice of husbands and limited possibilities for escaping unwanted marriages. Colonial officials considered uncivilized the customary practices of forced marriages, child marriages and betrothals, bride abduction and widow inheritance. They therefore sought to reform or abolish them through legal intervention. This was sometimes in response to pressure from missionaries and activist groups in Britain and the colonies seeking to prohibit these practices. Activist women's organizations such as the St. Joan's Social and Political Alliance and the British Commonwealth League were at the forefront of the campaign against forced marriages.[51]

---

[49] Momanyi Bwonwonga, *Procedures in Criminal Law in Kenya* (Nairobi: East African Publishers, 1994), 24.

[50] For a comprehensive discussion of forced marriage and social change in colonial Africa, see Annie Bunting, Benjamin Lawrance and Richard L. Roberts, eds., *Marriage by Force? Contestation over Consent and Coercion in Africa* (Athens: Ohio University Press, 2016).

[51] British Commonwealth League, *Annual Reports 1948–1961*, 7TBG/1/38a, The Women's Library, London School of Economics, London University.

By the 1920s, most colonial regimes had enacted laws to discourage these practices and give African women the legal status and right to pursue litigation in either the so-called Native Courts or European-style courts. As part of broader social transformation agendas, colonial authorities introduced laws that emphasized the rights of women to have a say in the choice of their husbands and to be able to seek divorce under certain conditions. In some cases, colonial laws entirely abrogated indigenous customs regarding marriage, divorce and custody of children, replacing them with practices that European officials regarded as moral and more in accordance with civilized practice.

Officials viewed marriage without consent and without the option of divorce as de facto slavery. For this reason, colonial courts were exceedingly liberal in their approach to requests from African women for divorce. This was often in defiance of the traditional code of behavior that made marital separation difficult and rare. In a 1930 white paper, "Welfare of Women in Tropical Africa," the British Colonial Office instructed that no women or girl under British juris-diction, irrespective of race, should be sold by her father or alleged proprietor to a polygamist or anyone else. Officials were also instructed to nullify marriage contracts made for girls under fourteen years, or over fourteen without her formal consent, and abolish the inheritance of widows by their husband's heirs.[52] Colonial courts became legal battlegrounds where African women challenged patri-archal authority by taking advantage of the new circumstances to assert their freedom and independence in matters of marriage and divorce. In Kenya, colonial marriage and divorce laws provided African women with new opportunities to assert their independence and escape traditional unwanted marriages. Under tight customary rules imposed on women's right to divorce, women sought in unprecedented numbers new legal avenues that governments made available. In colonial courts where they expected fairer hearing than traditional customary venues, they invoked official arguments about women's liberties and the need to change "immoral" customary marriage practices.[53]

---

[52] National Archives of the United Kingdom (NAUK) CO 847/11/12, "Status of Women in Africa 1938."

[53] Tabitha Kanogo, *African Womanhood in Colonial Kenya, 1900–50* (Oxford: James Currey, 2005), 54.

Following the establishment of native courts in French West Africa in 1905, waves of disputes regarding marriage divorce, bride wreath and child custody filled the courts. But by 1912, the French stepped back because they feared that increasing divorce would lead to female vagrancy, prostitution and social disorder. What surprised them is how quickly women understood and took advantage of colonial law. Concerns about forced marriages flared again in the mid-1930s following social and economic pressures arising from global economic depression. This resulted in the introduction of the Mandel Decree of 1939, which mandated the minimum age of marriage for girls at fourteen and boys at sixteen and required the consent of parties to be married.[54] Although social and economic barriers limited women's access to colonial courts and their claims were not always successful, colonial sensibilities with respect to marriage and divorce generally worked to the advantage of African women. In this sense, colonial legal reforms marked the expansion of the rights and liberties of certain vulnerable populations. These changes were not welcomed by everyone. Opposition to changes to customary marriage practices came mostly from senior African men concerned about the loss of patriarchal authority and the disruptive social effects of divorce. The sociologist N. A. Fadipe captured the dominant reaction to these changes in Nigeria when he wrote in 1933: "Women who wanted to renounce their husbands simply went up the hill to the officer or the court of the British Resident Commissioner to sue for divorce. Young girls have availed themselves of the opportunity offered by the law and courts to defy tradition by rejecting unwanted marriage proposals imposed on them by their parents."[55]

Opposition to the legal expansion of the right to divorce also came from conservative colonial officials who regarded the high rate of divorce as a serious threat to the social cohesion of African communities. In 1943, one British colonial judge decried the effects of colonial policy on indigenous customary marriage practices, pointing out that native custom regarding marriage, divorce and the custody of children had been almost entirely abrogated by administrative interventions. He noted that in native marriages, the "free will of the

---

[54] Richard Roberts, "Constrained Consent Women, Marriage, and Household Instability in Colonial French West Africa 1905–60," in *Marriage by Force? Contestation over Consent and Coercion in Africa*, 44, 50.

[55] N. A. Fadipẹ, *The Sociology of the Yoruba* (Ibadan: Ibadan University Press, 1970 [1933]), 92.

woman," which was a matter of little or no consideration under native custom, had suddenly become a cardinal principle. To secure a divorce in a Native Court, he noted disapprovingly, had become "as simple a matter as buying a railway ticket."[56] Concerns like these sometimes prompted review of the government policy toward divorce and official intervention in marital and other domestic affairs. Although the personal rights regimes introduced under colonial law were not always welcomed by those invested in maintaining the patriarchal status quo, these socially disruptive laws were mostly welcomed by women and other marginalized groups, such as former slaves and persons of lower castes, who took advantage of them to assert their freedoms. They used colonial arguments about individual rights and personal freedoms to challenge customary practices and escape restrictive social traditions.

Opposition to colonial reforms on marriage and divorce that expanded social rights for African women reminds us that the history of human rights is not simply a story of unremitting human progress. Rather, it is a more complicated story of progression and regression, inclusion and exclusion at different historical moments. Evident in colonial political restructuring and social reforms is a paradoxical process of rights exclusion and inclusion: exclusion through the repression and subordination of indigenous political authority, and inclusion through the expansion of social freedoms for women and other marginalized groups. We see in the ability of African women to take advantage of liberating divorce laws an example of the struggle for rights inclusion and expansion. But we also see in the opposition of conservative African men and colonial officials a story of opposition to rights expansion founded on concerns about maintaining social order and communal cohesion. This tension between struggles for rights inclusion and counter-efforts to maintain exclusionary status quo underlies the global human rights story.

Rights and Resistance

Resistance to colonial rule was at the core of rights struggles in Africa in the first half of the twentieth century. In resisting colonial violence, coercion and control, Africans used the same rhetoric of

---

[56] Quoted in Philip Igbafe, *Benin under British Administration: The Impact of Colonial Rule on an African Kingdom 1897–1938* (New York: Longman, 1979), 241.

rights and liberties that colonial authorities found so appealing on social issues. African opposition to colonial rule took many different forms ranging from armed resistance in the form of wars, revolts and insurrections to the rights-based intellectual resistance and anti-colonial movements for independence. I discuss the human rights dimensions of anti-colonial struggles and decolonization in the following chapter. Here, I am concerned primarily with earlier indigenous rights-based intellectual opposition struggles centered on the moral, legal and political obligations of the colonial state toward indigenous people.

From the earliest encounters with European colonists, African leaders resisted aspects of colonial rule that they found objectionable by drawing attention to the obligations of colonizers in treaty agreements and official statements. In a petition to the British Secretary of State in the 1930s, the elders of Buganda recalled the agreement of 1900 in which the king of England undertook to protect Buganda in return for their loyalty. They noted the promises of Winston Churchill, then British Under-Secretary of State for the Colonies, when he visited Buganda in 1907. Churchill, they recalled, had affirmed that under the Buganda agreement they would be guaranteed all their "rights and liberties ... lands, possessions, and ancient privileges."[57] They also recalled that under the agreement, the Buganda were guaranteed the preservation of "all the old grace and simplicity of their lives which have always so honorably distinguished them as a people."[58] The agreement provided that the justice of the British Crown would be evenly administered among all classes and all those who came under the authority of the king. Buganda leaders viewed this agreement as the "Buganda Charter of Rights" and the "Buganda Magna Carta," a treaty between two kingdoms under which the *Kabaka* (king) surrendered some (not all) of his sovereign rights in return for the protection of the British Crown.[59] These treaty provisions provided the basis for Buganda's long-standing demands for autonomy and self-rule.

---

[57] "Bataka Petitioners to Britain's Secretary of State for Colonies [1923]," in Donald Anthony Low, *The Mind of Buganda: Documents of the Modern History of an African Kingdom* (Berkeley: University of California Press, 1971), 182.

[58] Ibid., 182.

[59] John Mugambwa, "The Legal Aspects of the 1900 Buganda Agreement Revisited," *Journal of Legal Pluralism and Unofficial Law*, 25–26 (1987): 243, 245.

In West Africa, Western-educated African political leaders also invoked colonial legal obligations to challenge what they considered the excesses and abuses of colonial rule. Blaise Diagne, a pioneer of black African electoral politics and an early advocate for equal rights and non-discrimination, acquired a reputation throughout West Africa as a spokesman for the rights of all Africans against a demanding and authoritarian French colonial administration.[60] He encouraged African accommodation to French rule but also appealed to the legal and moral obligations of colonial rulers to demand the extension of equal rights to Africans. In 1916 he successfully convinced the French parliament to approve a law granting full citizenship to all residents of the Four Communes in Senegal. He subsequently argued for the extension of these rights to all Africans in Senegal.

Joseph Casely-Hayford and Herbert Macaulay played similar roles in British West Africa. Casely-Hayford, a prominent Gold Coast lawyer and nationalist, organized the National Congress of British West Africa in 1920, which attracted representation from across Britain's West African colonies. The Congress subsequently sent a delegation to the British Colonial Office to argue for elected representation in colonial administration and demanded administrative changes to allow for more African participation in their governance. Macaulay, an engineer, journalist and politician who rose to prominence in Nigerian politics of the 1920s and '30s was described in contemporary records as a "champion and defender of Native rights and liberties."[61] He led opposition against British policies that undermined the political and economic interests of Africans or violated their rights. He organized the first political party in the country, the Nigerian National Democratic party (NNDP), which provided a platform for several political demands including limited self-government, compulsory primary education, the indigenization of the colonial civil service and non-discrimination in economic enterprise. Owing partly to Macaulay's campaigns, British authorities introduced a new constitution in 1922 providing for limited franchise elections in Nigeria.

Early African opposition to colonial rule was not always explicitly articulated in terms of human rights. Traditional African leaders such as the Chiefs of the Fante Confederacy and Western-educated leaders

[60] Conklin, *A Mission to Civilize*, 156.
[61] Tekena Tamuno, *Herbert Macaulay: Nigerian Patriot* (Ibadan: Heinemann Educational, 1976), 31.

such as Diagne, Macaulay and Casely-Hayford did not initially express their political demands in terms of an inalienable right to self-determination as later anti-colonial nationalists would do. Rather, they anchored their claims on the political and social obligations of colonial rulers. However, even at this early phase of opposition to colonial rule, the movement for native rights had a transnational character. Organizations such as the Anti-Slavery and Aborigines' Protection Society and the League against Imperialism provided an early forum for African leaders and their metropolitan allies to articulate indigenous rights claims. The declared goal of the socialist-oriented League against Imperialism and its South African offshoot, the League of Native Rights, was to "protect African interests on all matters and to demand all rights to which Africans were entitled."[62] This was similar to the objective of the Gold Coast Aborigines' Rights Protection Society (ARPS), formed in 1897 by African leaders originally to protest colonial land laws that threatened African rights and traditional land tenure. The organization led sustained opposition against the colonial administration in the Gold Coast, laying the foundation for the more assertive anti-colonial nationalist movement in the 1940s and '50s. A related organization, the Lagos Auxiliary of the Anti-Slavery and Aborigines' Protection Society (ASAPS), was formed in Nigeria in 1911 with the support of the parent body in Britain. The organization was actively involved in campaigns to protect native rights. When the British government proposed assuming formal control of all lands in southern Nigeria in 1911, the Lagos ASAPS raised the alarm of an impending threat to customary land rights and sent a delegation of protest to London. These organizations were the precursors of present-day African human rights NGOs.

★★★

Despite the foregoing account, it would be wrong to assume that all political rights discourses and struggles in the early colonial period centered on claims by natives against colonists. Rights struggles in early colonialism were complex and multifaceted. In settler colonies such as Algeria, Kenya and South Africa, European settlers also articulated political demands in terms of their inherent rights as British or French citizens. These rights were synonymous with "civic privileges," claimed exclusively for settlers and not intended to extend

---

[62] Allison Drew, *Between Empire and Revolution: A Life of Sidney Bunting 1873–1936* (London: Pickering & Chatto, 2007), 189.

beyond that privileged group. These claims are also not congruent with present-day understanding of human rights as rights that pertain to everyone equally by virtue of their humanity. However, our task should not be simply to measure historical rights claims against today's standards. It should also be to understand how rights language has been historically invoked by various groups within colonial society to further divergent goals.

Early South African settler politics offer an example of such exclusionary invocation of rights language. Amid late nineteenth-century tensions between British emancipationists and Afrikaner slaveholders, a group of settler colonists in South Africa's Eastern Cape convened in 1824 to assert a distinctive form of expanded British colonial identity that might be extended to "deserving non-whites." The group set out to articulate the freedoms, rights and liberties to which British citizens and deserving non-white subjects should be entitled. The group established a newspaper, *The South African Commercial Advertiser*, with the mandate of asserting "the rights of free-born Britons in a new colony of settlements." When local authorities concerned about their factionalist agenda shut down the newspaper, the ensuing campaign for freedom of expression centered on "settler civic rights" while embracing the broader humanitarian struggle to improve legal and social conditions of the indigenous population.[63] This idea of extending certain civic rights to deserving non-whites reflected a liberal strategy of exclusion that viewed colonized peoples as potential rights-bearers, needing acculturation before the acquisition of equal political rights. "Equal rights for all *civilized men* south of the Zambezi," the slogan of Cecil Rhodes's pro-British South African League, came to encompass the liberal tradition of the British Cape Colony in the late nineteenth century. This vision of rights marked an expansion from the League's previous slogan of "equal rights for all whites."[64]

Rights claims were also asserted, challenged and negotiated in legal and social struggles between Africans. The language of individual liberties and property rights favored by the colonial state came to be increasingly deployed in competition over power and resources. Just

---

[63] Saul Dubow, *South Africa's Struggle for Human Rights* (Athens: Ohio University Press, 2012), 29.

[64] David Killingray, "'A Good West Indian, a Good African, and, in Short, a Good Britisher': Black and British in a Colour-Conscious Empire, 1760–1950," in *Ambiguities of Empire: Essays in Honour of Andrew Porter*, Robert Holland and Sarah Stockwell, eds. (London: Routledge, 2009), 31.

as colonial social reforms were framed in terms of native rights, the opposition to unfavorable political changes was often expressed in rights language. Buganda leaders opposed British plans for an East African federation in 1931 partly on the grounds that such a federation would infringe on the collective political rights of the Buganda people guaranteed under treaty agreements with the British. Buganda officials complained that closer union with other British territories would seriously impair Buganda rights and privileges.[65] A uniform native policy for East Africa would be impractical, they argued, because the various "tribes" differed vastly, and some tribes, like Buganda, had "reached a more advanced state of civilization than others."[66] Such assertions of Buganda paramountcy were increasingly articulated in terms of Buganda treaty rights and inherent Buganda rights more generally. As with British South African settlers, Buganda's notion of rights was restrictive and exclusionary. The use of rights language in this context was clearly based on an exclusionary agenda of difference and paramountcy rather than one of equity and equality.

My discussion of rights and resistance so far has centered on discourses and struggles of men – indigenous, settler and metropolitan male elites. It reflects the reality that colonialism was essentially a male project shaped largely by the intersection of African and European patriarchies. However, rights struggles under colonial rule were not limited to male elites. African women also played an important part in these early struggles even if their roles have not received due attention in human rights histories. In South Africa, women played key roles in the early struggle against racial oppression. They protested pass laws that controlled their employment and freedom of movement into towns. One of the earliest anti-pass demonstrations occurred in the Orange Free State in 1913 when the authorities began requiring women to have a permit to live in urban areas. Women sent petitions to authorities, including the king of England. A key figure in this early anti-segregation movement was Charlotte Maxeke, who, as president of the Bantu Women's League and the National Council of African Women (NCAW), led oppositions against the pass laws. Drawing from her experience and education in the United States where she attended a segregated "Negro college," she worked within political, labor and church organizations to advocate for the rights and welfare of

---

[65] Low, *The Mind of Buganda*, 66.   [66] Ibid., 88.

Africans. In 1918 she led a deputation to put the women's case to the Prime Minister, Louis Botha. This early protest against pass laws was successful, as passes were not issued to women until decades later.[67]

Perhaps the most well-known incident of women's resistance in West Africa is the 1929 Aba Women's Revolt, or Igbo Women's War, in southeastern Nigeria. A unique aspect of the movement that produced the revolt is that its leadership was composed entirely of rural women determined to redress social, political and economic grievances. It was a protest against an unjust colonial regime that sought to impose taxes on women without consulting them. Igbo women demanded an end to this form of taxation and recognition of women's traditional rights. The revolt spread quickly throughout the region, catching British colonial authorities by surprise and ultimately resulting in the death of fifty-five women. One historian who has studied the testimonies of women given at the Commission of Inquiry established by British authorities characterized the Aba Women's war as "a feminist movement in the sense that the women were very conscious of the special role of women, the importance of women to society, and the assertion of their rights as women vis-à-vis the men."[68] Women were also active in early anti-colonial protests and later liberation movements in eastern and southern Africa. Working within both women's groups and larger political organizations, they struggled on two fronts as they fought simultaneously for African political control and the inclusion of women in governance.[69] These discourses of women's rights and the role of women in broader political struggles constitute an integral part of the history of human rights in colonial Africa.

Segregation and Apartheid

Policies and practices of racial prejudice, discrimination and segregation deserve special attention in the history of human rights in colonial

---

[67] Cherryl Walker, *Women and Resistance in South Africa* (London: Onyx Press, 1982), 27–28.

[68] Nina Mba, *Nigerian Women Mobilized: Women's Political Activity in Southern Nigeria, 1900–1965* (Berkeley: University of California, 1982), 91. For a comprehensive history of the revolt, see Toyin Falola and Adam Paddock, *The Women's War of 1929: A History of Anti-Colonial Resistance in Eastern Nigeria* (Durham: Carolina Academic Press), 2011.

[69] Kathleen Sheldon, *Historical Dictionary of Women in Sub-Saharan Africa* (Lanham: Scarecrow Press, 2005), 8.

Africa. Colonialism was everywhere premised on racism. Assumptions about hierarchies of civilization shaped all aspects of the colonial enterprise, ultimately determining the scope of civic, economic and social rights that members of each group could enjoy within the colonial state. As subordinated subjects, colonized Africans occupied the lowest rung of the colonial social ladder. French colonialism, for example, was founded on the *Code de l'indigénat*, creating, in practice, an inferior legal status for natives of French colonies from 1887 until the 1940s. However, the most extreme of racial exclusion was in the settler colonies of southern Africa where discrimination based on race was firmly institutionalized through segregationist policies. Racially discriminatory policies shaped the everyday lives of Africans living in these areas and became the core rights issues in later liberation struggles. In the Portuguese colonies of Angola and Mozambique, an equally virulent form of paternalistic racism was central to the exploitation of an African migrant labor force in colonial mines and plantations.[70]

South Africa offers a unique case for historians of human rights. Its extended colonial history offers insights into the development and maintenance of several competing rights regimes –British liberal, Afrikaner, and African nationalist – that have shaped present-day political, social and economic realities in this region.[71] In many settler territories such as the Afrikaner-dominated colonies of Transvaal and the Orange Free States, the franchise was limited to whites. This developed as part of a broader segregationist policy of the Afrikaner-dominated National Party that became apartheid in 1948.

Racially discriminatory and segregationist policies introduced to protect the political and economic interests of the minority white population affected Africans' rights to own land or enjoy job security and restricted their freedom to live or travel unhindered. This was achieved through a series of restrictive laws introduced in the early twentieth century, including the 1911 Mines and Works Act, which effectively restricted Africans to mostly menial and unskilled labor, excluding them from skilled categories of work in mines and thereby reserving the jobs for whites. The related Natives Land Act of

---

[70] For a detailed study of Portuguese colonial labor policies, see Jeanne Penvenne, *African Workers and Colonial Racism: Mozambican Strategies and Struggles in Lourenco Marques, 1877–1962* (Portsmouth: Heinemann, 1994).
[71] Dubow, *South Africa's Struggle for Human Rights*, 11.

1913 confined blacks to land ownership within the boundaries of government-designated reserves. Subsequent laws introduced in the 1930s placed further restrictions on the access of blacks to land. Similar restrictive laws were introduced by the white minority regime in neighboring Rhodesia, reserving huge shares of land for the country's white minority, which made up only about 2 percent of the population. Racially repressive laws also constrained the rights of blacks to live or work where they chose. The Native Labor Regulation Act controlled African working conditions, imposing restrictions on "native workers" recruited in rural areas who were required to be fingerprinted, issued passes to enter cities and confined to staying in urban areas only when they could prove that they had legitimate work. Under the provisions of the Act, Africans violating these working conditions could be arrested and imprisoned for months.

The introduction of an institutionalized system of racial discrimination under the banner of apartheid by the Nationalist government in 1948 consolidated these long-standing policies of segregation and race-based discrimination. It is significant that the policy of apartheid was introduced in 1948, the same year that the Universal Declaration of Human Rights was adopted by the UN General Assembly. The discourse of self-determination and universal human rights at the United Nations during this period stood in deep contrast to the politics of racial exclusion and repression in South Africa. The South African Prime Minister, Jan Smuts, a staunch advocate for racial segregation at home, was one of the world leaders who drafted the UN Charter and was a key figure at the San Francisco Conference where the charter was adopted in 1945. He is credited with being the driving force behind the inclusion of the notion of human dignity in the UN Charter and specifically with writing the defining words that affirm "faith in fundamental human rights, in the dignity and worth of the human person."[72] But even as he led discussions about human rights at the UN, Smuts worked strenuously at home to prevent the extension of these fundamental rights to non-whites. Nonetheless, he was defeated in 1948 because most Afrikaner voters believed that he intended to liberalize social controls.

Apartheid policies institutionalized state-sanctioned racism in almost every facet of life. The Group Areas Act, passed in 1950 along

---

[72] Stefan-Ludwig Hoffmann, *Human Rights in the Twentieth Century* (Cambridge: Cambridge University Press, 2010), 16.

with several other apartheid laws, delineated where black Africans could live. Described as "the very essence of apartheid" by Smuts's Afrikaner Nationalist successor, Daniel Malan, the Group Areas Act established "homelands" for South Africa's blacks and authorized the government to displace and transfer black communities to create exclusive white residential zones. Apartheid's political repression and social exclusion were reinforced with laws such as the Population Registration Act, which required individuals to register their ethnic identity with the government. This established a divisive and exclusionary mechanism for classifying residents into racial categories of white, colored, Asian (Chinese, Indian) and native (Bantu). People were issued with identity cards displaying their "assigned races," which affected everyday life including residence, education, employment, social services and voting rights.

At an economic level, the goal of apartheid was to regulate black working conditions in ways that served the interests of the white minority population. On a social level, the objective was to place people into easily defined racial categories that hierarchically kept them apart. Apartheid policies restricted interracial interaction not only in public spaces but also in private life. Laws such as the Prohibition of Mixed Marriage Act of 1949 and Immorality Act of 1950 forbade sexual relations between races, while the Group Areas Act and the Reservation and Separate Amenities Act divided the entire country into geographical areas based on race. Severe penalties were prescribed for transgressing these racial laws. Africans considered the Bantu Education Act of 1953 particularly repressive because it sought to affect black education and prospects by providing separate educational facilities for them under the control of the minister of Native Affairs rather than the Ministry of Education.

Throughout the history of South Africa, Africans and other marginalized groups resisted the violence and repression of white minority rule. In 1912 a group of African leaders formed the South African Native National Council (SANNC), mainly in response to the Native Land bill of 1913 but also as a reaction to other injustices perpetrated by the government. The formation of the SANNC, which evolved into the African National Congress (ANC), represented a shift from tribal resistance to organized opposition led by a Westernized elite. Resistance to repression and segregation took the form of public protests and strikes despite laws forbidding them. The formation of the SANNC and other activist political organizations marked the progressive shift toward the expression of African resistance as rights struggles. Resistance against racial oppression would expand significantly in the 1960s in response to the intensification of apartheid and events such as the Sharpeville massacre of 1960. By the 1980s, the activities of political groups such as the ANC and the international campaigns of anti-apartheid activists would coalesce into a global human rights movement.

★★★

What were the defining trends in rights discourses and struggles in colonial Africa? One discernible trend is that colonial rule was premised on a legitimizing discourse of "native rights" founded on the notion of the civilizing mission. Colonial rule meant the loss of African political autonomy and the imposition of wide-ranging restrictions on the rights and liberties of indigenous people. Colonial economic and labor policies, driven as they were by overriding imperial interests, narrowed the scope of everyday civil and social freedoms for many Africans. Forced and compulsory labor, coercive and repressive laws and discriminatory social policies and practices became the central issues in early African resistance struggles against colonial governments. However, rights struggles were not limited to encounters between natives and colonists. The language of rights was also used by other groups within the colonial state. It was invoked by European settlers challenging government restrictions on their activities and by Africans in competition for political power and economic opportunities. Colonial social policies sometimes had the salutary effect of expanding the scope of legal rights for women and other traditionally marginalized groups. The history of human rights in colonial Africa is certainly a story of profound human rights restrictions and violations in the political and civil spheres, but it is also a story of tentative rights expansion in certain social spheres. Ultimately, however, it was the discontent arising from colonial authoritarianism and political subjugation that would shape mid-twentieth-century anti-colonial rights struggles for self-determination and independence.

5

Nationalists and Anti-Colonists

The peoples of the colonies know precisely what they want. They wish
to be free and independent, to be able to feel themselves ... equal with
all other peoples, and to work out their own destiny without interference, and to be unrestrained to attain an advancement that will put
them on a par with other technically advanced nations of the world.

– Kwame Nkrumah[1]

As World War II gathered pace in 1941, President Roosevelt and
Prime Minster Churchill signed the Atlantic Charter, a document
expressing the war aims of the United States and Britain, and their
allied goals for the post-war political-economic world order. Two
years later, a delegation of West African journalists traveled to London
partly with the intent of clarifying the application of the Charter to the
colonies in Africa. The journalists considered the Charter crucial to
the fate of those living under colonial rule in Africa. Their main
interest was the third clause of the Charter, which affirmed "the right
of all peoples to choose the form of government under which they
will live." In a statement to the House of Commons shortly after
the agreement was signed, Prime Minister Churchill stated that
the right to self-determination outlined in the Charter would apply
to those living under Nazi occupation in Europe but not to Britain's
colonial subjects still in need of "progressive evolution" toward

---

[1] Kwame Nkrumah, *Revolutionary Path* (London: Panaf Books, 1973), 40.

self-government.[2] Churchill would later add that the existence of the Atlantic Charter did not compel him "to preside over the liquidation of the British Empire"[3] and that allies proposing self-rule in colonies should take their "hands off the British Empire."[4]

The leader of the delegation of West African journalists, Nnamdi Azikiwe, submitted to the British Secretary of State for the Colonies a memorandum entitled "The Atlantic Charter and British West Africa." In it, the delegates sought clarification of British policy on self-determination in the colonies and proposed, based on the Atlantic Charter, policy changes toward African independence. These included the abrogation of the Crown colony system, the immediate "Africanization" of the colonial government and the institution of representative government in the colonies with the goal of full responsible government.[5] Invoking the third clause of the Atlantic Charter, the delegates envisioned that by 1958 all West African territories under colonial rule would be independent and sovereign political entities.[6] These proposals did not receive immediate response from the Colonial Office. Disappointed, members of the delegation returned to West Africa where they expressed their frustrations at the hypocrisy and indifference of British officials.[7]

Even after the departure of the West African delegates, concerns over the political implications of the Atlantic Charter for European colonies in Africa lingered in Britain and the colonies. The West African Students Union, a politically active organization of West African students in London, kept the issue alive by working with sympathetic groups such as the Colonial Bureau of the Fabian Society

[2] Robert E. Sherwood, *Roosevelt and Hopkins: An Intimate History* (New York: Enigma Books, 2008), 363.

[3] *The Times* (United Kingdom), November 11, 1942. Prime Minister Churchill was not alone in seeking a restrictive interpretation of the principle of self-determination in the Atlantic Charter. The Soviet leader Josef Stalin, who saw the Charter as an "anti-Soviet tract," also asserted that it did not apply to regions of Soviet influence.

[4] Winston Churchill, "Hands Off the British Empire," quoted in William Roger Louis, *Imperialism at Bay: The United States and the Decolonization of the British Empire 1941–1945* (Oxford: Oxford University Press, 1977), 356.

[5] National Archives of the United Kingdom (hereinafter NAUK) CO 554/133/3, "Memorandum on the Atlantic Charter and British West Africa by the West African Press Delegation to the United Kingdom, 1 August 1943,"

[6] NAUK CO554/133/3, "Memorandum on the Atlantic Charter and British West Africa."

[7] James Coleman, *Nigeria: Background to Nationalism* (Berkeley: University of California Press, 1971), 240.

and concerned members of the British Parliament.[8] The organization was eventually able to extract a public statement from Britain's Deputy Prime Minister Clement Attlee, who affirmed that the principles espoused in the Atlantic Charter applied to everyone.[9] Pushing back against Churchill's restrictive interpretation of the Atlantic Charter from across the Atlantic, President Roosevelt would also later assert that the ideals of the Charter applied not only to Europe but to all people. His insistence echoed his "Four Freedoms" speech of January 1941, which reflected his belief that the future of global security depended on the universal applicability of the principles of self-determination.[10]

Discussions over the interpretation of the Atlantic Charter and the right to self-determination became central to post–World War II international anti-colonial politics. Colonized Africa was at the center of these debates. Writing in 1943, the American historian Lawrence Reddick posited that Africa would be the test of the Atlantic Charter and the ultimate vindication of US involvement in World War II.[11] "What happens in Africa," Reddick wrote, "will reveal to the submerged masses everywhere, and to ourselves, whether our stirring declarations have meaning or whether this is just one more indecent war."[12] Discussions about the Atlantic Charter became linked to the legitimacy of colonialism and the shape of post-war internationalism. Most significantly, the Atlantic Charter would become a cornerstone of the post-war international human rights movement. The Charter, which was subsequently endorsed by forty-four additional countries, referred to human rights and fundamental freedoms, galvanizing popular support globally for social justice on issues concerning race relations, women's rights and colonial rule.[13] For these reasons, the Atlantic Charter has been described as the first major document of

---

[8] Gabriel Olakunle Olusanya, *The West African Students' Union and the Politics of Decolonisation, 1925–1958* (Ibadan: Daystar Press, 1982), 15.

[9] Ashley Jackson, *The British Empire and the Second World War* (New York: Hambledon Continuum, 2006), 224.

[10] Robert E. Sherwood, *Roosevelt and Hopkins: An Intimate History* (New York: Grosset and Dunlop, 1950), 353–363.

[11] L. D. Reddick, "Africa: Test of the Atlantic Charter," *Crisis*, 50, 7 (1943): 202.

[12] Ibid., 202.

[13] Susan Eileen Waltz, "Universalizing Human Rights: The Role of Small States in the Construction of the Universal Declaration of Human Rights," *Human Rights Quarterly*, 23, 1 (2001): 51.

global significance to affirm the right to self-determination in both humanistic and universalistic terms.[14]

How and why did African colonies and anti-colonial activism become so central to international debates about the Atlantic Charter and Allied visions of a post-war world? In this chapter, I examine debates over self-determination within post–World War II internationalism and the political struggles for independence in the colonies. I explore the links between anti-colonial nationalism, decolonization and human rights in Africa from two perspectives. The first interrogates the argument – contested but still dominant in human rights scholarship – that anti-colonialism was not a human rights movement. I assess this claim by examining how African independence activists used the Atlantic Charter in struggles for self-determination and deployed an emergent human rights lexicon to strengthen long-standing demands for independence. I query the historicity of delinking struggles for self-determination within anti-colonialism from the post–World War II human rights movement, and argue for the integral connections between both movements.[15]

The second perspective that I bring to linking anti-colonialism with human rights centers on the relationship between anti-colonialism and two distinct phases of the African struggle for political self-determination. The first phase of the self-determination struggle was aimed at achieving national liberation from *external* European imperial rule. The second phase of self-determination struggles involved *internal* subnational agitations for autonomy by minority groups within the colonial or post-colonial state. Both movements for self-rule drew on the language of human rights and self-determination, even though

[14] Although the UDHR does not explicitly assert the right to self-determination in the same terms as articulated in the Atlantic Charter, the principle is implied in its article 21, which upholds the right to participate in government and asserts that the "will of the people shall be the basis of the authority of government." For a general treatment of the Atlantic Charter, see Douglas Brinkley and David R. Facey-Crowther, eds., *The Atlantic Charter* (New York: St. Martin's Press, 1994).

[15] This chapter draws on some of my arguments presented elsewhere: Bonny Ibhawoh, "Testing the Atlantic Charter: Linking Anti-Colonialism, Self-Determination and Universal Human Rights," *International Journal of Human Rights*, 18, 7–8 (2014): 1–19; Bonny Ibhawoh, "Colonialism: Legacy for Human Rights," in *Encyclopedia of Human Rights*, David P. Forsythe, ed. (New York: Oxford University Press, 2009), 360–372; Bonny Ibhawoh, "Human Rights and National Liberation: The Anti-Colonial Politics of Nnamdi Azikiwe," in *Leadership in Colonial Africa*, Baba G. Jallo, ed. (New York: Palgrave Macmillan, 2014).

nationalist anti-colonialism often drowned out minority subnational struggles. In the era of decolonization, leaders of anti-colonial movements privileged national liberation over competing demands for subnational autonomy and equitable distribution of power and resources in the state.

Studies in the nexus between decolonization and human rights have, for the most part, been preoccupied with the *externalist* human rights impulse centered on how anti-colonial activists used human rights in struggles for national liberation.[16] Largely missing from these narratives are contemporaneous accounts of how anti-colonial activists addressed internal struggles for self-determination by minority groups and other marginalized constituencies within the decolonizing state. These internal rights struggles are essential to understanding the links between African anti-colonialism and human rights in the age of decolonization. They are also crucial to understanding why human rights language, which was so resonant in anti-colonial debates, seemed to dissipate in nationalist discourse once independence was attained. My goal here is not only to shed light on the discourse of human rights within African anti-colonial struggles, but also to trouble conventional notions and histories of the links between anti-colonialism and the post–World War II international human rights movement.

Anti-Colonialism and Human Rights

Anti-colonial struggles for self-determination had a significant impact on the international human rights movement. Colonized peoples all over the world drew on an emergent human rights lexicon in their political and ideological struggles against imperial powers and demands for independence. Anti-colonial movements in Asia and

---

[16] See, for example, Fabian Klose, *Human Rights in the Shadow of Colonial Violence: The Wars of Independence in Kenya and Algeria* (Philadelphia: University of Pennsylvania Press, 2013); Roland Burke, *Decolonization and the Evolution of International Human Rights* (Philadelphia: University of Pennsylvania Press, 2010); Charles Parkinson, *Bills of Rights and Decolonization: The Emergence of Domestic Human Rights Instruments in Britain's Overseas Territories* (Oxford: Oxford University Press, 2007); Bonny Ibhawoh, *Imperialism and Human Rights: Colonial Discourses of Rights and Liberties in African History* (Albany: State University of New York Press, 2007); A. W. B. Simpson, *Human Rights and the End of Empire: Britain and the Genesis of the European Convention* (Oxford: Oxford University Press, 2001); Samuel Moyn, *The Last Utopia: Human Rights in History* (Cambridge, MA: Belknap Press of Harvard University Press, 2010).

Africa were among the first mass movements to use post-war language of universal and inalienable human rights in struggles for political autonomy. Yet the notion persists in some quarters that anti-colonialism was not a human rights movement because its primary aim was collective liberation rather than the reduction and regulation of state power over the individual.[17] This explains the relative neglect of anti-colonialism and decolonization in historical accounts of twentieth-century human rights.

The argument against reading anti-colonial movements as human rights movements hinges on three main premises. The first is the claim that anti-colonialism was already fully formed before the post-1945 human rights rhetoric had a chance to have a serious impact on it. Proponents of this argument point out that there were only minor and occasional uses of the term "human rights" in anti-colonial discourse. Historian Samuel Moyn argues, for example, that in the era of decolonization, self-determination and human rights were mutually exclusive. For him, anti-colonialism at the UN emerged as its own distinctive tradition, one that the rise of human rights in their more contemporary sense would have to displace.[18] This is the foundational premise of what I have described as the "anti-colonialism as non-human rights" argument.[19]

The second premise for delinking anti-colonialism from human rights is the claim that anti-colonialism privileged popular liberation and collective self-determination over individual rights and liberties. In his study *Human Rights and the End of Empire*, Brian Simpson argues that the primary aim of anti-colonial activists was to liberate collective national entities from the grip of imperial arms and not to reduce the power of the state over the individual, which is "the defining character of all human rights activism."[20] According to Simpson, the real connection between the human rights movement and anti-colonialism lies in a common commitment to the notion of human dignity.[21] Within this conceptual framework, human rights are

---

[17] Moyn, *The Last Utopia*. In particular, chapter 3: "Why Anti-Colonialism Wasn't a Human Rights Movement," and Samuel Moyn, "Imperialism, Self-Determination, and the Rise of Human Rights," in *The Human Rights Revolution: An International History*, Akira Iriye et al., eds. (New York: Oxford University Press, 2012), 159–178.

[18] Moyn, *The Last Utopia*, 86.   [19] Ibhawoh, "Testing the Atlantic Charter."

[20] A. W. Brian Simpson, *Human Rights and the End of Empire: Britain and the Genesis of the European Convention* (Oxford: Oxford University Press, 2004), 301.

[21] Simpson, *Human Rights and the End of Empire*, 301.

essentially about curtailing *state* power over the individual, not the quest for the collective political freedom. In other words, for colonial states at the threshold of independence, self-determination took precedence over "human rights," narrowly defined as individual rights.

The final premise for delinking anti-colonialism from human rights is what may be termed the "human rights as political strategy" argument. This position claims that in rare situations when anti-colonial activists invoked human rights, they did so only as a discursive political strategy to achieve national liberation.[22] The broader implication here is that their invocation of human rights was born out of sheer political expediency rather than deep ideological commitment. This is perhaps the most contentious of all three premises because it ascribes exclusively to anti-colonialism what we know to be true of all human rights struggles. The history of twentieth-century human rights is a story of human dignity, equality and justice. But it is also as much a story of how individuals, groups, nations and regional blocs have used human rights language and ideology to further self-interested agendas. The politics of human rights isn't unique to anti-colonialism; it is integral to human rights history.

There are obvious analytical pitfalls in any blanket inclusion or rejection of human rights within anti-colonialism.[23] Delineating the place of human rights in the history of anti-colonialism is complex and ambiguous, requiring the use of a scalpel rather than a cleaver. Rather than generalized claims, careful contextual studies of specific anti-colonial struggles offer the most promising answers to these questions. Such studies have shown tangible connections between international human rights and the radicalization of colonial violence in Africa's wars of decolonization after 1945.[24] These wars of decolonization became the first major challenge and the testing ground for newly established international human rights norms. While colonial powers tried to deny the universal character of human rights in the colonies,

---

[22] Moyn, *The Last Utopia*, 117.

[23] Jan Eckel, "Human Rights and Decolonization: New Perspectives and Open Questions," *Humanity: An International Journal of Human Rights, Humanitarianism, and Development* 1, 1 (2010): 111–135; Meredith Terretta, "We Had Been Fooled into Thinking That the United Nations Watches over the Entire World: Human Rights, United Nations Trust Territories, and Africa's Decolonization," *Human Rights Quarterly*, 34, 2 (2012): 329–360.

[24] Klose, *Human Rights in the Shadow of Colonial Violence*; Burke, *Decolonization and the Evolution of International Human Rights*.

the anti-colonial movements deliberately exploited reports about massive violations of basic rights such as forced resettlement, torture and summary killings to win the support of international public opinion.[25]

★★★

The human rights idea evolved very quickly in the first two decades after World War II. We can point to at least two distinct and defining phases in this evolution. The first was a decidedly Euro-American phase beginning with the Atlantic Charter in 1941, the establishment of the UN in 1945 and ending with the adoption of the UDHR in 1948. International human rights discourse during this early phase centered mainly on the crisis of nationalism in post-war Europe. Human rights as debated at the UN tended to focus on atomized individualism and civil liberties centered on personalized entitlements and state obligations. These characteristics were largely shaped by the atrocities in wartime Europe and the imperatives of constraining state power over individuals in the post-war period. In this early iteration of "universal human rights," there was a prominent place for individual rights but not the collective rights of peoples. More attention was also given to civil and political liberties than to economic, social or cultural rights. This would change significantly with the emergence of what has been described as the "global United Nations" or the "post-colonial United Nations" as formerly colonized nations became independent and gained voices at international forums. These voices, mostly from the Global South, would play a transformative role in the debate on economic, social and cultural rights. This marked the second phase of the evolution of the human rights idea.

The European imperial powers that championed the establishment of the UN and adoption of the UDHR in first phase of the development of international human rights had an entrenched interest in defending their sovereignty and evading the contradictions between colonialism and the new doctrine of universal human rights. The denial of the franchise to colonial subjects came up often in discussions of the draft UDHR at the UN General Assembly, forcing British and French officials to defend their colonial policies.[26] While the

---

[25] Fabian Klose, "Debating Human Rights and Decolonization." Available at www.imperialglobalexeter.com/2014/02/18/debating-human-rights-and-decolonization. Accessed March 17, 2014.

[26] United Nations General Assembly Official Records (UNGAOR), Third Session, Third Committee (1948): 142.

human rights doctrine held great promise for the millions of people living under colonial rule, European colonial powers were much less sanguine about the universal extension of this empowering concept. The notion that the right to vote is a basic, universal right was particularly worrying to European countries presiding over undemocratic empires.[27] With concepts such as racial equality and self-determination, the European countries were faced with an emerging conception of international law that undercut the very foundations of the colonial relationship on which empire depended. British and French statesmen involved in the early debates about human rights at the UN strenuously sought to construct emergent international human rights in ways that could accommodate the social relationships and political hierarchies of their colonial systems. For them, delinking self-determination struggles in the colonies from human rights idealism at the UN was a matter of political expedience. They viewed the principle of sovereignty and the concept of human rights as being fundamentally opposed to each other – one having to do with the rights of states and the other with the rights of individuals. The *anti-colonialism as non-human rights* argument echoes this distinction of political convenience.

The history of the human rights movement cannot be based entirely on textual analysis of writings by a narrow group of political actors. There is deeper historical knowledge to be gained from locating, unpacking and assessing those ideas and practices that produced and sustained such discourses. Discourse does not exist in an apolitical vacuum; it is co-constituted by ideational and material contexts. Leaders and followers in the anti-colonial movement drew not only on the language of human rights but also on the ideas behind that language. The post-war human rights idea was essentially the promise of an immutable universal humanity upheld through international consensus and multilateral agreements. African independence activists captured this idea when they spoke about transitioning from imperial subjects to self-governing citizens of the world. In East Africa, nationalists proclaimed *Uhuru* (freedom) in their Kiswahili mother tongue, linking it to the promise of the Atlantic Charter, the equality of all humans and races, and the debates about fundamental freedoms taking place at the UN. Even if these activists did not speak or write

---

[27] Christopher Roberts, *The Contentious History of the International Bill of Human Rights* (Cambridge: Cambridge University Press, 2015), 129.

in the metropolitan languages of their colonial overlords, or use the voguish term "human rights," their engagement with the human rights idea is evident. The fixation with the metropolitan lexicon risks silencing other articulations of the human rights idea.

The Right to Self-Determination

Although the discourse of "native rights" provided a rationale for European imperialism from the beginning, the political and economic upheavals unleashed by the world wars accentuated debates over the rights and liberties of colonial subjects. Opposition to colonial rule increasingly became anchored on rights. During World War I, US President Woodrow Wilson gave the concept of national self-determination prominence in his Fourteen Points speech, which outlined principles for the end of war and for world peace. Wilson's Fourteen Points included proposals for securing the independence and self-determination of several European states that would form the basis of the Treaty of Versailles, which ended the war, and the League of Nations. Wilsonian idealism inspired many people in the colonized world who sought self-determination or representation in colonial governance. The end of the war signaled the beginning of the great upsurge of anti-colonial nationalism, which reached its fruition after 1945.

Following the strategies of Indian anti-colonial leaders such as Mohandas Gandhi and Jawaharlal Nehru, African leaders began to articulate their demands for political representation and self-rule not simply as concessions from their European colonial overlords but as earned entitlements for their contributions to imperial war efforts. European powers relied extensively on their colonies for material, bureaucratic and manpower contributions to fight the war. French colonies in Africa contributed an estimated 235,000 soldiers to the war efforts and French West Africa provided 94 battalions for the European front. These contributions engendered a sense of entitlement among colonial subjects in Africa and elsewhere. African leaders increasingly articulated their political demand as a moral entitlement justified by their war-time loyalty. Prominent among these early political leaders were Joseph Casely-Hayford in the Gold Coast, Blaise Diagne in French West Africa, Herbert Macaulay in Nigeria and Harry Thuku in Kenya.

FIGURE 5.1 Blaise Diagne

The interwar years marked a defining moment in the anti-colonial movement as continental and diasporic African leaders came together at Pan-African forums to address issues of colonialism, racial discrimination and exploitation affecting peoples of African descent globally. The first Pan-African congress in Paris attracted delegates representing fifteen countries and colonies, including Liberia and the West African colonies, Haiti, the British West Indies and the United States. Two key organizers of the congress were the African American intellectual W. E. B. Du Bois and the Senegalese politician Blaise Diagne (see Figure 5.1). The objective of the congress, which was held on the fringes of the 1919 Versailles Peace Conference marking the end of World War I, was to influence the political agenda of the Peace Conference and the fate of black people in the post-war era. The congress adopted a *charter of rights* for peoples of African descent and passed a resolution calling for the protection of Africans and people of African descent from abuse, exploitation and colonial violence. In the following decade, more Pan-Africanist congresses addressed issues of rights, justice and empowerment of Africans and African descendant peoples in London in 1921, in Lisbon in 1923 and in New York in 1927. Delegates at these congresses demanded independence for the colonies of West Africa and the British West Indies;

the abolition of white minority rule in Kenya, Rhodesia and South Africa; and coordinated intervention to end the lynching of blacks and mob law in the United States.

Even more than World War I, World War II marked a period of renewed international debates over democracy, self-determination and fundamental human rights. These debates resonated deeply with colonized people in their struggles for independence. Although nationalist claims had been mounting in African colonies for several decades, wartime international politics made self-determination a living principle. Allied propaganda presented the war as a fight between the ideals of freedom, democracy and self-determination against the tyranny of Nazism, authoritarianism and Fascism. As the war progressed, however, it became apparent that the principles of self-determination, so forcefully espoused by the Allies, would not be extended beyond the confines of occupied Europe or to colonial subjects in the non-Western world. To independence activists, Prime Minister Wilson's Churchill's restrictive interpretation of the Atlantic Charter provided the clearest evidence of this limited vision of self-determination.

Post-war discontent with colonial rule in Africa found expression in anti-colonial rebellions that broke out across the continent in the 1940s and '50s. Protests against French rule in Madagascar and against British rule in Nigeria and the Gold Coast (Ghana) forced colonial governments to undertake reforms that allowed for greater representation of indigenous people in governance. Anti-colonial agitations were legitimized by the principle of self-determination expressed in the UN Charter, which urged member states with colonies to develop self-government and take due account of the political aspirations of the natives. Unlike the League of Nations, which had essentially been a club of European powers unconcerned with colonial problems, the more broadly based UN progressively became embroiled in colonial issues. Although European colonial powers opposed the idea that the UN should be actively engaged in the so-called colonial question, the UN Charter ultimately endorsed the right to self-determination of all peoples. This signaled that old colonial systems could not be sustained within the postwar international order.

The human rights provisions of the UN Charter were further strengthened by the UN's adoption of the Universal Declaration of Human Rights (UDHR) in 1948. The UDHR marked the international recognition of certain fundamental rights and freedoms as the inalienable universal entitlement of every person by virtue of their humanity. At its adoption, the UDHR was heralded as a world mile-stone in the long struggle for human rights. US First Lady Eleanor Roosevelt, one of the drafters of the Declaration, famously proclaimed that the Declaration might well become the Magna Carta of all man-kind. This optimism was in spite of the reality that a third of the world's population was, at the time, still under colonial rule. This was also in spite of the fact that most colonized peoples were unrepre-sented at the UN and had no opportunity to contribute to the inter-national debates about fashioning a global human rights document. The exclusion of the voices and perspectives of colonized peoples in the process of drawing up the UDHR would remain one of the most potent limitations of its claim to universality.

Paradoxes of Rights Talk

Anti-colonial activists highlighted the contradictions in the discourse of human rights by European imperial powers at the UN and the realities of state repression and violence in the colonies.[28] They noted, for example, that the emergent doctrine of international human rights did not have any significant impact on the British military campaigns against the Mau Mau or the French war in Algeria. Both conflicts come up only marginally in discussions about human rights and the colonial question. Even less impactful on colonial conditions was the European Convention on Human Rights (ECHR), which Britain ratified in 1951 and Belgium in 1955. Although the Convention came into effect in Kenya in 1953, just over a year into the Mau Mau insurgency, it had little impact on the conflict. It pitted an enthusiastic British Foreign Office, responsible for signing the Convention, against a cynical and suspicious Colonial Office. Officials at the Colonial Office mostly saw the convention as unnecessary because Britain, they believed, already had laws and policies that protected the freedoms of citizens at home and subjects in the colonies. Local colonial adminis-trators were equally dismissive of the Convention, seeing it as hin-drance to effective governance. In the end, concerns about Britain's human rights obligations under the UDHR and the ECHR, tepidly expressed by Foreign Office diplomats, had limited impact on British

---

[28] Klose, *Human Rights in the Shadow of Colonial Violence*, 6.

military campaigns in Kenya.[29] However, the atrocities committed by British agents during the Mau Mau insurgency would remain a contentious legacy of colonial human rights violations in Kenya. In 2012 a British high court ruled that 400 Kenyan victims could sue the British government for compensation for torture, rape, wrongful detention, forced labor and other human rights violations that they suffered in the hands of British officials during the Mau Mau insurgency.

The Algerian war held more direct relevance to the post–World War II international human rights movement. The atrocities of the Algerian war became a reference point in debates about the enforcement of universal human rights in the colonies. Faced with growing international outrage over wartime atrocities by French police and military forces, the French government in 1957 ordered an official investigation into complaints of torture and other abuses prohibited under the UDHR, the 1949 Geneva Convention on the Conduct of War and the provisions of the French Penal Code. The report of the "Committee for the Safeguard of Individual Rights" confirmed the extensive use of torture by French security forces in Algeria. In addition to facilitating Algeria's independence, one significant outcome of the Algerian war and the human rights debates it provoked was the affirmation of the right to national self-determination, which was subsequently laid out in the two major UN human rights covenants: the International Covenant on Economic, Social and Cultural Rights and the International Covenant on Civil and Political Rights.

Although anti-colonial activists drew on an emergent lexicon of universal human rights in their struggles for self-determination, they were also deeply skeptical of its transformative potential. They were not alone in their skepticism. The UN's creators envisioned a world organization that would address rights violations but also protect the interests of empire. The acceptance of human rights at this moment was conditioned by pessimism among the great powers that it would have little practical effect.[30] The South African statesman Jan Smut, who introduced the concept of human rights into the UN Charter, remained a firm believer in the supremacy of the British Empire and could not countenance extending the human rights principles he so

---

[29] Huw Bennett, *Fighting the Mau Mau: The British Army and Counter-Insurgency in the Kenya* (Cambridge: Cambridge University Press, 2013), 80.

[30] See Mark Mazower, *No Enchanted Palace: The End of Empire and the Ideological Origins of the United Nations* (Princeton: Princeton University Press, 2009), 30–35.

vigorously championed at the UN to his own country. Delegates of the white minority–ruled South African government at the UN strongly opposed discussions about racial discrimination in their country, seeing it as an undue interference in their internal affairs and a violation of sovereignty. When, in 1946, India's UN delegate Vijaya Lakshmi Pandit portrayed South Africa's policies of racial discrimination and segregation as human rights violations that contravened the UN Charter, General Smuts responded sternly that his country was protected by the provisions of the Charter, which precludes the UN from interfering with those internal matters concerning the domestic jurisdiction of states.[31] The treatment of Indians, "coloreds" and mixed races in South Africa, he stated, was a matter of domestic jurisdiction. Smuts warned that if the UN intervened in what he considered his country's domestic affairs, it would be setting a "dangerous precedent" that could undermine national sovereignty everywhere.[32]

In the colonies, doubt and cynicism also arose from the sense that it took the suffering of "whites" during World War II to jolt world powers into action, whereas the atrocities of colonialism had left the world indifferent. It did not escape independence activists that colonial massacres of indigenous people did not garner enough global outrage and indignation to trigger an international rights movement.[33] Wilsonian rhetoric of self-determination and the promising human rights impulses of post–World War I internationalism did not coalesce in a rights movement. That would wait until Europe encountered its own era of tyranny and atrocities. As historian Mark Mazower puts it, "such was the shock of being subjected to a regime of unprecedented and unremitting violence that in the space of eight years following the war, a sea-change took place in European's political attitudes, and they *rediscovered* the virtues of democracy."[34]

Indeed, the main concern for European statesmen in human rights discussions at the UN was post-war European geopolitics. The work of the UN Human Rights Commission in its early days consisted of underlying struggles over which rights to include and which ones

---

[31] United Nations, "Charter of the United Nations," Article 2(7). Available at www.un .org/en/documents/charter/index.shtml. Accessed May 14, 2014.

[32] Paul Gordon Lauren, *The Evolution of International Human Rights: Visions Seen* (Philadelphia: University of Pennsylvania Press, 1998), 200–201.

[33] *West African Pilot*, March 13, 1945, 8.

[34] Mark Mazower, *Dark Continent: Europe's Twentieth Century* (New York: Vintage Books, 2000), 140.

to leave out.[35] Discussions about colonies or "non-self-governing territories," in official UN jargon, occasionally became a source of embarrassment for imperial powers, but that did not deter resolute rejection of human rights proposals that were considered political interference in colonial affairs. For example, a 1953 proposal by Arab and Asian states for Tunisian independence on the basis of the UN principle of the right to self-determination was rejected as an interference into France's domestic affairs.[36] Low-key discussions took place within the context of information from non-self-governing territories, but there could be no serious debate on political issues such as the liberation war in Algeria. Despite compelling evidence of gross human rights violations, Western powers at the UN supported the French position that the North African conflict fell under France's domestic jurisdiction. South Africa's racism would be debated mainly in terms of the treatment of people of Indian origin because apartheid was viewed as an internal problem. Anti-colonial activists were therefore keenly aware of the politics of imperial self-interest in discussions about human rights at the UN. Nevertheless, they drew on the emergent human rights doctrine in their struggles for civil liberties and self-determination.

Nationalist Rights Discourse

Unlike earlier generations of African political leaders who were assimilationist and favored political and economic collaboration between the colony and metropole, the generations of leaders who came of age in the 1940s and '50s were more assertive and insistent on full independence. The emergence of a new group of Western-educated African elites strengthened nationalist movements and intensified local opposition to colonial rule. Prominent among this group of assertive pro-independence political leaders were Sékou Touré of Guinea, Kwame Nkrumah of Ghana, Nnamdi Azikiwe of Nigeria, Julius Nyerere of Tanzania, Kenneth Kaunda of Zambia, Jomo Kenyatta of Kenya and

[35] Johannes Morsink, *The Universal Declaration of Human Rights: Origins. Drafting and Intent* (Philadelphia: University of Pennsylvania Press, 1999), 12–14; A. W. B. Simpson, *Human Rights and the End of Empire*, chapter 5, "Human Rights and the Structure of the Brave New World."

[36] United States Department of State, *The Department of State Bulletin*, Office of Public Communication Bureau of Public Affairs, 28 (1953): 396.

Ferhat Abbas and Ahmed Ben Bella of Algeria. Some other political leaders, notably in the French colonies, were content at first with greater participation in the French Union.

In Algeria, the nationalist leader Ferhat Abbas drew on the wartime discourse of the right to self-determination to articulate political demands for independence. In his manifesto *Manifeste du Peuple Algérien*, published in 1943, Abbas referred directly to the Atlantic Charter. After France's defeat in 1940, he asked the new Vichy government to implement comprehensive reforms in Algeria in line with new global norms that warranted the redefining of the relationship between France and its colonies. In response to pressure by French authorities on Muslim Algerians to actively participate in the fight against Hitler for the liberation of their "Arabian brothers" in Tunisia, Abbas stated that if the war was indeed being fought for the liberation of people of all races and religions as proclaimed by the Allied leaders, Muslim Algerians would be willing to commit themselves wholeheartedly to this endeavor. However, he linked participation in the war to specific political demands, one of which was the convening of a conference where elected Muslim representatives would negotiate political, economic and social equality for the Muslim population. Abbas also demanded the abolition of colonial repression, the right of self-determination for all peoples and an Algerian constitution anchored in human rights.[37] Thus, while the promises implied in the Atlantic Charter helped to mobilize support of the colonized populations for the Allied Cause, it also served to reinforce and legitimize long-standing demands for equality and independence.

In the Gold Coast (Ghana), a vigorous anti-colonial nationalist campaign led by the charismatic Kwame Nkrumah rejected British war-time reforms and demanded complete independence from British rule. Nkrumah's Convention People's Party took as its motto: "We prefer self-government with danger, to servitude in tranquility." A central theme in Nkrumah's anti-colonialism was universal equality. In the course of Ghana's struggle for independence, he wrote that "[t]he peoples of the colonies know precisely what they want. They wish to be free and independent, to be able to feel themselves ... equal with all other peoples, and to work out their own destiny without interference."[38] Responding to critics who questioned his emphasis

---

[37] Klose, *Human Rights in the Shadow of Colonial Violence*, 24–25.
[38] Nkrumah, *Revolutionary Path*, 40.

on political independence over economic and social development, Nkrumah famously urged his countrymen: "Seek ye first the political kingdom and all other things shall be added unto you."[39] Nkrumah's quest for the political kingdom not only represented a normative statement but also symbolized a propensity to view the political struggle as the paramount human rights question in the colonial state.[40] In his words, "self-determination is a means of further realization of our social, economic and cultural potentialities. It is political freedom that dictates the pace of economic and social progress."[41] To this end, Kwame Nkrumah took up the issue of the application of the principle of self-determination espoused in the Atlantic Charter to African colonies. The clear emphasis in his anti-colonial nationalist rights discourse was on the collective right to self-government, which he considered to be a prerequisite to fulfilling other rights aspirations.

The political ideas of Nnamdi Azikiwe, who became the first president of independent Nigeria, also epitomized the connections between anti-colonial struggle and the human rights movement. Azikiwe's experiences of colonial rule in Africa and racial segregation in the United States, where he studied at black universities in the 1920s and 1930s, shaped his political ideology and understanding of human rights. He drew on an eclectic tradition of rights ideas and was deeply aware of the contradictions in imperial rights discourses. His human rights ideas were influenced by traditional African thought, Christian theology, Enlightenment liberalism, American republicanism and post-war universal human rights doctrine. Azikiwe was among the first in a steady stream of African students studying in the United States who would return to lead the anti-colonial movement in Africa. For many of these students, the United States represented both the promises and failures of rights idealism. On one hand, their experiences of racial discrimination intensified racial consciousness and fostered an uncompromising determination to achieve equality at home. On the other hand, they "shared a loyalty to the American ideal, the confident expectation of improved status, and the admiration for a dynamic society."[42]

[39] Kwame Nkrumah, *The Autobiography of Kwame Nkrumah* (Nelson: London, 1957), 146.
[40] Kenneth Grundy, "Nkrumah's Theory of Underdevelopment: An Analysis of Recurrent Themes," *World Politics*, 15, 3 (1963): 438.
[41] *The Gold Coast Weekly Review*, July 20, 1955. Quoted in Martin L. Kilson, "Nationalism and Social Classes in British West Africa," *Journal of Politics*, 20 (1958): 380.
[42] Coleman, *Nigeria: Background to Nationalism*, 245.

Perhaps more than any other African political leader of his era, Azikiwe came to represent a strand of African intellectual nationalism that challenged the legitimacy of colonial rule both domestically and internationally. He established two newspapers, *West African Pilot* and *Daily Comet*, which became platforms for his anti-colonial activism. *West African Pilot* became one of the most widely circulated newspapers in sub-Saharan Africa in the 1940s and 1950s. His connections with intellectuals and institutions in the United States also provided an international forum for Azikiwe's anti-colonial activism. At Howard University he was exposed to the Black Nationalist movement of Marcus Garvey and encountered the African-American intellectual and activist George Padmore. Azikiwe and Padmore cooperated later on several projects, including founding the Pan-African Federation and organizing the Pan-African Congress in Manchester in 1945, which called for universal implementation of the principles of the Four Freedoms and self-determination in the Atlantic Charter.[43]

In a speech delivered to the graduates of Storer College in the United States on the occasion of his being given an honorary doctorate degree in 1947, Azikiwe linked the struggles for self-determination in the colonies with President Roosevelt's "Four Freedoms," the Atlantic Charter and universal human rights, stating:

> According to the leaders of the Allied Nations, we fought the last war in order to revive the stature of man and to make the Four Freedoms a living reality. I interpret those war and peace aims to mean the enjoyment of political freedom, social equality, economic security, and religious freedom, everywhere in the world ... [but] when we demand to exercise elementary *human rights*, not only are we silenced by our self-appointed rulers, but the outside world seems to close its eyes, stuff its ears, and seal its mouth on the subject of what is to us a righteous cause.[44]

The Memorandum on "The Atlantic Charter and British West Africa," which Azikiwe and other West African leaders submitted to the British Secretary of State in 1943, was part of a strategy of assailing the legitimacy of colonial rule by showing the inconsistencies and contradictions of Britain's position on the right to self-determination.

---

[43] "Pan-African Congress Resolution, Manchester 1945," in *African Intellectual Heritage: A Book of Sources*, Molefi Asante and Abu Shardow Abarry, eds. (Philadelphia: Temple University Press, 1996), 518.

[44] Nnamdi Azikiwe, *Zik: A Selection from the Speeches of Nnamdi Azikiwe* (Cambridge: Cambridge University Press, 1961), 82.

Following Prime Minister Churchill's statement that the Atlantic Charter applied only to Europe and not to British colonies, Azikiwe wrote that it was imperative for Africans to prepare their own political blueprint rather than rely on "those who are too busy preparing their own."[45] In 1943 he published his *Political Blueprint of Nigeria*, in which he outlined a rights-based vision for Nigeria's independence. He referred to the Atlantic Charter and Woodrow Wilson's Fourteen Points, using both to support his uniquely anti-colonial human rights agenda. After the adoption of the UDHR in 1948, Azikiwe increasingly drew on it and the idea of universal human rights in his political speeches and writings. He referenced Eleanor Roosevelt's vision of a post-war world where individuals all over the world would have freedom. "World peace," he stated, could be assured only if this vision of universal rights was "true for men all over the world ... regardless of race and religion."[46] At a time when colonial powers sought to drive a wedge between self-determination in the colonies and discussions about universal human rights at the UN, Azikiwe insisted on the fundamental interrelatedness of both ideas. He strenuously countered British attempts to delink anti-colonial movements from universal human rights.

Azikiwe's *Political Blueprint* listed the basic rights that should be guaranteed to every "commonwealth subject." These included the right to health, education, social equality, material security and the right to recreation. It also included provisions for religious freedom, the protection of life and property, collective bargaining and the rights to public assembly, discussion and demonstration.[47] Azikiwe recommended that the Virginia Bill of Rights of 1776, which served as a model for the American Constitution, should also serve as a model for preparing Nigeria's constitution. The Virginia Bill of Rights, he argued, was ideal, because "it embodies all the basic rights for which democratic-loving humanity had fought to preserve in the course of history."[48] He also idealized the Declaration of Independence of Liberia of 1847 for its affirmation of the "inalienable rights of all men."[49] Azikiwe's vision of human rights appears to have hinged more

---

[45] Nnamdi Azikiwe, *Political Blueprint of Nigeria* (Lagos: African Book Company, 1945), 72. My emphasis.

[46] Azikiwe, *Zik: A Selection from the Speeches of Nnamdi Azikiwe*, 7.

[47] Azikiwe, *Political Blueprint*, 2.   [48] Ibid., 40.

[49] Nnamdi Azikiwe, *Renascent Africa* (London: F. Cass, 1968 [1937]), 174.

FIGURE 5.2 Nnamdi Azikiwe
Credit: Dr. Nnamdi Azikiwe, Urualla, Nigeria. Photograph by Eliot Elisofon,
1959 EEPA EECL 1645. Eliot Elisofon Photographic Archives, National Museum
of African Art Smithsonian Institution.

on the Enlightenment liberal rights tradition than on the uncertain
promise of the Atlantic Charter.

Azikiwe also led the drafting of the *Freedom Charter*, which served as
a manifesto for his political party, the National Council for Nigeria and
the Cameroons in 1948.[50] The Charter affirmed a wide range of political, economic and social rights, including the right to life, freedom of
opinion, freedom of association and the right to self-determination. It
called for the establishment of states on ethnic and linguistic bases as a
guarantee of political representation and minority rights. Alluding to
the Atlantic Charter, the Freedom Charter affirmed the right of all
peoples to choose the form of government under which they may live.
It also included a condemnation of slavery, servitude and imperialism;
an affirmation of the equality of all persons; the right to basic education
and healthcare; and even the right to recreation and leisure.[51]

---

[50] National Council for Nigeria and the Cameroons "Freedom Charter," reprinted in
West African Pilot, January 4, 1949 (hereinafter *Freedom Charter*)
[51] Ibid.

The Uganda National Congress under the leadership of Ignatius Musaazi adopted a similar manifesto, *Freedom Charter and the Manifesto of the Uganda National Congress* (UNC) in 1952. The Charter also drew extensively from the language of international human rights that had, by the 1950s, become fully intertwined with nationalist anti-colonial discourse. The Charter asserted: "Freedom is the birth right of all peoples, irrespective of color or race; a right to choose their own government which would guarantee the human rights of peoples to choose and practice any religion, trade and occupation, to protect the sanctity of the home and to respect individual liberty and parliamentary opposition." The Manifesto also outlined several rights that the UNC believed should constitute the foundations of an independent and democratic Uganda. These include the right of adult men and women to vote, the guarantee of equal status in relation to government institutions, the right of free enterprise, the right to form trade unions and a reaffirmation of the rights outlined in the UN Charter.[52]

In Tanganyika, Julius Nyerere referred frequently to the repression and injustices of colonial rule as derogations from basic human dignity and fundamental human rights. "Our struggle," he stated, "will always be a struggle for human rights ... Our position is based on the belief in the equality of human beings, in their rights and duties as citizens."[53] Similarly, the Kenyan nationalist leader Jomo Kenyatta accused the British government of denying Africans the "most elementary human rights of self-expression, freedom of speech, the right to form social organizations to improve their conditions, and above all, the right to move freely in their own country."[54] He claimed that these were the rights that the Gikuyu people enjoyed from time immemorial before the arrival of the British. Instead of advancing the African toward a higher intellectual, moral and economic level as colonists had promised, colonial rule had reduced him to a state of serfdom, subjected him to an inferior position in human society and denied his social, economic and political initiatives.[55]

---

[52] Donald Anthony Low, *The Mind of Buganda: Documents of the Modern History of an African Kingdom* (Berkeley: University of California Press, 1971), 182.

[53] Julius Nyerere, *Freedom and Unity: Uhuru na umoja; A Selection from Writings and Speeches, 1952–65* (London: Oxford University Press, 1967), 76.

[54] Jomo Kenyatta, *Facing Mount Kenya: The Tribal Life of the Gikuyu* (New York: Vintage Books, 1965), 189.

[55] Kenyatta, *Facing Mount Kenya*, 190.

It is clear, therefore, that African political leaders and anti-colonial activists were engaged in debates about international human rights as it emerged in the mid-twentieth century. They coopted the new language of universal human rights to reinforce long-standing demands for self-rule. Their struggles, along with other global developments, precipitated the eventual collapse of European imperialism in the continent. The voices of indigenous political leaders and activists in the margins of Empire were not always heard in early international human rights debates or at the early UN, where a new international order was being defined. When the UDHR was adopted at the UN in 1948, most of Africa's population was still under colonial domination. However, it would be mistaken to interpret this as signifying the absence of human rights ideas in African anti-colonial movements. The tendency to overlook the experiences and perspectives of indigenous anti-colonial activists in twentieth-century human rights histories is largely a consequence of the privileging of Western and metropolitan narratives in the scholarship.

Trusteeship and Grassroots Activism

The role of grassroots activists has not been given enough attention in histories of anti-colonialism in Africa. Anti-colonialism has mostly been constructed as an elite-led movement, and the place of human rights within it has largely been framed around the high politics of nationalism and independence. Recent studies, however, have expanded the discussion to include grassroots networks and activities where anti-colonial human rights ideology also found expression.[56] These studies show that the appeal to human rights within anti-colonial struggles was not limited to national political leaders and high officeholders. Ordinary people and local grassroots activists also mobilized the idea and language of human rights in opposition to colonial rule. In order to construct a fully representative history of human rights and decolonization, it is essential to pay attention to the grassroots impulses that shaped anti-colonialism. This requires

---

[56] For example, Meredith Terretta, *Petitioning for Our rights, Fighting for Our Nation: The History of the Democratic Union of Cameroonian Women, 1949–1960* (Bamenda, Cameroon: Langaa Research & Publishing, 2013), and Burke, *Decolonization and the Evolution of International Human Rights*.

attending to local anti-colonial political contexts and social settings in which the historical actors deployed the language of human rights. Given the objective of human rights ideology to give voice to the disenfranchised, it is crucial that histories of human rights be written not only from the perspectives of dominant actors in mainstream political processes, but also from bottom-up perspectives that take account of grassroots activities. A history of human rights centered solely or predominantly on actors and institutions at the highest echelons of politics risks becoming itself a narrative of power and exclusion, and the antithesis of human rights ideology.

In many parts of Africa, decolonization was a grassroots movement. Mid-twentieth-century mass mobilization against colonial rule was possible because of the involvement of ordinary people, such as woman artisans who protested oppressive tax policies, workers who organized strikes to protest unfair labor conditions, peasants who demanded fair prices for their produce and demobilized soldiers who fought in imperial armies during the world wars. The global political upheavals unleashed by the world wars provided ordinary Africans with opportunities to express discontent and opposition to colonial rule in international arenas such as the League of Nations Mandate Commission and, later, the UN Trusteeship System.

With the defeat of Germany and the Ottoman Empire in World War I, their Asian and African possessions, considered not yet capable of being self-governing, were distributed among the victorious Allied powers through the League of Nations mandate system. German colonies in Africa were put under the control of Great Britain and France with the mandate to administer Togoland (both), the Cameroons (both), Ruanda-Urundi (Belgium) and Tanganyika (Britain), while South West Africa (Namibia) was put under the control of Britain and South Africa. With the creation of the UN following World War II, the mandated territories of the League of Nations became trust territories of the United Nations. Under the League's mandate system, mandating powers were required to report periodically on the "welfare of the natives under their rule" to the League's Mandate Commission in Geneva. This reporting obligation provided opportunities for colonial subjects and their allies to present their grievances at an international forum. Between 1920 and 1946 the Mandates Commission received thousands of appeals against French mandatory rule in Africa from Duala elites in Cameroon and Ewe traders in Togo.[57] Similar appeals were brought against British mandatory rule in Tanganyika and South West Africa.

African petitions expressed a wide range of grievances. They denounced racial discrimination and repressive policies, objected to the corporal punishment of laborers, demanded the reinstatement of deposed chiefs, and protested unfair taxation and land expropriation. Metropolitan humanitarian organizations such as the *Ligue des Droits de l'Homme* (the League of the Rights of Man), founded in France in 1898, worked with local activists in French mandate territories to bring petitions before the Mandates Commission.[58] The most transformative aspect of the mandates system, from a human rights standpoint, was the level of international publicity and scrutiny that it brought to the conditions of indigenous people under colonial rule. Although the League of Nations mandate system did not explicitly reference human rights, it was founded on a notion of native rights and liberties that also informed the colonial "civilizing mission" – the obligations of imperial powers to administer their colonies with the aim of improving the welfare of natives. By instituting international oversight and providing a platform for missionaries, humanitarians and nationalists to expose the repression and brutalities of imperial rule, the League's mandate system made imperial governance more burdensome and brought independent statehood nearer.[59]

The UN trusteeship system created after World War II provided a similar international platform for airing anti-colonial grievances. Of the eleven former German territories placed under UN trusteeship at the end of World War II, six were in Africa. The main objective of the trusteeship system was to promote the political, economic and social advancement of the trust territories and to facilitate their development toward self-government. The UN Trusteeship Council was also specifically mandated to promote "respect for human rights and fundamental freedoms and recognition of the interdependence of peoples of the world."[60] This provided a platform for African independence activists to engage directly with an emergent discourse of international

---

[57] Susan Pedersen, *The Guardians: The League of Nations and the Crisis of Empire* (Oxford: Oxford University Press, 2015), 3.

[58] Meredith Terretta, "Cause lawyering et anti-colonialisme: activisme politique et Etat de droit dans l'Afrique française, 1946–1960," *Politique Africaine*, 138, 2 (2015): 25–28.

[59] Pedersen, *The Guardians: The League of Nations and the Crisis of Empire*, 4.

[60] United Nations, "The United Nations and Decolonization: International Trusteeship System." Available at www.un.org/en/decolonization/its.shtml. Accessed September 23, 2016.

human rights. Africa's UN Trust Territories were therefore pivotal sites for the conception and definition of human rights; as historian Meredith Terretta has argued, they were a "birthplace of the postwar international human rights project."[61] Anti-colonial activists in the trust territories believed that the UDHR, the UN Charter and the UN Trusteeship Agreement gave them moral and legal grounds to redress the injustices they faced at the hands of European administrators. Working through NGOs such as the New York–based International League of the Rights of Man, the American Committee on Africa and the Movement for Colonial Freedom in London, Africans drew on the human rights doctrine to further their anti-colonial agenda at the UN and other international forums. A few examples of such engagement will suffice here.

In the early 1950s, the UN Trusteeship Council received several petitions from Africans living in the UN trust territories of the Cameroons, Tanganyika and Togoland. Many of these petitions were framed in the language of international human rights. African petitioners invoked assurances of civil liberties and self-determination in the UDHR and the ECHR. In northern Togoland, marginalized groups challenged British administrative authority by putting forward their own chiefs while simultaneously appealing to the UN Trusteeship Council to protect their rights. In one collective petition to the Trusteeship Council, the Nawuri community complained that they had "suffered untold hardships" under local British administrators and that the issues involved were not merely political but involved a "violation of fundamental legal rights of the people of Togoland."[62]

It is noteworthy that the majority of these petitions to UN bodies were from ordinary people – market traders and farmers, civil servants, artisans, women, youth groups and rural peasants. In French Cameroon, petitioners appealed to human rights not only in the call for self-determination but also for the protection of individual rights codified in international law. They sent a list with the names of people whom French and British administrators had deported, arrested or killed, appealing to the international community to protect specific

---

[61] Terretta, "We Had Been Fooled," 333.

[62] Northern Region of Ghana Public Records, Tamale, 8/2/210, Petition from Nawuri leaders to the administering authority and the Trusteeship Council, 3 Nov. 1954. Cited in Paul Stacey, "'The Chiefs, Elders, and People Have for Many Years Suffered Untold Hardships': Protests by Coalitions of the Excluded in British Northern Togoland, United Nations Trusteeship Territory, 1950–7," *The Journal of African History*, 55, 3 (2014): 423.

individuals.[63] In Tanganyika, Africans petitioned the UN Trusteeship Council to demand the protection of their human rights against violations by British officials and European settlers. Petitioning the Council in 1951, one group of African workers complained that the practice of pay discrimination "based on skin color" contravened the UDHR. Invoking the anti-discrimination provisions of the UDHR, they stated: "African employees are, according to the Universal Declaration of Human Rights born free and equal in dignity and rights, entitled to all the rights set forth in the Declaration ... If these are indeed human rights, and if Africans are regarded as human beings, surely they are entitled to them."[64] In Zanzibar, anti-colonial activists formed the Human Rights League, an organization whose primary objective was to advocate for national self-government. Although the organization promoted a narrow exclusionary nationalism that was anti-Arab and anti-Indian, its leaders drew on the language of international human rights to justify their cause.[65] Declaring the organization a threat to public order, British authorities banned the League even though they worried that the ban might cause adverse criticism abroad because of the "high sounding title of the organization."[66]

Petitions to the Trusteeship Council came not only from trust territories. Africans in non-trust territories also took advantage of the platform that the Trusteeship System offered to protest colonial rule and policies. In 1953, a group of Chiefs in Nyasaland petitioned the Trusteeship Council about the creation of the Central African Federation. They claimed that the lack of consultation in the process of creating the Federation amounted to a violation of their right to self-determination.[67] Concerned that this might open a floodgate of petitions from its colonies, Britain threatened to withdraw cooperation from the Trusteeship Council if it considered the petition. Britain, France and Belgium also strongly opposed proposals to establish petition

---

[63] Terretta, "We Had Been Fooled," 345.

[64] Tanzania National Archives (hereinafter TNA), Foreign Affairs (FA) 37681/5/3. Petition of the African Government Employees Association, Mwanza to the Visiting United Nations Trusteeship Council Mission to Tanganyika, August 10, 1951.

[65] Jonathon Glassman, *War of Words, War of Stones: Racial Thought and Violence in Colonial Zanzibar* (Bloomington: Indiana University Press, 2011), 345.

[66] NAUK CO 822/2193, "The Human Rights League, Zanzibar," anonymous confidential memorandum, November 8, 1961.

[67] NAUK CO 936/99. The Chiefs transmitted their petition to the Committee through the British anti-apartheid activist Reverend Michael Scott. *Times*, October 27, 1953.

mechanisms for colonized peoples, forcing the UN to adopt a compromise complaints procedure that accommodated imperial interests.[68]

★★★

Women played important roles in grassroots anti-colonial struggles. African workers organized in labor unions and women organized in advocacy groups mobilized mass support for anti-colonial campaigns. In some cases, they explicitly linked their struggles to international human rights. Perhaps the most prominent female anti-colonial grassroots activist of this era in West Africa was Funmilayo Ransome-Kuti, an unrelenting advocate of self-determination, women's rights and a wide range of other civil and socioeconomic rights. The Abeokuta Women's Union (AWU), which Ransome-Kuti formed in 1946, was an eclectic group that comprised elite and artisanal market women. The organization played an active role in local protest politics and grassroots mobilization of women in support of nationalist causes. In 1949, it embarked on a major protest against an authoritarian chief who, as the local "Native Authority" under the British indirect rule system, was seen as a symbol of colonial sexism and oppression. The protest campaign ultimately forced the chief's abdication. In a letter to a British newspaper in 1947, Ransome-Kuti argued that under colonialism, African women had lost their traditional economic and political rights. Not only were they denied suffrage and any role in government, they were forced to pay taxes they could not afford and were denied basic amenities, leaving many of them impoverished.[69] She appealed to British women to help free African women from political, social and economic "slavery," stating: "Your country is responsible for the state of ours; can you let this state of things continue?"[70]

Beyond her local activism, Ransome-Kuti was also active in several international women's organizations, including the Women's International Democratic Federation, a post-war women's organization that grew out of European resistance movements and was connected to the Communist International. Ransome-Kuti's anti-colonial human rights activism in the 1940s and '50s took her across colonized

---

[68] James P. Hubbard, *The United States and the End of British Colonial Rule in Africa, 1941–1968* (Jefferson, NC: McFarland, 2011), 169–170.

[69] Jeremiah I. Dibua, *Modernization and the Crisis of Development in Africa: The Nigerian Experience* (Burlington, VT: Ashgate, 2006), 69.

[70] Funmilayo Ransome-Kuti. "For Women: She Speaks for Nigeria – We Had Equality till Britain Came," *Daily Worker* (London), August 18, 1947.

Africa and beyond, including travels to Austria, China (where she met with Mao Tse-tung), Czechoslovakia, Denmark, England, Germany, Hungary, Poland, the Soviet Union and Switzerland. She had contacts with women's organizations in South Africa, Trinidad, Korea, India, Vietnam and Bulgaria. In a Cold War era when any affiliation with communist or socialist-leaning organizations or individuals was seen as dangerous by Western bloc governments, Ransome-Kuti, as a women and colonial subject, came under heavy pressure from British colonial authorities, intent on suppressing her local and international activism.[71] In 1956 British authorities in Nigeria denied her a travel passport to curtail her efforts to "influence women with communist ideas and policies."[72]

Like many other independence activists of her era, Ransome-Kuti did not see any distinction between her demands for political self-determination and other human rights claims. Rather, she considered collective liberation and individual rights to be interrelated. African independence activists who assigned great importance to the protection of individual human rights recognized that independence from European rule was an essential prerequisite for other rights. Active in anti-imperialist, anti-racist and anti-sexist struggles for most of her life, Ransome-Kuti dedicated herself to issues of woman suffrage and representation in government, considering herself as "primarily an advocate for human rights."[73] She was part of a long tradition of women activists across the continent who did not isolate their oppression as women from their oppression as colonial subjects and as Africans. They well understood that their liberation as women was as connected to colonialism as it was to racism and sexism. These oppressions were intersectional and could not be disaggregated. The history of human rights and decolonization in the twentieth century is incomplete without the stories of activists such as Ransome-Kuti and African petitioners to the League of Nations and the UN, who worked to connect grassroots mobilization with international activism.

---

[71] Cheryl Johnson-Odim, "For Their Freedoms: The Anti-Imperialist and International Feminist Activity of Funmilayo Ransome-Kuti of Nigeria," *Women's Studies International Forum*, 32 (2009): 53.

[72] Cheryl Johnson-Odim and Nina Emma Mba, *For Women and the Nation: Funmilayo Ransome-Kuti of Nigeria* (Urbana: University of Illinois Press, 1997), 147.

[73] Johnson-Odim, "For Their Freedoms," 51.

Anti-Apartheid

The anti-apartheid movement and the larger struggle against white minority rule in Southern Africa marked a defining moment in the history of human rights in Africa. Long after other African countries achieved independence, South Africa and Rhodesia (Zimbabwe) remained under the grip of white minority governments founded on racial segregation and rights exclusion. Nowhere else during the post-colonial era were there a majority of blacks denied basic freedoms for such an extended period.[74] In the case of South Africa, some scholars have suggested that although the struggles against British imperialism, Afrikaner nationalism and white supremacy were configured broadly to achieve "rights" (or to redress "wrongs"), the ANC and other anti-apartheid organizations did not actively engage human rights until the 1980s. This is supposedly because the phrase "human rights" seldom features in either the texts or the indexes of key works of history.[75]

While it is true that the language of human rights within anti-apartheid gained prominence in the 1980s with the sanctions and boycott movement, the history of human rights in South Africa – or indeed in any part of Africa more generally – cannot be reduced to the textual frequency or infrequency of the specific phrase "human rights." As I have argued throughout this book, such privileging of the metropolitan lexicon risks silencing other expressions of the human rights idea especially among indigenous people who did not or could not express themselves in dominant colonial languages. Few indigenous languages had phraseological equivalents of the term "human rights." Human rights ideas were conveyed in a multiplicity of phrases and idioms that convey local understandings of the ideas underlying human rights. A more useful history of *human rights* can emerge if we pay attention not to particular phraseologies but to the normative and legal ideas about human rights conveyed in local parlance. These include the claims hinged on the universalist notion of human dignity, non-discrimination and fundamental freedoms that gained international prominence in the mid-twentieth century. Considered from this perspective, it becomes apparent that the long-standing struggles against white supremacy and black oppression in South Africa were essentially human rights struggles. As noted by the jurist Ismail

[74] Brian Baughan, *Human Rights in Africa* (Philadelphia: Mason Crest, 2007), 43.
[75] Saul Dubow, *South Africa's Struggle for Human Rights* (Athens: Ohio University Press, 2012), 11.

Mahomed, South African history was for several decades dominated by a deep conflict between a minority who reserved for itself all control over the political instruments of the state and a majority who sought to resist that domination. "Fundamental human rights became a major casualty of this conflict ... the legitimacy of the law itself was deeply wounded as the country hemorrhaged in the face of this tragic conflict."[76]

Political opposition to apartheid repression and injustices was frequently framed in terms of human rights. The African National Congress (ANC), which led opposition against white minority rule, issued a *Bill of Rights* in 1923 that expressed the political aspirations of the organization. The Bill called for the dignity of all people, equality, property rights and justice for all. A more detailed Bill issued in 1943 called for full citizenship, an end to discrimination, and access to education and employment.[77] By the 1950s, the ANC was expressing its political demands even more explicitly in terms of international human rights and international discourses of self-determination. Of particular significance in this regard was the Atlantic Charter. Inspired by the Atlantic Charter, the ANC adopted its own *Freedom Charter* in 1955, which referenced international human rights. Repudiating apartheid, the Freedom Charter declared that "South Africa belongs to all who live in it, black and white, and that no government can justly claim authority unless it is based on the will of all the people." It proclaimed that "All shall enjoy equal human rights."[78] As Nelson Mandela would recall in his autobiography:

> Change was in the air in the 1940s. The Atlantic Charter of 1941, signed by Roosevelt and Churchill, affirmed the faith in the dignity of each human being and propagated a host of democratic principles. Some in the West saw the Charter as empty promises, but not those of us in Africa ... We hoped that the government and ordinary South Africans would see the principles they were fighting for in Europe were the same ones we were advocating at home.[79]

---

[76] Quoted in the Truth and Reconciliation Commission of South Africa Report, vol. 1 (Pretoria: 1998), 24. Available at www.justice.gov.za/trc/report/finalreport/Volume%201.pdf. Accessed September 12, 2016.

[77] African National Congress, "The African Bill of Rights," in *Resolutions of the Annual Conference of the African National Congress, 1943* (Johannesburg: ANC Department or Information and Publicity, 1943).

[78] Nelson Mandela, *Long Walk to Freedom: The Autobiography of Nelson Mandela* (Boston: Little Brown, 1995), 95–96.

[79] Mandela, *Long Walk to Freedom*, 83.

However, there was opposition to this inclusive vision of rights that was also expressed in the language of rights. In what is perhaps the most disingenuous appropriation of rights discourse, the South African government deployed the language of "native rights" to rationalize its segregationist policies. Justifying apartheid land policy in 1956, Minister of Native Affairs and later Prime Minster Hendrick Verwoerd described apartheid as a policy of "good neighborliness" that was beneficial to all racial population groups because it respected their respective right to self-determination and separate development. He stated: "The European enjoys rights and privileges in one part of the country, the European area, and the Native has similar rights and privileges in the Native areas, i.e. the Reserves."[80] This perverse notion of "native rights" also informed the Promotion of Bantu Self-Government Act of 1959, which purported to promote self-determination for the ethnic black communities (Bantustans) by establishing boundaries for them and letting them exercise some political autonomy within an overarching national structure of white supremacy. Far from fostering African self-determination and native rights, the black homelands and the Bantustan system maintained black oppression and preserved the white supremacist status quo.

Throughout the 1950s and 1960s, the ANC led a grassroots anti-apartheid coalition that included other political groups such as the South African Indian Congress, the Congress of Democrats, the Colored People's Congress and the South African Communist Party (SACP). This period also witnessed the rise of black nationalist organizations such as the Pan African Congress (PAC), which organized an effective campaign against restrictive pass laws. Following the Sharpeville massacre in which scores of demonstrators were killed by security forces, the South African government banned the PAC and ANC, forcing many of their members into exile. Increased government repression ushered in a new era of anti-apartheid activism. Abandoning its policy of non-violence, the ANC and the SACP jointly founded *Umkhonto we Sizwe* (the Spear of the Nation), an armed paramilitary wing of their anti-apartheid movement. The Sharpeville massacre and the subsequent banning of the PAC and ANC drew global condemnation and galvanized international grassroots support for the anti-apartheid movement. Anti-apartheid activists drew world attention

---

[80] Hendrik Verwoerd, *Verwoerd Speaks: Speeches 1948–1966* (Pretoria: APB Publishers, 1966), 128.

to apartheid brutalities including torture; arbitrary arrests and detentions; and restrictions on movement, free speech and political activities.

The ANC's turn to militancy and sabotage was a contentious issue in human rights debates among anti-apartheid activists. When Nelson Mandela was jailed in 1962 for inciting workers to strike, Amnesty International, the international human rights organization founded in London a year earlier, adopted him as a "prisoner of conscience" – its designation for those unfairly jailed for their political views. However, after the Rivonia trial in 1964 where Mandela faced charges of sabotage and armed struggle against the apartheid government, Amnesty International took the controversial decision to no longer consider Mandela a prisoner of conscience and, as such, did not demand his release.[81] However, Mandela himself explicitly invoked human rights to justify his actions. In his famous closing speech at the trial, he offered a defense of the ANC's sabotage campaign and its defiance of the ban imposed by the government. He stated that the ANC had resorted to sabotage tactics because the government had closed all lawful modes of expressing opposition. "We believed," he said, "in the words of the Universal Declaration of Human Rights that the will of the people shall be the basis of authority of the government." To accept the ban on the ANC was equivalent to accepting to "silence the African for all time."[82]

By the 1970s, apartheid had become universally synonymous with the worst form of racial discrimination and race-based human rights violations. It was frequently condemned by the UN General Assembly and Security Council as contrary to the UN Charter and the international bill of human rights.[83] Apartheid became part of international human rights vocabulary in 1966 when the UN General Assembly labeled it as a crime against humanity. Two decades later, the UN Security Council delineated apartheid as a universal crime.[84] The UN Special Committee against Apartheid played a key role in the UN's opposition to apartheid.

---

[81] Ann Marie Clark, *Diplomacy of Conscience: Amnesty International and Changing Human Rights Norms* (Princeton: Princeton University Press, 2010), 14.

[82] Nelson Mandela, *No Easy Walk to Freedom: Articles, Speeches and Trial Addresses of Nelson Mandela* (London: Heinemann Educational, 1973), 189.

[83] The International Bill of Rights consists of UDHR (adopted in 1948), the International Covenant on Civil and Political Rights (1966) and the International Covenant on Economic, Social and Cultural Rights (1966).

[84] For a detailed history of anti-apartheid debates at the United Nations during this period, see Jeremy Brown Shearar, *Against the World: South Africa and Human Rights at the United Nations 1945–1961* (Pretoria: UNISA Press, 2011).

From 1948 to 1994, the UN issued more than two hundred documents on the eradication of apartheid, including several General Assembly resolutions and reports condemning apartheid as a violation of international law. Other international and regional organizations such as the Organization of African Unity and the International Olympic Committee supported the movement to isolate South Africa from the international community. The Convention on the Suppression and Punishment of the Crime of Apartheid, also known as the Apartheid Convention, was the ultimate step in the condemnation of apartheid as a violation of international human rights law.

In 1974, the UN expelled South Africa as the South African regime faced increasing international sanctions and boycotts. However, there was not always consensus on how far the UN should go in its condemnation of the South African government. When the Apartheid Convention was adopted by the UN General Assembly in 1973, 91 countries voted in favor, 26 abstained and four voted against it. South Africa, the United Kingdom, the United States and Portugal voted against the convention. The combination of international sanctions, a global grassroots anti-apartheid movement and domestic resistance ultimately forced the South African government into negotiations with the ANC and other opposition groups, eventually leading to the collapse of apartheid and the end of white minority rule in the 1990s. A symbolic moment in this process was the release of Nelson Mandela, who had been imprisoned for twenty-seven years. Contemporary debates at the UN and elsewhere regarding the utility and legitimacy of imposing military, economic and cultural sanctions when a state violates international law illustrate the impact of anti-apartheid movement on international human rights law.[85] By imposing a military embargo on the South African apartheid government, the Security Council, for the first time, invoked Chapter VII of the UN Charter, which outlines the obligations of the UN with respect to threat to international peace and security.

Shaping the Post-Colonial Order

After 1945, colonialism was in retreat across Africa despite the efforts of European imperial powers to hold on to their colonies. With the

---

[85] Penelope Andrews, "South Africa," in *Encyclopedia of Human Rights*, David P. Forsythe, ed. (New York: Oxford University Press, 2009), 486–487.

charter of the UN affirming the interest of colonized peoples and their goal of self-determination, colonialism progressively lost international acceptance. It became clear that old arguments of "civilizing missions" and enlightened imperialism were no longer acceptable and that nationalist struggles for independence could no longer be held back. Britain was among the first to begin the process of dismantling its colonial empire. Having earlier partitioned its Indian empire into India, Pakistan and Sri Lanka, Britain eventually gave in to the demands and activism of Indian nationalists, formally granting India independence in 1947. This marked the beginning of the first wave of decolonization processes that swept across Asia and Africa in the 1950s and '60s. It ushered in the dawn of a new world order that challenged the legitimacy of old colonial empires and asserted the right of self-determination of colonized people. At the UN, the emergence of the Asian and African blocs of newly independent nations – the G77 – radically changed the landscape of international politics and the discourse of international human rights.

A defining event in the post-war decolonization process that shaped international human rights was the Asian-African Conference of 1955, also known as the Bandung Conference, which brought together a group of newly independent Asian and African countries including Egypt, Ethiopia, Liberia, the Gold Coast (Ghana) and Sudan to discuss Afro-Asian cooperation and state their collective opposition to colonialism. Among the primary concerns of delegates at the conference were national sovereignty, racism, nationalism and struggles against colonialism. Delegates reaffirmed loyalty to the UN Charter and the UDHR, but they also condemned colonial rule in Asia and Africa and, in particular, the repression of French colonial rule in Algeria where nationalists had launched a war for independence. The Bandung Conference was vital to the development of ideas of non-alignment and Afro-Asian solidarity. It also served as a key point of origin for the human rights agenda that would be pursued by newly decolonized states at the UN.[86]

Colonial rule unraveled rapidly. Perhaps the most symbolic decolonization process was in the Gold Coast where Kwame Nkrumah's Convention People's Party led a mass nationalist movement for the independence of the country, which was renamed Ghana in 1957. The

---

[86] Burke, *Decolonization and the Evolution of International Human Rights*, 13.

independence of Ghana marked the beginning of the era of decolonization in sub-Saharan Africa. One year after Ghana's independence,
political leaders from across Africa met at the All-African People's
Conference in Ghana where they passed a resolution on "Imperialism
and Colonialism." The resolution drew extensively from the post-war
international human rights lexicon to demand an end to European
colonization in the continent. Delegates at the conference condemned
colonial oppression and subjugation, which denied Africans their
fundamental human rights, and demanded that these rights and universal adult franchise be extended to all parts of Africa. The conference also established a human rights committee to look into
complaints of human rights abuses across Africa and to work toward
formally redressing them. Tom Mboya, the Kenyan trade unionist
and independence activist who chaired the conference, proposed the
conference slogan, "European scram out of Africa," in refutation of
the European scramble for Africa in the nineteenth century, which
marked the beginning of colonial rule in the continent.

The 1960s saw the end of European colonial rule in Africa as
several countries became independent – Nigeria, Senegal and
Cameroon in 1960; Algeria, Uganda and Rwanda in 1962; Kenya in
1963 and Tanzania and Zambia in 1964. The notable exceptions were
the Portuguese colonies of Angola, Guinea Bissau and Mozambique
and the settler colonies of Eastern and Southern Africa – Rhodesia,
Namibia and South Africa – where white minority governments held
on to political power until the 1970s to 1990s. Decolonization became
explicitly linked with international human rights in 1960 when the UN
General Assembly issued the "Declaration on Granting Independence
to Colonial Countries and Peoples."[87] The declaration reaffirmed the
fundamental human rights, dignity and worth of all humans and the
equal rights of peoples of all nations to self-determination. It asserted
that all peoples have an inalienable right to complete freedom, the
exercise of their sovereignty and the integrity of their national territory. It also acknowledged that the process of liberation of colonized
peoples was "irresistible and irreversible." These principles were subsequently included in the International Covenant on Civil and

---

[87] United Nations, "Declaration on the Granting of Independence to Colonial Countries and Peoples," General Assembly Resolution 1514 (XV) of 14 December 1960.
Available at www.un.org/en/decolonization/declaration.shtml. Accessed June 8,
2016.

Political Rights in 1966, article 1 of which states: "All peoples have the right of self-determination. By virtue of that right they freely determine their political status and freely pursue their economic, social and cultural development." The same provision was included in the International Covenant on Economic, Social and Cultural Rights adopted by the UN General Assembly in 1966.

Majority Rule, Minority Rights

The link between anti-colonialism and human rights is evident not only in the ways African independence activists used human rights doctrine to legitimize struggles for self-determination, but also in the ways colonial powers deployed human rights to ensure the orderly transfer of power. In many African countries, constitutional human rights first emerged in the context of decolonization. After signing the ECHR in 1950, the British government sought to extend its operation to its dependencies. In order to meet Britain's obligations under the Convention, the Colonial Office mandated local administrators to file annual reports on human rights conditions in their respective territories and to explain "derogations" from the provisions of the Conventions in cases of violations or emergency rule.[88] The Colonial Office also encouraged the enactment of a bill of rights in colonial territories where there was no opposition to such bills being implemented.

Across British Africa, constitutional conferences leading to independence addressed the question of whether and how to incorporate human rights guarantees modeled after the ECHR and the UDHR into independence constitutions. Much of these discussions turned on the question of how best to protect ethnic, religious and racial minority groups from domination and oppression after the transfer of power to indigenous leaders. These concerns were similar to post–World War II anxieties about protecting the rights of national minorities in Europe, which influenced the enactment of the ECHR. The provisions of the ECHR influenced Britain's outlook on minority rights

---

[88] NAUK CO 936/535, Council of Europe Convention on Human Rights: Derogations in Respect of Nyasaland Use of Collective Punishment; NAUK CO 936/492, Council of Europe Convention of Human Rights: Derogations in Respect of Northern Rhodesia 1957–1957; NAUK CO 963/536 Council of Europe Convention on Human Rights in Respect to Kenya; NAUK CO 936/865 Council of Europe Convention on the Human Rights: Deposition in Respect to Mauritius 1965.

protections in its dependencies.[89] British authorities wanted to transfer power to strong centralized governments, yet local and metropolitan officials were keenly aware of the need to provide legal safeguards for minority groups within ethnically and racially diverse independent states. Their mantra was "majority rule, minority rights."

In Nigeria, where Britain had adopted separate administrative policies for the Muslim-dominated northern region and the Christian-dominated southern region, officials set up a "Minorities Commission" in 1957 to look into the complaints of minority ethnic groups and recommend ways to alleviate their fears of being oppressed by majority groups at independence. The Commission recommended the inclusion of a bill of rights, fashioned on the ECHR, into the independence constitution. While leaders of minority ethnic groups welcomed this recommendation, others rejected it. Political leaders in the Muslim northern region, for example, objected to a bill of rights out of concern that government policies aimed at preserving land and public service jobs for ethnic groups in the educationally disadvantaged northern region would be nullified by constitutional anti-discrimination provisions. Colonial officials also worried about conflicts between a European-style bill of rights and indigenous customary and Islamic laws.[90]

The constitution eventually adopted at Nigeria's independence in 1960 included a bill of rights with elaborate provisions for fundamental human rights including the right to life; freedom of expression; peaceful assembly and association; protection against inhuman treatment, slavery and forced labor; and protection against discrimination on grounds of tribe, place of origin, religion or political opinion. The bill was, however, notably silent on gender discrimination.[91] To address concerns that these wide-ranging constitutional human rights guarantees would hinder effective governance, the bill also included certain limitations or provisos on these rights. One such proviso was that the bill of rights did not invalidate state laws that are "reasonably justifiable in democratic society."[92] This nebulous phase provided assurances that constitutional human rights guarantees would not hamstring executive power. The Nigerian bill of rights

---

[89] Simpson, *Human Rights and the End of Empire*, 8.
[90] NAUK CO 554/153, Parliamentary Discussion on the Review of Nigerian Constitution 1957–1959.
[91] Constitution of the Federal Republic of Nigeria, 1960, Section 17–32.
[92] Ibid., Section 27(2) d.

became a model for the bill of rights introduced in other British dependencies in Africa and the Caribbean. In Sierra Leone, colonial administrators pushed for a constitutional bill of rights as a way of protecting the creole minority population, who feared oppression by the majority indigenous African population. Some officials cautioned, however, that the bill of rights provisions must be sufficiently loosely drawn to avoid paralyzing the government in times of crisis.[93]

In the settler colonies of Eastern and Southern Africa – notably Kenya, Botswana, Nyasaland and Uganda – constitutional bills of rights primarily served to reassure the European minority population. Botswana's 1966 independence constitution included a bill of rights that enshrined a human rights regime founded on individual liberties, democratic rights and private property protections. The protection of private property rights was meant to reassure the European minority population, who feared the loss of economic interests in an independent state.[94] By enshrining a set of protections suited to the European population within the bill of rights, the dominant African political party, the Bechuanaland Democratic Party, was able to acquire favorable compromises in other areas. Europeans gave up their reserved seats in the legislature and became a political minority after independence, while the African population began to enjoy the fulfillment of a broad set of new democratic rights under majority rule and a multiparty system.

In Kenya, the bill of rights also emerged out of political compromise. At the Lancaster House Conferences where the constitutional framework for self-government was negotiated, the British Government faced pressure from European settlers, who wanted to maintain their political control, and from African politicians, who wanted majority rule. The minority European settler community under the auspices of the New Kenya Party wanted a bill of rights that protected their political and economic interests enacted before the handover of power to an African majority government. Representatives of the Asian and Arab "middleman minorities" also demanded constitutional guarantees with specific provisions for property rights

---

[93] NAUK CO 554/1673, Sierra Leone Constitutional Conference: Fundamental Human Rights 1960.

[94] James Kirby, "Conditional on a Bill of Rights: The Constitutional and Political Foundations of Botswana's Non-Racial Democracy," *Law & History*, 3 (2017), 30.

protection. These competing demands shaped the bill of rights included in Kenya's pre-self-government constitution of 1960.

Comparatively, constitutional human rights debates took a different turn in Tanganyika where the dominant African party, the Tanganyika National Union, opposed the inclusion of a bill of rights in the independence constitution on the grounds that, unlike many other African colonies, Tanganyika did not have "a minority problem." Opponents of the bill of rights argued that parliamentary democracy and enlightened public opinion were enough to safeguard minority rights in the new state. The rights of the individual in any society, they insisted, depended more on the ethical sense of the people than on formal guarantees in the law. They noted the example of England, which had "an enviable respect for human rights" based not on a bill of rights but on enlightened public opinion.[95] Tanganyika was therefore one of a few British dependencies to achieve independence without a bill of rights.

In French Africa, discourses of rights within decolonization centered on the issue of democratic rights. While British common law systems produced explicit and in-depth constitutions, French territories tended to adopt shorter constitutions that set a general outline of governmental organization that was fleshed out through organic law.[96] As colonialism and paternalism gave way to the idea of a community based on partnership between colonial powers and their former colonies, French official policy emphasized democratic self-rule. Frances's war burden had been intensified by the conflict between the Vichy regime and the Free France forces of General de Gaulle, which relied heavily on French colonies, particularly those of North Africa. Although de Gaulle was imbued with a strong sense of French nationalism and imperial destiny, he also recognized the need to dismantle the old colonial system. France had fallen victim to Nazi expansionism in Europe, and in the drastically changed post-war climate, France was no longer in a position to hold on to its colonies in Africa. Decolonization in the French colonial empire was therefore framed around the right of indigenous people to self-determination and democratic rule. This approach was influenced by the post-war international human rights movement. The constitution of the Fifth

---

[95] Parkinson, *Bills of Rights and Decolonization*, 191.
[96] B. O. Nwabueze, *Constitutionalism in the Emergent States* (Rutherford: Fairleigh Dickinson University Press, 1973), 31.

Republic acknowledged the free determination of peoples and pledged the commitment of France to guide its colonial dependencies toward freedom to govern themselves and toward democratic institutions of their own affairs.[97]

In enacting constitutional bills of rights in the colonies and framing decolonization in terms of democratic rights, the British and, to a lesser extent, the French government had two related goals. The first was to ensure the smooth and peaceful transfer of power in their colonies. The second was to create stable and viable long-term civil societies in the new states. Minority groups also saw the bill of rights as a means of protecting their political and economic interests under majority rule at independence. In most British and French territories, the first goal of using human rights doctrine to facilitate orderly political transition was largely achieved. But whether the enactment of constitutional bills of rights achieved the second goal of protecting human rights, and creating stable and democratic civil societies in Africa with the attainment of independence, is a question that I address in the next chapter.

★★★

My central argument in this chapter is that the relationship between anti-colonialism and human rights in the age of decolonization is more complex than extant studies have presented. International human rights shaped decolonization, but anti-colonial struggles also influenced international human rights. Initial post-war articulations of individual-centric, state-centric "universal human rights" were neither settled nor paradigmatic. Later, "Third World" articulations and contestations of this insular human rights idea expanded the frontiers of the human rights doctrine by highlighting its contradictions and questioning its universalist claims. It is mistaken to interpret these developments as marking simply the succession, displacement or abandonment of the human rights idea. To do so is to read the relationship between human rights and anti-colonialism in terms of a one-directional ideological encounter. The underlying premise is problematic: that anti-colonial activists appropriated and deployed human rights language in their struggles for self-determination but that these activists contributed nothing to an emergent universal human rights movement. I argue instead that anti-colonialism did not develop in isolation of the post–World War II currents of

---

[97] Ibhawoh, "Colonialism: Legacy for Human Rights," 369.

international human rights. Anti-colonial struggles were integral to the mid-twentieth-century emergence of the doctrine of universal human rights. Our focus should be not only on how human rights impacted anti-colonialism but also on how anti-colonialism shaped an emergent and evolving human rights ideology. Colonized peoples not only drew on universal human rights in their struggles against imperialism; they also shaped the global meanings of human rights.

What is also evident, however, is that many African anti-colonial activists consciously privileged the collective political right to self-determination over other rights such as individual civic rights, women's rights and subnational minority rights. This strategy of prioritizing political collective rights at the moment of decolonization may be understood in terms of Gayatri Spivak's notion of *strategic essentialism*, a political and discursive strategy that nationalities and subaltern groups have historically used to present themselves in moments of conflict with dominant groups. While differences of identities and ideologies may exist between members of subjugated groups (internal differentiation), it sometimes becomes advantageous for them to temporarily emphasize their group identity and aspirations into a more cohesive way in order to achieve specific goals.[98] The emphasis on collective interests as a short-term strategy to affirm a political identity or movement can be effective, as long as that identity does not get fixed as an essential category by a dominant group.

In the context of African anti-colonialism, the strategic prioritizing of national liberation, framed as the collective right to self-determination over individual rights, would indeed ultimately become self-serving. Anti-colonial leaders such as Sékou Touré of Guinea and Kwame Nkrumah of Ghana, who championed the right to self-determination in anti-colonial struggles, showed little interest in the rights of workers as workers, or in issues of equality across gender or ethnic lines. Both leaders sought instead to persuade workers of the virtues of order and productivity, in the name of a bigger cause, fighting imperialism and developing the economy.[99] Nnamdi Azikiwe expressed the right to self-determination more in terms of national liberation than protecting minority rights within the independent state. Even as he advocated for Nigeria's independence, he opposed

---

[98] Donna Landry and Gerald MacLean, *The Spivak Reader* (New York: Routledge, 1996), 214.
[99] Frederick Cooper, *Decolonization and African Society: The Labor Question in French and British* (New York: Cambridge University Press, 1996), 438.

constitutional reforms that would have granted minority ethnic groups regional autonomy at the expense of centralized political authority.[100] He was also ambivalent about subnational demands for self-rule.[101]

In many independent African countries, the language of sovereignty, collective rights and "solidarity rights" ultimately became excuses for suppressing opposition politics and restricting individual liberties in efforts to consolidate political power. By articulating self-determination exclusively in terms of national liberation from European colonial rule, independence activists could dismiss or suppress equally legitimate aspirations for internal self-determination by minority groups within the state. Like European statesmen at the UN who, for political expediency, sought to narrowly define universal human rights to exclude self-determination in the colonies, some African independence activists sought to restrict the right to self-determination to national liberation from colonial rule. Subnational self-determination aspirations and struggles were often dismissed as distractions from the paramount cause of national liberation.

The paradox of essentializing the right to self-determination as collective national liberation is that it soon shifted from being a strategy for resisting domination to a means of consolidating political power. With independence, national solidarity and collective political rights came to be expressed in opposition to individual liberties. State policies were cast in terms of the paramountcy of the collective rights and aspirations of nation over the rights of individual citizens or groups within the state. Post-colonial political leaders such as Julius Nyerere of Tanzania, Modibo Keita of Mali, Léopold Senghor of Senegal and Kwame Nkrumah of Ghana framed the ideology of African socialism in terms of the collective social and economic rights of the people in ways that tended to undermine individual civil liberties. The rhetoric of collective solidarity rights thus became a means by which ruling regimes and ascendant elites sought to legitimize statist ideology and consolidate power. Ultimately, human rights would become deeply contested, as a doctrine of collective solidarity rights used by governments to legitimize power and as principles of individual liberties and democratic rights invoked by opposition groups to challenge state power. This tension between statist and oppositional rights discourses underscores the history of human rights in independent Africa.

---

[100] Azikiwe, *Zik: A Selection from the Speeches of Nnamdi Azikiwe*, 7.
[101] Coleman, *Nigeria: Background to Nationalism*, 347.

6

Dictators and Dissidents

Human rights begin with breakfast.

  – Léopold Senghor, President of Senegal (1960–1980)

Soon after Ghana gained independence in 1957, the government of
Kwame Nkrumah arrested and imprisoned Joseph Danquah, the
leading opposition politician in the country. Like Nkrumah, Danquah
had been active in the anti-colonial movement against British rule. He
was a leading advocate for constitutional reforms that allowed for
greater African representation in the colonial government and was
one of the founders of the United Gold Coast Convention (UGCC),
which led demands for self-government in the 1940s. In 1948 the
British authorities had arrested and imprisoned Danquah and Nkrumah
for their anti-colonial activities. Although both men worked together
in the anti-colonial movement, ideological difference made them political rivals. Nkrumah eventually split from the conservative Danquah-led
UGCC to form the more radical and mass-oriented Convention
People's Party in 1949. In the partisan politics of independence,
Danquah lost out to the more popular and charismatic Nkrumah,
who became president. But although politically sidelined, Danquah
remained relevant in Ghanaian politics. He became a prominent
opposition figure, speaking out against the progressively authoritarian
posture of the Nkrumah regime. Danquah's uncompromising oppositional politics led to his imprisonment in 1961 under Ghana's
Preventive Detention Act, which was a relic of colonial emergency
law. He was released in 1962 but imprisoned again in 1964 on the

charge of plotting to overthrow the government. He died in prison a year later and was eulogized as a "great champion of fundamental human rights."[1]

In a letter to Nkrumah from prison shortly before he died, Danquah decried the injustice of his detention without due process, stating, "I am tired of being in prison on preventive detention with no opportunity to make an original or any contribution to the progress and development of the country ... I am anxious to resume my contribution to the progress and development of Ghana."[2] He went on to compare his imprisonment under Nkrumah's government to the fate they both had suffered under British imprisonment. The comparison is poignant. "You will recall," he wrote to Nkrumah, "... that when in 1948 we were arrested by the British Government and sent to the North for detention, they treated us as gentlemen, not as galley slaves, and provided each of us with a furnished bungalow (two or three rooms) with a garden, together with opportunity for reading and writing." Under Nkrumah's imprisonment, Danquah complained, he was locked up in a tiny prison cell under the most inhumane conditions, denied access to medical treatment and cut off from communication with his family. He also noted that under British detention they were promptly brought before a court for trial, whereas under Nkrumah's detention he was denied the due process of being presented before a properly constituted court of law.[3] For Danquah, the oppositional language of human rights that anti-colonial activists used so effectively to challenge British colonial repression and demand justice remained acutely relevant in the independent state. For Nkrumah, now at the helm of state power, that human rights language had become irrelevant.

This encounter between two key figures in Ghanaian politics shows that independence did not usher in a golden age of human rights. For all the talk about human rights within anti-colonialism and a constitutional bill of rights within decolonization, political independence in the 1950s and 1960s did not mark the ascendancy of human rights.

---

[1] Nnamdi Azikiwe, "Statement on the Death of J. B Danquah," quoted in Francis L. Bartels, *The Persistence of Paradox: Memoirs of F. L. Bartels* (Accra: Ghana Universities Press, 2003), 225.

[2] A. Adu Boahen, *The Ghanaian Establishment: Its Constitution, Its detentions, Its traditions, Its justice and Statecraft, and Its Heritage of Ghanaism* (Accra: Ghana Universities Press, 1997), 329.

[3] Ibid., 329.

Once in power, many African political leaders seemed to turn their backs on human rights, at least in the sense of individual civil liberties. The proliferation of authoritarian regimes in newly independent African countries signaled that the promising adaptation of rights ideas in anti-colonial struggles had faltered. Rights talk, once wielded vigorously and effectively by independence activists to challenge colonial subjugation and negotiate independence, was soon overshadowed by a discourse of sovereignty and national solidarity. From the dictatorships of Idi Amin in Uganda, Mobutu Sese Seko in Zaire, Jean-Bédel Bokassa in the Central African Republic, Ben Bella in Algeria and Gaafar Nimeiry in Sudan, to one-party rule in Jomo Kenyatta's Kenya, Kwame Nkrumah's Ghana and Julius Nyerere's Tanzania, the decades following independence marked an era of "big men" and authoritarian rule.

With independence, African political leaders who had championed self-determination in anti-colonial struggles began to advance new arguments about the constraints of human rights norms on governance. The central thrust of these arguments was that individual rights come at the expense of collective rights and national solidarity. Unrestrained individual liberties, some leaders argued, imposed limits on the capacity of governments to govern, weakened sovereignty and threated national unity. As one Tanzanian official report put it, the bill of rights limits the capacity of government to take measures necessary to suppress subversion and "serves only to protect those whose aim it was to subvert and destroy democracy."[4] Human rights talk became increasingly seen not as enhancing democracy and strengthening civil society but as a threat to the fragile post-colonial state. Introducing rights-based governance into state structures and institutions would not be the primary task that faced new independent governments. Rather, building viable states where none had really been built before was considered the first step toward rights-based governance.[5]

Rights discourse at independence also came to be increasingly marked by differentiation between individual rights and collective rights. Individual rights centered on citizenship came to be differentiated

---

[4] *Report of the Presidential Commission on the Establishment of a Democratic One-Party State* (Dar es Salaam: Government Printer, 1965), 31.

[5] Martin Chanock, "Human Rights and Cultural Branding: Who Speaks and How," in *Cultural Transformation and Human Rights in Africa*, Abdullahi A. An-Na'im, ed. (New York: Zed Books, 2002), 56–57.

from collective rights centered on the nation. The ideals of national unity manifested by centralized political power, common language and culture, and economic and geographical limits tended also to express themselves in intolerant and repressive attitudes toward those who were perceived or perceived themselves as "others."[6] This paradox reflects the double-sided nature of African nationalism: its capacity to inspire expressions of unity while at the same time narrowing the scope of political debate and participation.[7]

As more African countries gained independence in the 1960s, there was less of a focus on human rights, except as a tool in the fight against colonialism and white minority rule where it persisted in the continent. When the Organization of African Unity was created in 1963, a few token references to human rights were included in its charter, but it was evident that the human rights language that had been so central to anti-colonial struggles held less urgency to ruling regimes. To the extent that any attention was given to human rights by African political leaders, their priority was on socioeconomic rights tightly framed and differentiated from civil and political rights.[8] Post-colonial ruling elites argued the cultural relativism of human rights and the primacy of collective economic and social rights over individual liberties in Africa. The African values debate coincided with the Asian values debate, both of which challenged the dominant Western individual and civil rights–centered premise of international human rights. Colonel Acheampong, the Ghanaian head of state who took over power in a military coup, famously stated that "one man, one vote is meaningless unless accompanied by the principle of one man, one bread."[9] The Senegalese leader Leopold Senghor expressed the same sentiment when he asserted that "human rights begin with breakfast."[10]

---

[6] Patrick Thornberry, "Is There a Phoenix in the Ashes? International Law and Minority Rights," *Texas International Law Journal* 15 (summer 1980), 421.

[7] Gregory Maddox and James Leonard Giblin, eds., *In Search of a Nation: Histories of Authority and Dissidence in Tanzania* (Athens: Ohio University Press, 2005), 63.

[8] Magnus Killander, "African Human Rights Law in Theory and Practice," in *Research Handbook on International Law*, Sarah Joseph and Adam McBeth, eds. (Cheltenham: Edward Elgar, 2010), 390.

[9] I. K. Acheampong, *Speeches and Interviews*, vol. 1 (Accra: Information Services Department, 1973), 29.

[10] Quoted in William Felice, "The Viability of the United Nations Approach to Economic and Social Human Rights in a Globalized Economy," *International Affairs*, 75, 3 (1999): 569.

These statist arguments for prioritizing certain rights over others challenged the notion of the interdependence and indivisibility of human rights. A particularly resilient line of argument was that the fledging post-colonial state could ill-afford the unrestrained license of individual-centered human rights. Forging viable nation-states out of the arbitrary colonial geopolitical entities inherited at independence required placing certain pragmatic limits on individual liberties in the larger collective interest of the nation. As President Samora Machel of Mozambique proclaimed soon after his country's independence: "For the nation to live, the tribe must die."[11] In other words, tribes and ethnic identities were atavistic, denoting primordial stasis and primitive sectarianism that had no place in the brave new world of nation-states.[12]

In human rights debates at the UN, delegates representing newly independent African states forcefully pushed these arguments. They stressed collective rights over individual rights, and social and economic rights over civil and political rights, and positioned the state as the custodian of these collective rights. Pushing back against proposals to allow individual human rights petitions to the UN in 1966, a Zairean delegate argued that newly independent African states required "strong governments" and warned against an international human rights regime, which had the effect of weakening the authority of national governments. Concurring, his Togolese counterpart argued that allowing individual petition would negatively impact the authority of government over its citizens. This, he argued, is undesirable because recently independent states required strong governments to consolidate new structures and address the challenges of underdevelopment.[13] These positions challenged the restraints on state power over citizens imposed by international human rights doctrine.

African political leaders also made arguments for socioeconomic and cultural relativism in interpreting human rights, as a way of asserting state authority. The relativist claim was that human rights

---

[11] Quoted in Mahmood Mamdani, *Citizen and Subject: Contemporary Africa and the Legacy of Late Colonialism* (Princeton: Princeton University Press, 1996), 135.

[12] Richard Reid, "Ghosts in the Academy: Historians and Historical Consciousness in the Making of Modern Uganda," *Comparative Studies in Society and History*, 56, 2 (2014): 351.

[13] Summary Records of Third Committee, 1456th meeting, November 30, 1966, A/C. 3/SR. 1429. Cited in Ronald Burke, *Decolonization and the Evolution of International Human Rights* (Philadelphia: University of Pennsylvania Press, 2010), 77.

needed to be interpreted and applied in ways that reflect the unique socioeconomic conditions and cultural traditions of African societies. This familiar argument for socioeconomic and cultural relativism had earlier been used by European colonial administrators to resist calls to extend international human rights standards to their colonies. Their claim was that the cultural traditions of natives and prevailing socioeconomic conditions in the colonies made it difficult to fully implement international human rights. For example, in 1949 British administrators in Nyasaland resisted pressure from the Colonial Office to repeal the Forced Labor Ordinance to keep Britain compliant with the new Human Rights Covenant being drafted at the UN. Local colonial administrators argued that the unique socioeconomic and cultural conditions in Nyasaland made forced labor necessary. Existing restrictions on worker's rights were necessary, one official stated, because in "this predominantly agricultural country, sufficient able bodied males are required, without whom there would be famine and possibly pestilence and riots."[14] It is therefore ironic that in the era of independence, African political leaders used similar arguments for social and cultural relativism to resist international human rights constraints on state power. In this regard, some anti-colonial activists who championed universal human rights in struggles for self-determination shifted away from the language of *universalism* toward a language of *relativism* and national sovereignty.

What do we make of post-colonial statist contestations of international human rights? Some scholars have attributed this shift to the emergence of a new wave of post-colonial nationalist leaders in Asia and Africa who denounced human rights as a Western imposition and emphasized the need for a different rights agenda in "Third World" countries.[15] This is partly true. However, to read these developments simply as the abandonment of traditional human rights by nationalist elites misses a key point. The language of "abandonment" tends to be too generalizing and does not adequately reflect how local political dynamics engendered the vagaries of post-colonial human rights movement. It is not enough to identify the political shifts in human rights that followed decolonization and the proliferation of authoritarian

---

[14] BNAUK CO 963/5/7 Economic and Social Council: Commission of Human Rights. Confidential Memorandum from the Governor of Nyasaland, November 26, 1949.
[15] Burke, *Decolonization and the Evolution of International Human Rights*, 5.

regimes across Africa. It is also important to understand the complex sociopolitical circumstances that compelled and shaped these shifts.

By the 1960s, international human rights had come to mean more than just atomized individual rights. As with the discourse of self-determination within anti-colonialism, post-colonial leaders sought to expand the scope of international human rights to include collective solidarity rights. Their articulation of human rights in collective terms, and in ways that did not adversely constrain state power, cannot simply be dismissed as a refutation of traditional human rights principles. Rather, statist rights discourses reflected attempts by new ruling elites to reprioritize international human rights norms in politically convenient ways. In addition, post-colonial rights discourse was not monolithic, and African political leaders did not speak with one voice on these issues. Not every African political leader who appealed to human rights within anti-colonialism abandoned it at independence. By the same token, post-colonial leaders who advanced statist rights arguments were not all instinctively opposed to traditional individual-centered human rights. The positions of some of these leaders on human rights were shaped by deeper cultural and ideological considerations.

To be sure, ascendant African political leaders who inherited colonial power at independence moved away from individual-centered human rights, speaking instead a language of sovereignty and collective solidarity rights. However, many other anti-colonial activists and politicians who lost out in political succession contests at independence continued to embrace individual-centered human rights in their opposition to abuses of state power. These activists found renewed relevance in the language of universal human rights, individual liberties and minority rights. For post-colonial dissidents and opposition activists such as J. B. Danquah in Ghana, Odinga Odinga in Kenya, Ferhat Abbas in Algeria and Vera Chirwa in Malawi, human rights took on a new relevance in struggles against authoritarian regimes, one-party rule and military dictatorships.

In the following pages, I explore the shifts and turns in human rights struggles in the post-colonial African state, juxtaposing state authoritarianism with a resurgent oppositional rights movement. I go beyond the narrative of abandonment to examine the political, economic and social contingencies that shaped the shifts in human rights discourses and practices. I am concerned here not only with the objective human rights conditions in independent Africa, but also with the contestations over the meanings and scope of human rights as reflected in statist and oppositional rights discourses.

Rights and Repression

International human rights doctrine, as it emerged at the UN in the mid-twentieth century, held three distinct revolutionary promises. It held the promise of a revolution of *self-determination*, a revolution of *democracy* and a revolution of *equality*. Although each revolution held the promise of ushering in the next one, this did not always materialize. By the 1970s, most African countries had gained political independence, marking in some measure a fulfillment of the first human rights promise of self-determination. These countries gained independence with democratic governments and constitutional human rights guarantees, which suggested a democratic revolution in the continent. Many independence constitutions affirmed international human rights principles and specifically the UDHR, including the right to life, liberty and security of person; prohibition of inhuman or degrading treatment; freedom of thought, conscience and religion; freedom of expression and association; and the rights-related duties of citizens.[16] In some cases, constitutional protections even extended to economic and social rights and the collective right to development. Some revised constitutions such as Ethiopia's went further to explicitly link human rights with democracy, making the proclamation that "the human and democratic rights of citizens and peoples shall be respected."[17]

The end of colonial rule marked the triumph of the revolution of self-determination, and national constitutions promised democratic rights. The first two decades of self-rule did not fulfill the full promise of human rights, however. Many African governments imposed severe restrictions on human rights as state security became synonymous with the security of the regime in power. The state and its agents acted with impunity, often with no accountability for human rights violations. Constitutional bills of rights and other human rights laws adopted at independence failed to hold governments legally or politically accountable to citizens. In some cases, constitutional human

---

[16] For example, the Mozambican constitution links human rights with duties by outlining the duties of citizens toward fellow human beings, the community and the state Constitution of Mozambique (1990). Art. 44, 45, 46.

[17] Constitution of Federal Democratic Republic of Ethiopia (1994), Article 10.

rights provisions were suspended or altered by military usurpers and one-party states within a few years of independence. Political developments in several African countries in the decades following independence provide evidence of this gradual erosion of human rights idealism. One early example of what would become a trend was Ghana under Kwame Nkrumah.

As the first sub-Saharan African country to attain independence in 1957, Ghana represented the aspirations of many Africans and the promise of democracy in post-colonial Africa. On the eve of the country's independence, Kwame Nkrumah as leader of the new government affirmed his commitment to protecting human rights and civil liberties in a country founded on democracy, equal opportunity and the rule of law. Speaking before the National Assembly in 1956, he stated that individual citizens ought to be guaranteed their civil liberties by law, including freedom from arbitrary arrest or arbitrary search and confiscation of property. He expressed his commitment to press freedom, freedom of speech, freedom of religion and the freedom of political association. These rights, he proclaimed, were an essential part of Ghana's new democracy.[18] However, Nkrumah's rights idealism did not always translate into practice. Once enthroned, Nkrumah, the once vociferous champion of constitutional rights and the right to self-determination, immediately began to deconstruct the constitution to consolidate political power. His regime repealed human rights protection clauses of the constitution and abolished regional assemblies. Repressive laws such as the Deportation Act, the Emergency Powers Act of 1957 and the Preventive Detention Act were introduced to enable the government and its security agencies detain citizens without legal recourse. These laws proved useful in governance by stifling opposition parties as well as harassing and intimidating political opponents.

Like other African leaders of his era, Nkrumah justified repressive state policies in terms of sovereignty, security and national solidarity. In a national broadcast in 1964, he stated ominously that the government "demands that everyone within our society must either accept the spirit and aims of our revolution or expose themselves as the deceivers and betrayers of the people."[19] That same year, Ghana was declared a one-party state and effectively ceased to be a liberal democracy.

---

[18] Afari Gyan, *The Political Ideas of Kwame Nkrumah* (New York: African Heritage Studies Publishers, 1976), 94.
[19] Akwasi Afrifa, *The Ghana Coup, 24th February 1966* (London: Cass, 1966), 135.

Between 1960 and 1965, hundreds of people were taken into preventive detention, including J. B. Danquah, a leading member of the main opposition party and a presidential candidate who stood against Nkrumah. Danquah was released after ten months in prison, then was rearrested and detained until his death in prison in 1965. A year later, the Nkrumah government was overthrown in a military coup, ushering a period of political instability and military rule in Ghana.

The military officers who ousted Nkrumah justified their coup as a last resort for overthrowing an unpopular government. They claimed that Ghana was sliding into a dictatorship and that Nkrumah had foreclosed all constitutional means of offering political opposition to the one-party government imposed on the country. Under such circumstances, the armed forces had to reassert themselves as the official opposition to the government.[20] Military rule did not improve human rights conditions in Ghana, however. If anything, the era of military dictatorship brought greater restrictions on civil rights and liberties, which were justified as necessary interventions to prevent the fragile post-colonial state from disintegration. One Ghanaian military ruler, Ignatius Acheampong, justified the incessant military coups in Africa on the grounds that Africa had not yet found a system of democratic governance suited to its unique circumstances. Until it did, he argued, Africa needed governments with "the strength of its convictions and the courage to take the most difficult decisions if they are in the interest of the people."[21]

Events took a similar turn in neighboring Nigeria, a country whose complex ethnopolitics made governance difficult even for its British colonizers. The ethno-religious tensions that necessitated the enactment of a constitutional bill of rights as part of decolonization process worsened with independence. Minority ethnic groups who had clamored for a bill of rights found their fears justified as the dominant political parties became platforms for majority ethnic groups. Leaders of dominant ethnopolitical groups were often unsympathetic to the complaints of marginalization by leaders of minority groups and their demands for subnational autonomy. Nnamdi Azikiwe, once the vocal anti-colonial advocate of self-determination, was ambivalent about

[20] Ibid., 31.
[21] Interview with Ignatius Acheampong, Africa, March 19, 1973, reprinted in Martin Minogue and Judith Molloy, eds., *African Aims and Attitudes: Selected Documents* (London: Cambridge University Press, 1974), 352.

constitutional proposals that would have allowed for the autonomy of minority ethnic groups within independent Nigeria.[22] Azikiwe, whose name and newspaper articles were emblematic of the unremitting struggle against British colonial curbs on press freedom, no longer saw anything wrong with the sort of laws he once criticized. During his tenure as president of Nigeria, the repressive Newspaper Ordinance of 1917, which he once pilloried as a repressive reactionary measure for curtailing press liberties and which he rejected as being "overdue for repeal," was dusted off and applied to restrict press freedom in the independent state.[23]

Only six years after Nigeria gained independence, a military coup overthrew the elected government and the new military rulers suspended the constitution. Violence between the predominately Christian Igbo of Eastern Nigeria and Hausa/Fulani Muslims of Northern Nigeria triggered the Nigeria-Biafra War and decades of military dictatorships that were characterized by widespread human rights violations. It is noteworthy that in Biafra, the right to self-determination that Nigerian nationalists asserted in anti-colonial struggles for independence from British colonialism was recast in the new secessionist struggle for independence from Nigeria. Biafra's leaders framed the conflict as a matter of human rights and national survival, not unlike the anti-colonial struggle, and appealed to international human rights law.[24] Justifying the Biafran cause as a struggle for self-determination, its leader Chukwuemeka Ojukwu claimed that the secession movement was based on democratic ideals, human rights and self-determination, stating: "When the Nigerians violated our basic human rights and liberties, we decided reluctantly but bravely to found our own state, to exercise our inalienable right to self-determination as our only remaining hope for survival as a people."[25] In contrast, political leaders in Nigeria, some of whom

---

[22] Azikiwe opposed constitutional reforms introduced by the British colonial government in Nigeria in 1950 that allowed for regional legislative autonomy. Azikiwe, *Zik: A Selection from the Speeches of Nnamdi Azikiwe*, 7.

[23] Ndaeyo Uko, *Romancing the Gun: The Press as Promoter of Military Rule* (Trenton: Africa World Press, 2004), 40.

[24] Arua Oko Omaka, *The Biafran Humanitarian Crisis, 1967–1970: International Human Rights and Joint Church Aid* (Madison: Fairleigh Dickinson University Press), 53, 76.

[25] Cited in Raphael Chijoke Njoku, "The Ahiara Declaration and the Fate of Biafra in a Postcolonial/Bi-Polar World Order," in *Writing the Nigeria-Biafra War*, Toyin Falola and Ogechukwu Ezekwem, eds. (Suffolk: James Currey, 2016), 76.

had eagerly canvassed the right to self-determination in anti-colonial struggles, resisted Biafran framing of the conflict in terms of self-determination. Instead, they advanced counter-arguments for sovereignty, national solidarity and the territorial integrity of the Nigerian state. I return to the topic of human rights in war and other armed conflicts later in this chapter.

In Kenya, ethnic factionalism did not spiral into civil war but had significant repercussions for human rights nonetheless. Like most former British colonies, Kenya's independence constitution contained a comprehensive bill of rights that guaranteed equality before the law and personal freedoms, including the freedom of belief and conscience, freedom of movement and free choice of domicile, the rights to property and even the unique "right to leave Kenya."[26] The constitution prohibited slavery, forced labor, torture and inhuman and degrading treatment. Human rights protection was also officially espoused as state policy. A 1965 Kenyan government policy paper on the application of African socialism to national planning stated that African socialism differed politically from communism because it ensures every citizen equal *political rights*. It also differs from capitalism because it prevents the exercise of disproportionate political influence by economic power groups.[27] However, in the years following independence, these human rights guarantees were routinely flouted by the government and its agents. If anything, human rights rhetoric was used more for legitimizing statist agendas than promoting individual liberties.

The alliance between ethnic Luo and Kikuyu politicians that hastened Britain's retreat fell apart once independence was attained. Prime Minister Jomo Kenyatta and the Kikuyu elite consolidated their hold on power at the expense of the Luo-dominated opposition. By 1969, Kenya had become a one-party state with shrinking political and participatory space for minorities and opposition groups. The power of executive detention once used by British officials to suppress the Mau Mau rebellion was retained in the statute books and was used

[26] Report of the Kenya Constitutional Conference, 1962: Presented to Parliament by the Secretary of State for the Colonies by Command of Her Majesty, April 1962, Colonial office, H.M. Stationery Office, 1962, 22.

[27] Government of Kenya, "African Socialism and Its Application to Planning in Kenya," Kenya Government Sessional Paper No. 10 of 1965 (Nairobi, n.p: 1965), reprinted in Minogue and Molloy, eds., *African Aims and Attitudes*, 131.

against opponents of the emergent oligarchy.[28] Justifying the adoption of one-party rule, Kenyatta pushed a familiar relativist argument. He argued that multiparty systems of government were unsuitable for new African states because under such systems, the machinery of political parties is concerned primarily with defeating opponents at the polls rather than serving the interest of the people.[29] Single-party rule, which he considered more suitable, would however come with significant restrictions on civil liberties and human rights. Another African leader, Prime Minister Albert Margai of Sierra Leone justified single-party rule on similar terms. Multiarty politics, Margai argued, caused division and dissension among citizens, whereas under a single national party, national unity is restored and citizens "speak with one mind."[30]

The language of national solidarity was also mobilized to legitimize socialist policies in Tanzania, Zambia and Uganda in ways that sometimes undermined individual rights. Governance came to be defined by an authoritarian and hegemonic developmentalism that framed economic development as a state prerogative. In Tanzania, Julius Nyerere's African Socialism or *Ujamaa* involved forced villagization in the 1960s, which resulted in the mass displacement of indigenous nomadic communities such as the Massai, Barabaig and Mbulu from their ancestral lands. This resulted in protracted legal battles between indigenous communities and the state, centering on the restrictions imposed by state policy on minority rights.[31] In 1963, the ruling party, the Tanganyika African Union (TANU), declared Tanganyika a one-party state, ensuring that many of the party's candidates ran unopposed in local and national elections.

Nyerere's positions on human rights epitomize post-colonial statist rights discourse that tended to prioritize collective economic and social rights over individual civil liberties. The Arusha Declaration, a policy document issued by the ruling TANU party in 1967, linked Ujamaa, as an indigenous political philosophy inspired by African traditions, to international human rights. Referencing the UDHR,

---

[28] Caroline Elkins, *Imperial Reckoning: The Untold Story of Britain's Gulag in Kenya* (New York: Henry Holt, 2005), 361.

[29] Jomo Kenyatta, *Suffering Without Bitterness: The Founding of the Kenya Nation* (Nairobi: East African Publishing House, 1968), 298.

[30] Quoted in K. A Busia, *Africa in Search of Democracy* (New York: Praeger, 1967), 123.

[31] A. Madsen, *The Hadzabe of Tanzania: Land and Human Rights for a Hunter-Gatherer Community* (London: International Working Group for Indigenous Affairs, 2002), 85.

the Arusha Declaration affirms the equality of all human beings and the inherent dignity all individuals.[32] However, the vision of human rights expressed in the Arusha Declaration also centered on the rights and *duties* of citizens as members of a national community. It emphasized equality, collective work for the common good and the need to prevent exploitation within the community. Nyerere argued that political freedom could be meaningful and the right to human dignity could be fulfilled only when poverty is reduced and communal well-being is achieved.[33] For Nyerere, human rights were essentially about collective empowerment.

In articulating Ujamaa, Nyerere drew on a radical human rights tradition rooted in "Third World" anti-colonial activism, which was positioned in contrast to an atomizing, depoliticizing movement for individual human rights championed by the West.[34] "What do we mean when we talk of freedom?" Nyerere asked in one of his many treatises on Ujamaa. His answer expressed a hierarchy of rights and freedoms in which "national freedom" and collective economic and social well-being clearly took precedence over individual civil liberties. He stated:

> First, there is national freedom; that is, the ability of the citizens of Tanzania to determine their own future, and to govern themselves without interference from non-Tanzanians. Second, there is freedom from hunger, disease, and poverty. And third, there is personal freedom for the individual; that is, his right to live in dignity and equality with all others, his right to freedom of speech, freedom to participate in the making of all decisions which affect his life, and freedom from arbitrary arrest because he happens to annoy someone in authority – and so on. All these things are aspects of freedom, and the citizens of Tanzania cannot be said to be truly free until all of them are assured.[35]

---

[32] Tanganyika African Union (TANU), *The Arusha Declaration and TANU's Policy on Socialism and Self-Reliance* (Dar es Salaam: TANU Publicity Section, 1967).

[33] Julius Nyerere, "Stability and Change in Africa," *Africa Contemporary Record*, 2 (1970), cited in Issa Shivji, *The Concept of Human Rights in Africa* (London: Council for the Development of Economic and Social Research in Africa-Codesria, 1989), 26.

[34] Priya Lal, "African Socialism and the Limits of Global Familyhood: Tanzania and the New International Economic Order in Sub-Saharan Africa," *Humanity: An International Journal of Human Rights, Humanitarianism and Development*, 6, 1 (2015): 22.

[35] Julius Nyerere, *Man and Development: Binadamu Na Maendeleó* (Oxford: Oxford University Press, 1974), 25.

President Kenneth Kaunda of Zambia deployed a similar notion of human rights in his philosophy of "Zambian humanism," which the country adopted as the state ideology at independence. Official policy statements on Zambian socialism, shaped by Kaunda's humanist ideas, affirmed commitment to "promoting human rights and human dignity" and transforming Zambia to become progressively a country in which there is equality and respect for human dignity.[36] However, like Nyerere, Kaunda's human rights vision centered on collective, rather than individual, rights. Writing in 1967, he proclaimed that one of the goals of Zambian humanism was to abolish all forms of discrimination and segregation based on color, tribe, clan and creed and to promote understanding and unity among the people of Zambia "by removing individualism, tribalism and provincialism."[37] A similar vision of human rights founded on communal solidarity was expressed in the *Common Man's Charter*, adopted by the Uganda People's Congress (UPC) in 1969. The Charter, which foreshadowed the imposition of one-party rule in the country, set out the basic principles of a socialist policy of government. Although it expressed the UPC's commitment to promoting justice, equality and liberty for all Ugandans, it also stated that in the enjoyment of these rights and freedoms, "no person shall be allowed to prejudice the rights and freedoms of others and the interests of the state."[38] Often, the "interests of the state" were considered synonymous with those of the government in power.

The shift toward one-party rule and the rise of a statist, collectively oriented discourse of rights was not limited to sub-Saharan Africa. In the Maghrebi states of Morocco, Tunisia and Algeria, the decades following independence did not bring the halcyon days that many in the anti-colonial movements had hoped for. If anything, governance was characterized by autocratic personalist rule and the repression of political opposition groups. Governments and their agents were responsible for blatantly contrived political trials, disappearances, political assassinations and the torture and imprisonment of opponents. Wide-ranging human rights violations, spanning civil rights abuses and socioeconomic restrictions, raised concern both at home and

[36] Kenneth Kaunda, *Zambian Humanism: A Guide to the Nation* (Lusaka: Zambia Information Services, 1967), excerpts reprinted in Minogue and Molloy, eds., *African Aims and Attitudes*, 108.

[37] Kaunda, *Zambian Humanism*, 105.

[38] Apollo Milton Obote, *The Common Man's Charter* (Kampala: Government Printer, Kampala, 1970), 3.

abroad.[39] In Tunisia, the lawyer and journalist Habib Bourguiba, who led the nationalist movement and spent many years as a prisoner of the French, became the leader of the country at independence. Upon attaining power, Bourguiba proclaimed himself president for life and ruled with a rigid authoritarian hand until his forcible removal from office in 1987. Under his rule, political opponents were subject to arbitrary arrest and institutionalized torture; several leading opposition Islamists were sentenced to death by secretive state security courts.[40]

In Algeria, the ruling National Liberation Front (FLN), which gained power after the independence war with France, faced an internal political power struggle that divided the party and the country. Amid the political turmoil, President Ben Bella took steps to concentrate power in the executive arm of government, establishing a one-party state and limiting the role of Parliament. He believed that the main task of his regime was establishing law and order after a disruptive war of independence and rebuilding autonomous state institutions. By presidential decree, he banned all other major political groups, leaving the FLN as the sole political party. Political opponents were selectively arrested, including the veteran nationalist and independence activist Ferhat Abbas. As head of the Constituent National Assembly, Abbas opposed constitutional changes that allowed the FLN to handpick members of Parliament. He saw Parliament as an important source of authority in Algeria's political system and advocated for the separation of powers, with Parliament playing an active role in government. Abbas was ultimately forced to resign, expelled from the FLN and placed under house arrest.[41]

The story was similar in Egypt where Gamal Nasser's ascendancy to the presidency in 1954 ushered in an era of pan-Arabism and socialism. Nasser led the overthrow of the country's constitutional monarchy in 1952 and introduced land reforms aimed at curtailing the political influence of major land owners. Political and economic change came with a wide range of restrictions on civil liberties and property rights. Although Nasser's populist socialism fostered a sense of secular

---

[39] Susan Waltz, *Human Rights and Reform: Changing the Face of North African Politics* (Berkeley: University of California Press, 1995), vii.

[40] Susan Waltz, "North Africa," in *Encyclopedia of Human Rights*, David Forsythe, ed. (New York: Oxford University Press, 2009), 113.

[41] Azzedine Layachi, *Economic Crisis and Political Change in North Africa* (Westport: Praeger, 1998), 8–9.

nationalism in the country, it also undermined some of the progressive policies of his predecessor, President Mohammed Naguib, who had presented himself as a campaigner for enhancing human rights.[42] Under Nasser, opposition political groups such as the Muslim Brotherhood faced a hostile environment with the creation of a one-party state in 1953, the dissolution of all political parties and the creation of the Arab Socialist Union (ASU) in 1963 as the single ruling party. Nasser and the country's ruling elites saw a need for a "transitional authoritarianism," considering Egypt's poverty, illiteracy and lack of a large middle class.[43] As elsewhere in Africa, developmentalist aspirations became the main justification for state restrictions on human rights and civil liberties. The successor regimes of Anwar Sadat and Hosni Mubarak did not fare significantly better in terms of their human rights record. Human rights conditions in Egypt deteriorated significantly during the three decades of Mubarak's dictatorship.

Muammar Gaddafi's four-decade rule in Libya was characterized by political repression and a cult of personality. Seizing power from the ruling monarchy in a coup in 1969, Gaddafi rode a wave of popular discontent and populist politics to assert power. Like many military rulers of the era, he positioned himself as a modernist and reformer adopting an anti-Western and anti-imperialist stance. Ruling by decree, he nationalized Libya lucrative oil industry and declared Libya a *Jamahiriya*, or "socialist state of the masses." His political philosophy was outlined in his "Green Book," which charted a homegrown, Islam-inspired political ideology framed as an alternative to socialism and capitalism. Like Nasser, he advocated pan-Arabism, and in the later years of his rule pushed a vigorous pan-Africanist political agenda. With Libya's oil wealth, Gaddafi implemented major social welfare projects that transformed housing, education and healthcare, making Libya among the highest ranked African countries in the UN Human Development Index.[44] However, oil wealth also provided Gaddafi with the means to suppress opposition at home and interfere politically aboard through support for foreign militants.

---

[42] Benjamin MacQueen, "The Reluctant Partnership between the Muslim Brotherhood and Human Rights NGOs in Egypt," in *Islam and Human Rights in Practice: Perspectives across the Ummah*, Shahram Akbarzadeh and Benjamin MacQueen, eds. (New York: Routledge, 2008), 76.

[43] Kirk Beattie, *Egypt during the Sadat Years* (New York: Palgrave, 2000), 4.

[44] United Nations Development Programme, *Human Development Report 2010: The Real Wealth of Nations – Pathways to Human Development* (New York: UNDP), 142.

This resulted in conflicts with neighboring Egypt and Chad in the 1970s and '80s. Domestic and international human rights groups reported frequently on widespread abuses including detentions, torture and disappearances. Gaddafi's human rights record came under particular international scrutiny because of accusations of his government's sponsorship of international terrorism, including the bombing of an American civilian aircraft over Lockerbie, Scotland, in 1988. This garnered him international condemnation and isolated Libya on the international stage until he was killed in 2011 during the civil war following a wave of popular uprisings that swept across the Arab world.

When assessed comparatively, these developments point to a common trend in post-colonial African politics. From Ghana to Algeria, and from Tanzania to Egypt, ruling regimes abandoned multiparty democracy founded on constitutional rights and moved toward military dictatorships and one-party rule founded on socialist idealism, national solidarity and a restrictive statist discourse of collective rights.

The Era of Dictatorship

The most egregious human rights violations in Africa in the decades following independence occurred under regimes that can best be described as kleptocratic dictatorships. Even in an era of military usurpation of power, authoritarian regimes, one-party rule and "big men" politics, the human rights violations of kleptocratic dictators stood out. Perhaps the most infamous of these leaders was Idi Amin Dada, who ruled Uganda for most of the 1970s. Amin gained international notoriety for unleashing a reign of terror on his people and leaving an unprecedented record of human rights violations. A military officer who overthrew the elected government of Milton Obote in 1971, Amin came to symbolize the worst of post-colonial African despots. His regime was responsible for the death of tens of thousands of Ugandans through torture, assassinations and mass killings. Amin gained a reputation not only as a ruthless dictator but also as a bumbling megalomaniac. Upon seizing power and declaring himself president, he also promoted himself to the position of field marshal, dissolved the National Assembly and ruled by personal decree. His reign of terror in Uganda relied on the apparatus of state security agencies such as the notorious State Research Bureau, which was responsible for widespread intimidation, arbitrary imprisonment, torture and murder.

Amin's reign of terror possessed a uniquely ethnic and racial character. His rule was defined by bloody persecutions of opposing ethnic groups and those considered and political enemies. Many of his victims were from the Lango and Acholi ethnic groups, who were targeted because of suspicions of their loyalty to the ousted Obote regime. In 1972, Amin ordered the expulsion of thousands of Indo-Pakistani Asians from the country and seized their assets without compensation. This was part of a wider policy of so-called Africanization of the Ugandan economy. Up to 70,000 Asians, many of whom were born in Uganda and had lived their entire lives in the country, were given three months to leave the country. Amin's repressive policies drew the condemnation of the international community and human rights organizations such as Amnesty International, which reported extreme violations of human rights and flouting of the rule of law. Amnesty International identified the major violations as political imprisonment and the "disappearance" of opponents of the government. Human rights organizations reported widespread killings and torture by the security forces, affecting Ugandans from all socio-cultural strata. They published the names of hundreds of people who had disappeared under Amin's rule. These included prominent figures such as the chief justice of Uganda and the vice-chancellor of Makerere University.[45] In 1974, to take one example, Amnesty International reported that 600 Ugandans had been massacred near the eastern town of Moroto and called for an independent judicial inquiry into the killings and disappearances.[46] Amin's reign of terror also forced thousands of Ugandan refugees to flee to Kenya at the height of the killings in 1977.[47]

Following sustained pressure from international human rights groups, Amin's government became increasingly isolated from the international community until it was overthrown by a combination

---

[45] *Amnesty International Annual Report 1972–73* (London: Amnesty International Publications, 1974), 42.

[46] *Amnesty International Annual Report 1974–75* (London: Amnesty International Publications, 1976), 35; *Amnesty International Annual Report 1975–76* (London: Amnesty International), 58.

[47] *Amnesty International Annual Report 1976–77* (London: Amnesty International Publications, 1978), 109–112.

of Ugandan rebel forces and the Tanzanian military in 1979. Human rights and humanitarian organizations followed their campaigns against rights violations with an international fund-raising campaign in aid of the estimated one million widows and orphans of those tortured to death or otherwise murdered by Amin's security forces.[48] Although Amin's overthrow reduced the most extreme cases of human rights violations that characterized his rule, it did not bring political calm to Uganda. His deposition was followed by a series of short-term administrations and the return of Milton Obote, under whom political repression and state-sanctioned murder continued until he too was forced into exile in 1985 by Yoweri Museveni and his National Resistance Army. The legacy of authoritarianism and repression would continue under Museveni's rule, and Amin's legacy of torture and mass killings would persist in the wars that ensued between the government and rebel groups such as the Lord's Resistance Army.

The regimes of Mobutu Sese Seko in Zaire, Jean-Bedel Bokassa in the Central African Republic and Hastings Banda in Malawi provide further examples of the more extreme despotisms of the post-colonial era in Africa. Mobutu has been described as Africa's "King of Klepto-crats," whose tales pandered to the caricature visions of an African banana republic and fitted the Heart of Darkness clichés about the Congo.[49] His thirty-two-year rule in Zaire was characterized by cor-ruption and the use of state security forces to commit widespread human rights violations including torture, arbitrary detentions and extrajudicial killings. Mobutu fostered a culture of impunity that allowed even the worst forms of human rights abuses to go unpunished. International and local human rights organizations such as Amnesty International, Human Rights Watch, Article 19, the International League for Human Rights and the Human Rights League of Zaire all reported widespread human rights violations in Zaire under Mobutu's rule.[50] In one particularly brutal incident, the government violently suppressed student protests at the University of Lubumbashi, resulting

---

[48] *Amnesty International Annual Report 1980* (London: Amnesty International Publica-tions, 1981), 86.

[49] Alec Russell, *Big Men, Little People: Encounters in Africa* (London: Macmillan, 1999), 4.

[50] Article 19, *Freedom of Information and Expression in Zaire: Commentary on the Report Submitted to the U.N. Human Rights Committee by the Government* (London: Article 19, 1987); International League for Human Rights, *Human Rights Comments on the Govern-ment of Zaire's Official Report to the UN Human Rights Committee* (New York: ILHR,

FIGURE 6.1 Mobutu Sese Seko of Zaire
Credit: President Mobutu, Mont Ngaliema, Kinshasa, Congo (Democratic
Republic). Photograph by Eliot Elisofon, 1967 EEPA EECL 2450. Eliot Elisofon
Photographic Archives, National Museum of African Art Smithsonian Institution.

in the massacre of about 100 students and the destruction of the
campus.[51] Apart from its outright brutality, Mobutu's policies also
placed restrictions on economic and social rights. Political repression
and socioeconomic rights restrictions were justified in the name of
national security and indigenous culture. As part of his "Zairianization"
policy, Mobutu introduced the "obligatory civic work" program called
salongo. Salongo supposedly marked a return to traditional values of
communalism and solidarity. In practice, however, salongo had more
in common with the French colonial practice of corvée labor (forced
labor) than indigenous traditional labor practices (see Figure 6.1).

A similar scenario played out in the Central African Republic where
military officer Jean-Bedel Bokassa ousted the elected government

1987); Ligue Zaïroise des Droits de l'Homme (Human Rights League of Zaire), *Rapport
sur l'état des librtés au Zaire [Freedom Status Report in Zaire]* (Kinshasa, Zaire: 1990).
[51] Steve Askin, "The Lubumbashi Massacre," *The Tablet: International Catholic News
Weekly* (April 1992): 6; Lawyers Committee for Human Rights. *Zaire: Massacre of
Students al Lubumbashi. Fact-finding Report* (LCHR: New York, 1991).

and took over power in 1966. Bokassa appointed himself field marshall and later declared himself president for life with unlimited executive power. A megalomaniac who modeled himself after the French emperor Napoleon, Bokassa cultivated a cult of personality that severely restricted political participation and civil liberties. In 1977 he declared the country the Central African Empire and crowned himself the emperor in an extravagant ceremony that practically bankrupted the country. Bokassa's fourteen years in power were marked by large-scale human rights violations. Hundreds of people disappeared or were killed in prison, while thousands of political prisoners were detained without trial for long periods under appalling conditions. In 1979 Bokassa had hundreds of schoolchildren arrested for resisting his government's education policy on compulsory school uniforms. In the unrest that followed, 100 of these schoolchildren were killed by Bokassa's Imperial Guard forces. The killings caused a storm of protests and condemnation that led to an international inquiry into the incident.[52] International outrage and domestic resistance over this incident ultimately led to Bokassa's deposition by French military forces in September 1979.

Hastings Banda presided over an equally repressive regime in Malawi. Like Bokassa, he declared Malawi a one-party state and made himself president for life. His government routinely tortured and murdered both real and perceived political opponents. Human rights groups estimate that under Banda's rule, at least 6,000 people were killed, tortured or jailed without trial.[53] Social life was tightly controlled and civil liberties severely curtailed by a government that was particularly intolerant of dissent. All criticism of the president, his government or policies was effectively banned, as were long hair, short skirts and rock music. "Everything is my business," Banda famously declared, "Anything I say is law ... literally law."[54] Like Mobutu, Banda appealed to indigenous culture and morality to legitimize his authoritarian rule and sought to control even the most mundane aspects of social life. He utilized Malawi's "traditional courts," a

---

[52] *Amnesty International Annual Report 1980* (London: Amnesty International Publications, 1981), 51–52.

[53] *Human Rights Watch World Report 1992* (New York: Human Rights Watch, 1993), 12.

[54] Bon Drogin, "Malawi Tries Ex-Dictator in Murder. Africa: Aging Autocrat Is One of Few among Continent's Tyrants to Face Justice for Regime's Abuses," *Los Angeles Times* (May 21, 1995): 12.

carryover from colonial native courts, less to administer justice and more to suppress political opposition outside the regular legal system.

Ethiopia, one of only two African countries that did not come under European colonial rule, did not escape the era of dictatorships. The ascension to power of a military junta led by Mengistu Haile Mariam in 1974 ushered in a Marxist-leaning dictatorship characterized by political repression, economic restrictions and tight social control of the population. Mengistu's regime was responsible for widespread human rights violations that included political assassinations and mass killings. Among these were the executions of members of the royal family, including the deposed Emperor Haile Selassie.

In Chad, Hissène Habré, who seized power in 1982, led a regime that was notorious for egregious human rights abuses. His secret police terrorized his critics and those perceived as opponents of the regime. His campaign of repression and intimidation included widespread torture, mass killings and ethnic cleansing. After he was deposed in 1990, a truth commission in Chad found that more than 40,000 people were killed and thousands more tortured during his eight-year rule. Habré fled to Senegal where in 2016, he was tried and sentenced to life in prison for human rights violations by an international tribunal. Habré's trial and conviction has been described as a milestone for justice that could herald a new era of human rights accountability in Africa.[55] This marked the first time that a court in one country would try the former leader of another country for crimes against humanity. Significantly, this outcome took the concerted effort of the government of Senegal, the International Court of Justice at The Hague and the African Union working together to create a new "Extraordinary African Chambers" to try Habré.

What did dictators such as Mobutu, Bokassa, Banda, Mengistu Haile Mariam and Habré have in common? For one, they were all sustained by international Cold War politics. They thrived during an era when despots could count on the support of Western or Eastern bloc allies to prop up their regimes, enabling them to suppress dissent at home and deflect international criticism of their human rights record. Western governments justified their support for Mobutu and Banda in terms of Cold War realpolitik and turned a blind eye to their human rights violations. Checking the spread of communism took

---

[55] The Editorial Board, "A Milestone for Justice in Africa," *New York Times*, July 22, 2015, A26.

priority over any obligations to uphold international human rights norms. Habré seized power in Chad with the support of France and the United States. US President John Kennedy extolled Mobutu's role as commander-in-chief of Congolese armed forces in the Cold War struggle against communism while overlooking well-publicized reports of his atrocities.[56] When Mobutu eventually seized power in 1965, it was with the support of the US Central Intelligence Agency.

Similarly, the Soviet Union and other Eastern bloc countries positioned themselves as allies of newly independent African states in their struggles against exploitative Western capitalism and neo-colonialism. Mengistu Haile Mariam's dictatorship in Ethiopia was largely sustained by Soviet economic and military support, allowing for the creation of the largest army in sub-Saharan Africa. With Soviet military support, Mengistu could maintain an authoritarian grasp over the country and suppress Eritrean and Tigrean separatists.[57] The examples of Habré, Mobutu and Megistu lend credence to the claim that human rights were casualties of the Cold War. In Africa, the cost of the Cold War can be measured in terms of the hundreds of thousands of lives lost in proxy wars in Ethiopia, Congo, Angola, Mozambique and Namibia. But it can also be measured in terms of the millions of people whose human rights were violated under dictatorships sustained by the impunity engendered by international Cold War politics. The era of "big men" politics and kleptocratic dictatorships would dissipate only with the end of the Cold War in the 1990s, yet its legacy persists to today.

One final note should be added to the question of human rights and authoritarian politics in independent Africa. The restrictions on civil liberties that leaders such as Nkrumah and Nyerere imposed on their citizens were mostly driven by political ideology. While these restrictions evidently constituted human rights violations, it would be mistaken to group these violations into the same category as the mass atrocities committed by dictators such as Habré, Mobutu and Idi Amin. Nyerere was certainly not the megalomaniacal and murderous despot that Idi Amin was. In fact, Nyerere was one of the staunchest critics of Idi Amin and he consistently raised human rights objections

---

[56] Peter Schraeder, *United States Foreign Policy toward Africa: Incrementalism, Crisis and Change* (Cambridge: Cambridge University Press, 1994), 67.

[57] Robert Patman, *The Soviet Union in the Horn of Africa: The Diplomacy of Intervention and Disengagement* (Cambridge: Cambridge University Press, 2009), 305.

to the atrocities perpetrated by Idi Amin's regime. Nyerere would ultimately play a key role in the overthrow of Idi Amin with Tanzania's military intervention in Uganda.[58] Nyerere also supported self-determination struggles abroad, if not at home. Tanzania was the first country to recognize the separatist government of Biafra during the Nigeria-Biafra War. Nyerere believed that the cause of the Igbo people of Biafra was a justified struggle against oppression and for self-determination. At home, Nyerere played a moderating pro–human rights role with his principled opposition to the racially divisive Anti-European and Anti-Asian rhetoric of some politicians within his ruling TANU party. Instead, he pushed an inclusive non-discriminatory agenda by insisting on a non-racial citizenship bill in 1961 amid strong opposition from leaders within his own party.[59] Despite the authoritarian character of his socialist policies, Nyerere succeeded in bringing relative political stability to Tanzania in an era of turbulence across the continent. It is important therefore to recognize that despite the general inclination toward authoritarian rule, some African leaders of this period had a mixed and more complex human rights record.

A typology of African regimes based on their human rights record is possible.

I. *The movement to single-party regimes.* These include regimes headed by civilian anti-colonial nationalists such as Julius Nyerere (Tanzania), Kenneth Kaunda (Zambia), Sékou Touré (Guinea) and Kwame Nkrumah (Ghana) who inherited power at independence and positioned themselves as founders of the nation. Most of these leaders were motivated by a desire to carry out grand nation-building programs and saw single-party rule as means of achieving this. To varying degrees they used coercion, and to varying degrees they were prone to corruption.

II. *The military regimes*

    a. Reformist officer-led regimes such as those that emerged in Nigeria and Ghana following military coups in the 1960s. Some were motivated by a desire to correct the errors of civilians. Most, including Muammar Gaddafi of Libya, were authoritarian.

---

[58] Ralph Austin, "Colonial Boundaries and African Nationalism: The Case of the Kagera Salient," in *In Search of a Nation: Histories of Authority and Dissidence in Tanzania*, Gregory Maddox and James Leonard Giblin, eds. (Athens: Ohio University Press, 2005), 63.

[59] James Brenan, "A Short History of the Political Opposition and Multi-Party Democracy in Tanganyika, 1958–64," in *In Search of a Nation*, 258.

    b. Regimes led by brutal former non-commissioned officers such as Jean-Bédel Bokassa (Central African Republic) and Idi Amin (Uganda) who usurped power for personal aggrandizement and to settle political scores with adversaries. Their rule was the most ruthless, repressive and corrupt.

    c. The patriotic officer regimes. These regimes could be brutal, as in Mengistu Haile Mariam's Ethiopia, but were generally motivated by a desire for patriotic reconstruction as in Benin, Madagascar and Egypt.

  III. *Regimes created by guerilla movements.* These regimes came to power following liberation wars such as those in Guinea-Bissau, Angola, Mozambique, Namibia and Zimbabwe. They were authoritarian and tended to push a statist and collectivist interpretation of rights.

Within each of these types, there is much variety. Many of the military regimes were transitional and recognized a need to create political parties and return to democratic rule. Some had long-term goals and entrenched military governance. In some cases, the officers who led these regimes were simply interested in accumulating wealth and turned out to be even more corrupt than the politicians they deposed.

Oppositional Human Rights Struggles

The constrained political landscape in many African countries provides only one of many possible viewpoints for understanding how human rights developed in independent Africa. Although ascendant nationalist elites who inherited state power at independence tended to move away from the human rights principles they had espoused in anti-colonial struggles, human rights as both ideology and movement did not completely fizzle with independence. Rather, rights discourses came to be shaped by shifting political interests and agendas. With ruling regimes seeking to maintain their grasp on power and suppress opposition groups, political dissenters sought new platforms for human rights and pro-democracy struggles. They mobilized support through the press, formed new opposition political parties and civil society groups to resist repressive governments, and forged alliances with international human rights non-governmental organizations (NGOs). Thus, although political commitment to human rights waned in the corridors of state power, it persisted in oppositional discourses. More than simply the abandonment of human rights, these developments point to a recurrent pattern in the history of human rights movements – the opportunistic cooption of rights language, more to attain or enhance political power than to promote equality or alleviate human suffering.

A tendency toward politicizing human rights claims is evident in modern human rights history. In the colonial context, anti-colonial activists emphasized human rights as self-determination in independence struggles. As we have seen in the preceding chapter, independence activists challenged attempts by European colonists to delink national liberation struggles in the colonies from the emergent international human rights at the UN. Instead, anti-colonial activists framed self-determination as integral to universal human rights. They would be successful with the affirmation of the right to self-determination in several international human rights documents. With independence, African ruling elites once again essentialized human rights as collective claims to foster statist agendas. In contrast, independence activists who lost out in transitional politics appealed to individual-centered rights and civil liberties in opposition to state power.

This tension between statist and oppositional rights discourses is evident in the rivalry between Kwame Nkrumah and Joseph Danquah in early independent politics in Ghana. In the face of the government's repression, Danquah's oppositional politics and advocacy centered on upholding liberal constitutional and democratic rights. In a letter to Nkrumah in 1959, Danquah expressed concern that the government was sliding toward despotism with the wide restrictions imposed on individual liberties. "In the past twelve months," he wrote, "our country has witnessed a great display of the power of the State as against the individual. Laws have been passed or put into execution which have made it possible for the individual to be deprived of his liberty and imprisoned for five years without trial. Laws have been passed which have put the verdict of the Courts to nothingness and have elevated the power of the State above the right of the individual, even to the extent of depriving the individual of his property, even of his or her money."[60] Danquah's oppositional politics centered on individual rights, challenged Nkrumah's authoritarian rule and countered a statist rights discourse hinged on collective solidarity rights.

---

[60] Quoted in Minogue and Molloy, eds., *African Aims and Attitudes*, 29.

Similar patterns are evident in oppositional politics in Kenya. Odinga Odinga, a leading figure in Kenya's independence struggle, became the main opposition figure against Jomo Kenyatta's virtual single-party rule. He also positioned himself as an advocate for democratic rights. Ideological differences and underlying ethnic politics of Luo-Kikuyu rivalry exacerbated tensions between Kenya's political elites. In 1960 Odinga, an ethnic Luo, became vice-president of the main political party, the Kenya African National Union (KANU). When Kenya became independent in 1963, he was appointed as a minister in the government of Jomo Kenyatta and later became the vice-president. His socialist views, however, soon conflicted with Kenyatta's more centrist ideology, and in 1966 he broke away from KANU to form a left-wing opposition party, the Kenya People's Union (KPU). Although the KPU drew support mainly among the Luo, it also represented a more radical strand in Kenyan politics. The party criticized the government's infringements on constitutional rights and warned of the gradual erosion of individual freedoms and the establishment of a dictatorship. The KPU condemned the KANU's "capitalist policies" that it claimed had created a small class of rich people at the expense of the *Wananchi* (common people), who bore the brunt of the struggle against colonialism. The KPU therefore proclaimed its resolve to "struggle relentlessly to preserve guarantees of individual freedom and the right of political freedom contained in the Constitution."[61]

Seeking to suppress its oppositional activities, the Kenyatta government outlawed the KPU in 1969 and imprisoned its leaders, including Odinga. Although he later rejoined KANU, Odinga was politically sidelined and prevented from running for office. This effectively consigned him to oppositional politics. In opposition, he continued to denounce government corruption, spoke out against ethnic favoritism and pressed for improved human rights conditions and a multiparty political system. He was expelled from KANU in 1982 and placed under house arrest for several months by the government of Daniel arap Moi. He remained active in opposition politics and human rights advocacy on the platform of the Forum for the Restoration of Democracy (FORD), which he helped form in 1991.

Odinga's oppositional politics in Kenya reflect a pattern in postcolonial African politics. In newly independent states, opposition

---

[61] Kenya People's Union, *K.P.U. Manifesto for 1966 By-Elections* (Nairobi: KPU), 3.

politicians framed resistance to authoritarian rule in terms of constitutional rights and international human rights. In Algeria, Ferhat Abbas's opposition to the usurpation of legislative powers brought him into conflict with the government of Ben Bella and the ruling FLN party. Like Odinga in Kenya, Abbas was eventually expelled from the party and placed under house arrest by successive Algerian governments. A similar fate befell the Malawian politician Vera Chirwa, whose advocacy for multiparty democracy made her a target of the dictatorial regime of President Hastings Banda. For her oppositional politics, she was tried and convicted along with her husband for treason and sentenced to death. She spent twelve years on death row before her release following an international campaign by human rights organizations including Amnesty International.[62] Her husband, Orton Chirwa, who was the country's minister of justice, died in prison.

The oppositional politics of Ferhat Abbas in Algeria, Joseph Danquah in Ghana, Odinga Odinga in Kenya and Vera Chirwa in Malawi represent an aspect of the history of independent Africa that is rarely told as part of the global human rights story. The dominant narrative of ascendant African leaders who abandoned human rights at independence obscures the equally important story of the resilience of human rights principles in African oppositional politics and nascent pro-democracy movements. Before the rise of organized human rights NGOs in Africa, oppositional politicians and social activists framed their resistance to authoritarian governance in terms of constitutional and international human rights. These opposition politicians and activists sustained a human rights movement in independent Africa by building on strategies and discourses of anti-colonial struggles. When Danquah compared his incarceration by the Nkrumah government in independent Ghana to imprisonment under British colonial rule, he was making a deliberate statement about the continuity of oppression and the imperative of rights-based resistance. His denunciations of the elevated power of the state over the liberties of citizens represented an appeal to an internationalist individual-centered human rights norms to counteract a statist and collectivist discourse of rights.

My larger point here is that the story of human rights in Africa in the decades following independence defies confident generalizations

---

[62] Vera Chirwa, *Fearless Fighter: An Autobiography* (London: Zed Books, 2007), 208.

about the demise or abandonment of human rights. The discourse of human rights and democratic rights may have dimmed in the corridors of power, but it shone brightly in the oppositional politics of Joseph Danquah, Odinga Odinga, Ferhat Abbas and Vera Chirwa. Still, questions remain. Why did opposition politicians and activists continue to speak the language of human rights and democracy long after their triumphant comrades in anti-colonial struggles seemed to move away from it? Did opposition politicians and activists assert human rights only as a means of asserting relevance and redressing their own political marginalization? Were their invocations of human rights founded on deep commitment to democratic and human rights ideals? There can be no definitive answers to these questions. What is evident, however, is that changing political circumstances and ideological agendas influenced the shifts in human discourse among rival political elites in the era of independence.

Human Rights in War

The most egregious human rights violations in Africa have occurred in the context of wars and armed conflicts. In several African countries, violence has been used by ruling regimes as a means of asserting authority. Violence has also been used to challenge state authority through insurrection and secession. Human rights scholars have long drawn attention to the reciprocal relationship between human rights violations expressed in political repression and the outbreak of armed conflicts. Political repression and resistance to it triggers conflict, which, in turn, creates conditions of impunity and the breakdown in the rule of law that result in genocide, war crimes and other forms of gross human rights violations. This was certainly the case with the wave of armed conflicts that erupted across Africa in the first decade of independence.

Perhaps the most prominent of these early conflicts is the Nigeria-Biafra War, which broke out seven years into Nigeria's independence and led to one of the most significant global humanitarian crises in the post–World War II era. The ethnic Igbo of Eastern Nigeria, who felt marginalized and threatened within Nigeria, fought to establish an independent Biafra state. Nigerian leaders saw the conflict as a war to uphold the unity and territorial integrity of the newly independent country. Biafran leaders accused the Nigerian government of waging a genocidal war of starvation against the Igbo people, an allegation that elicited global concern. The language of human rights was effective in Biafra's war propaganda. Images of starving Biafran children horrified many people around the world and prompted an international humanitarian campaign that was framed largely around human rights. Human rights and humanitarian organizations reported summary executions, arbitrary arrests, ill-treatment and mass killings during and immediately after the war.[63] They organized intervention campaigns to stop the killing and suffering of civilians. A similar scenario had earlier played out in the Congo where civil war broke out following the secession of the region of Katanga, only eleven days after the country gained independence in 1960. That conflict triggered a chain of events that would lead to the rise of one of Africa's most ruthless dictators, Mobutu Sese Seko, and the outbreak of ethnopolitical civil conflicts in the 1990s.

In the southern African nations of Angola, Mozambique and Namibia, chaotic decolonization created opportunities for political instability and protracted civil wars fueled by Cold War international politics of the 1970s and 1980s. In Mozambique, resistance to Portuguese rule by the Front for the Liberation of Mozambique (FRELIMO), unlashed an insurgency war in which tens of thousands of Mozambicans lost their lives. Events took a similar turn in Angola where a protracted civil war was sustained by foreign military intervention in which the Western and Eastern blocs took opposing sides. While the People's Movement for the Liberation of Angola (MPLA) received military support from the Soviet Union and Cuba, the National Union for the Total Independence of Angola (UNITA) was supported by the United States and the apartheid regime in South Africa. The Angola war was characterized by flagrant human rights violations and acts of great cruelty. Armed groups perpetrated atrocities including extrajudicial executions, widespread use of torture and reprisals against civilians, including pregnant women, children and the elderly.[64] Successive peace accords that contained provisions for human rights protections broke down, and war raged on with devastating effects until the death of the UNITA's leader Jonas Savimbi in

[63] *Amnesty International Annual Report 1969–70* (London: Amnesty International Publications, 1971), 11; Omaka, *The Biafran Humanitarian Crisis*, 84.

[64] *Amnesty International Annual Report 1981* (London: Amnesty International Publications, 1982), 25–26.

2002. During the twenty-seven-year conflict, whole cities were reduced to ruins and hundreds of thousands of people were killed or died from war-related deprivation and disease. Tens of thousands of child soldiers were employed and underage girls abducted and abused. Between 1998 and 2002 an estimated 3.1 million people were forced from their homes as a result of indiscriminate tactics used by both government and UNITA forces against the civilian population.[65]

No region of Africa has been spared the devastating impacts of war and the toll in terms of lives lost, suffering inflicted on people and intergenerational trauma. In Burundi, Hutu-Tutsi ethnic rivalry and competition for political power resulted in mass killings in the 1970s and 1990s. The first of these mass killings has been described as Africa's first genocide.[66] Much better known is the Rwandan genocide of 1994. A good deal has been written about the issues of political upheaval, ethnic polarization, incitement and militarization that led to the genocide.[67] Those details need not be recounted here. It suffices for our purposes to highlight the human rights implications of the genocide.

Sporadic Hutu-Tutsi ethnic violence followed Rwanda's independence in 1962. This intensified in the 1990s with the rise of Hutu extremists who promoted a "Hutu power" ideology and an opposing military campaign by the Tutsi-backed Rwandan Patriotic Front (RPF). In the politics of independent Rwanda, the Hutu power movement represented a triumph of Hutu supremacists over moderates in liberal political parties committed to civil liberties and democratic institutions. Threatened by the prospects of losing power to an advancing RPF in the 1990s, radical Hutu extremists promoted a "final solution" to the Tutsi threat. The assassination of President Juvénal Habyarimana, who led a Hutu government, unleashed a wave of genocidal killings of both Tutsi and moderate Hutus, orchestrated by the Hutu majority government. An estimated 800,000 to one million Rwandans were killed within a three-month period in 1994, constituting up to 70 percent of the country's Tutsi population. The mass

---

[65] Sara Darehshori, *Selling Justice Short: Why Accountability Matters for Peace* (New York: Human Rights Watch, 2009), 66.

[66] For a detailed study of the mass killings in Burundi, see Patricia Daley, *Gender and Genocide in Burundi: The Search for Spaces of Peace in the Great Lakes Region* (Oxford: James Currey, 2008), 268.

[67] For accounts of the Rwandan genocide, see Samuel Totten and Rafiki Ubaldo, *We Cannot Forget: Interviews with Survivors of the 1994 Genocide in Rwanda* (New Brunswick: Rutgers University Press, 2011).

killings on an unprecedented scale were carried out by government-backed ethic militias such as Interahamwe, but also by professional elites and ordinary civilians. Political and military leaders promoted genocide as a means of securing their political power. Ordinary Hutus responded to state-promoted racist incitement and propaganda that portrayed the Tutsi as treacherous and subhuman. The genocide ended only when the RPF took the capital Kigali, stopping 100 days of systematic and well-planned violence. Apart from the deaths, many survivors were maimed and traumatized by the genocide. Hutu militia groups and the Rwandan military regularly used rape and gender-specific violence as weapons in their genocidal campaign.[68]

In the aftermath of the Rwandan genocide, there were recriminations about the failure of the international community to prevent the genocide and, specifically, the failure of the UN Assistance Mission to Rwanda (UNAMIR) charged with peacekeeping. Despite appeals from the UNAMIR's force commander, the Canadian lieutenant-general Roméo Dallaire, the world's major powers limited their intervention to diplomatic protest, minimal peacekeeping measures and evacuating their own nationals.[69] This lack of effective international response is significant from a human rights standpoint. International human rights emerged in the aftermath of World War II as a response to the Holocaust and the atrocities of war. Alongside the UDHR and its associated covenants, the UN adopted the Convention on the Prevention and Punishment of the Crime of Genocide in 1948. "Never again" was the sentiment that inspired the post-war international human rights system. Never again would the international community stand by and allow the mass extermination of people by virtue of their membership of a particular national, ethnic, racial or religious group. The Rwandan genocide demonstrated that the UN and the international community had fallen dismally short of this goal.

Since the Rwandan genocide, there have been other mass atrocities of genocidal proportions in Africa. In 2004 the attention of the international community was drawn to allegations of genocide being

---

[68] Binaifer Nowrojee and Human Rights Watch, *Shattered Lives: Sexual Violence during the Rwandan Genocide and Its Aftermath* (New York: Human Rights Watch/Fédération internationale des droits de l'homme, 1996). Available at www.hrw.org/legacy/reports/1996/Rwanda.htm. Accessed November 13, 2016.

[69] Roméo Dallaire's account of the events is told in Roméo Dallaire and Brent Beardsley, *Shake Hands with the Devil: The Failure of Humanity in Rwanda* (New York: Carroll & Graf, 2005).

committed by the government of Sudan in its war with rebel groups demanding regional autonomy in Darfur. Sudan's president, Omar al-Bashir, was accused of carrying out a campaign of ethnic cleansing against Darfur's non-Arabs, resulting in the deaths of hundreds of thousands of civilians. Al-Bashir's subsequent indictment for genocide, war crimes and crimes against humanity by the International Criminal Court (ICC) in The Hague proved controversial. While human rights groups welcomed the indictment as a victory against state impunity, several African leaders denounced it as a risky precedent that could undermine the sovereignty of African governments, engender political instability and jeopardize post-conflict peacebuilding efforts. South African officials condemned the ICC's issuance of an arrest warrant against Sudanese President Omar al-Bashir as a "regrettable step" that would impact negatively on the peace processes in that country.[70] These objections marked the beginning of the erosion of support by African countries for the ICC, an international tribunal established in 2002 to prosecute individuals for the international crimes of genocide, crimes against humanity and war crimes.

In West Africa, Liberia and Sierra Leone were plunged into civil wars for much of the 1990s and into the new millennium. These conflicts were also marked by brazen violations of basic human rights norms and wanton disregard for international humanitarian law. Both conflicts were characterized by indiscriminate attacks on civilians, who were targeted by different militias.[71] This included gender-based violence and the widespread use of rape as a weapon of war. One human rights group estimates that about 200,000 women and girls were victims of rape during the conflict in Sierra Leone.[72] Militant groups involved in these conflicts, such as the Revolutionary United Front (RUF) in Sierra Leone and the National Patriotic Front of Liberia (NPFL), committed heinous atrocities including systematic

---

[70] South African Government News Agency, "ICC Decision Will Impact on Sudan's Peace Process." Available at www.sanews.gov.za/south-africa/icc-decision-will-impact-sudans-peace-process-sa-0. Accessed August 2, 2016.

[71] For a detailed account of these conflicts, see Danny Hoffman, *The War Machines: Young Men and Violence in Sierra Leone and Liberia* (Durham: Duke University Press, 2011); Megan MacKenzie, *Female Soldiers in Sierra Leone: Sex, Security, and Post-Conflict Development* (New York: NYU Press, 2015).

[72] Physicians for Human Rights, *War-Related Sexual Violence in Sierra Leone: A Population-Based Assessment* (Washington, DC: Physicians for Human Rights, 2002), 3.

extrajudicial executions, amputations and the forced recruitment and abduction of child soldiers to strengthen their ranks and to terrorize civilian populations.

At the end of these conflicts, much international attention focused on protecting human rights within the framework of transitional justice and post-conflict peacebuilding processes. In post-genocide Rwanda, domestic and international efforts centered not only on bringing justice to victims and survivors, but also on reconciliation, conflict prevention and human rights protection. Recognizing that effective prosecution and punishment of war crimes can provide a meaningful deterrent, the UN established the International Criminal Tribunal for Rwanda (ICTR) in Arusha, Tanzania, to investigate and prosecute high-level members of the government and armed forces for their roles in the genocide. The government of Rwanda also established parallel judicial systems to prosecute lower-level leaders and local people. One of these systems was a participatory justice system known as the Gacaca Courts. The Gacaca court system, which traditionally dealt with conflicts within communities, was adapted to deal with genocide crimes, with mixed results. This was presented as a unique African experiment in transitional justice and post-conflict peacebuilding. Part of the goals of the Gacaca system was to halt the culture of impunity responsible for human rights violations, foster national unity and reconciliation and demonstrate the capacity of the Rwandan people to resolve their own problems.[73] The Rwandan government also established a Reconciliation Commission charged with promoting reconciliation and fostering a culture of peace and human rights.

Similar transitional justice measures were adopted in the aftermath of the wars in Liberia and Sierra Leone. The government of Sierra Leone, working with the UN, set up the Special Court for Sierra Leone in 2002 with a mandate to prosecute persons who bore the greatest responsibility for serious violations of international humanitarian law during the war. Charles Taylor, the warlord who later became president of Liberia, was tried and convicted by the special court for aiding and planning what the presiding judge described as "some of the most heinous and brutal crimes recorded in human

---

[73] National Service of Gacaca Courts, *Summary of the Report Presented at the Closing of Gacaca Courts Activities* (Kigali: Republic of Rwanda, National Service of Gacaca Courts, Kigali, 2012), 4.

history."[74] Transitional justice reforms in both Liberia and Sierra Leone also included the establishment of national truth and reconciliation commissions, the creation of national human rights commissions and the restructuring of the judiciary, police and electoral systems.

The scourge of war, militancy, insurgency and terrorism continued in many parts of Africa into the new millennium with adverse consequences for peace, security and human rights. In North Africa, the promise of human rights and democracy of the Arab Spring revolutions that toppled longstanding dictatorships in Egypt, Tunisia and Libya failed to materialize. Rather, these revolutions ushered a new era of political instability and violent militancy. The rise of militant Islamist groups such as the Islamic State and Al-Qaeda in North Africa, Al-Shabaab in East Africa and Boko Haram in West Africa has unleashed terror and indiscriminate violence against civilians. Other insurgent groups such as the Lord's Resistance Army (LRA) in Uganda have gained international notoriety for child abductions and the use of child soldiers in its insurgency campaign. Such indiscriminate militant violence against civilians perpetrated by both state and non-state actors has been responsible for the most egregious and large-scale violations of human rights in independent Africa.

The Second Liberation

In the 1980s and 1990s, the African continent witnessed widespread public unrest as citizens demanded political reforms, an end to military dictatorship and one-party rule, and the establishment of multiparty democracy. This was a period of transition led by new social movements and organized civil society. It was, as historian Paul Zeleza has noted, a period of "bewildering extremes, which saw the rise of mass movements and mass revolts driven by democratic and developmentalist ideals, as well as mass murder and mass poverty perpetrated by desperate regimes and discredited global agencies."[75] With the end of the Cold War, dictatorships in Africa and elsewhere lost the support of foreign governments that propped them up at a

---

[74] Charles Jalloh and Simon Meisenberg, eds., *The Law Reports of the Special Court for Sierra Leone*, vol. 3 (Leiden: M. Nijhoff, 2012), 4060.

[75] Paul Zeleza, "The Struggle for Human Rights," in *The Rule of Law and Development in Africa*, Paul Zeleza and Philip J. McConnaughay, eds. (Philadelphia: University of Pennsylvania Press, 2004), 1.

time when security concerns took priority over human rights principles. In the West African Republic of Benin, Mathieu Kérékou, who seized power in a military coup in 1972 and proclaimed a one-party Marxist state, presided over a peaceful transition from dictatorship to democracy. Under pressure from local and international pro-democracy forces, Kérékou held free elections in 1991 and gave up power when he lost. This ushered in an era of democratic reforms and transitions across West Africa. In Zaire and Malawi, the dictatorships of Mobutu Sese Seko and Hastings Banda also became vulnerable to internal opposition and external pro-democratic pressures. This post–Cold War wave of democratization and the popular struggles that brought it about ushered in an era of second independence or *second liberation* for Africa in the sense that it represented a renewed clamor for political freedom.

The pro-democracy and civil rights movements of this era were triggered partly by economic crises. As international financial institutions such as the International Monetary Fund (IMF) and the World Bank pushed an aggressive structural adjustment policy of trade liberalization and free market fundamentalism, many African governments were forced to adopt unpopular policies that incited social unrest and political strife. The structural adjustment agenda had roots in the continent's entanglement in the debt trap following the worldwide economic recession of the late 1970s and 1980s arising from the collapse of world commodity prices. In response to the debt crisis, the IMF and the World Bank increased the level of the conditions required for loans and credits to developing countries. By the end of the 1990s, the IMF's economic restructuring program was being implemented in thirty-six African countries. The key points of the programs included currency devaluation and the elimination of foreign exchange controls, curtailment of state expenditure to alleviate budget deficits, cuts in public wage bill and social sector programs, labor and trade liberalization and the elimination of state subsidies and price controls.

The 1980s and 1990s have been described as Africa's "lost decades" because structural adjustment programs compelled many African countries to devote much of their limited resources to satisfying the interests of external creditors at the expense of their own economies and the needs of their citizens.[76] Economic austerity

---

[76] John Hilary, "Africa: Dead Aid and the Return of Neoliberalism," *Race & Class*, 52, 2 (2010): 79.

measures and adjustment programs affected all aspects of political and social life, including human rights conditions. Studies have shown direct links between adjustment policies, the authoritarian character of their implementation by African governments and restrictions on human rights and democratic governance. By creating critical problems of legitimacy for African governments, adjustment economic policies eroded their political capacity to govern. This pushed regimes, some of which already exhibited authoritarian tendencies, to resort to even more repressive measures as a means of pushing through unpopular economic adjustment reforms.[77]

In Ghana, for example, early openings in a democratic direction in the 1980s were stifled in the interest of authoritarian control as structural adjustment policies gathered momentum. Restrictions on human rights in the form of arbitrary imprisonments and repression of civil society groups were justified on the grounds of maintaining order and national security in the face of opposition to unpopular economic policies. The government of Jerry Rawlings targeted civil society groups opposed to its economic policies. These included church organizations, labor unions and the Ghana Bar Association, which was targeted with pernicious legislation and harassment by state agencies.[78] Faced with similar cross-pressure from domestic political opposition, international financial institutions and aid agencies, the government of Zambia adopted repressive measures. In Senegal, the authoritarian features of governance were reasserted in the face of political tension precipitated by adjustment of economic policies. The situation was the same in Guinea and Nigeria where widespread opposition to structural adjustment policies was met with state repression and the cooption of opposition forces by ruling regimes.

Pushing through unpopular economic measures exacerbated the authoritarian character of some African governments, intensifying repression and human rights violations. However, the economic difficulties and political uncertainties arising from neoliberal policies also rallied civil society groups and emergent human rights and pro-democracy NGOs to oppose authoritarian governments. These NGOs took on a broader human rights agenda than the opposition politicians

---

[77] Bonny Ibhawoh, "Structural Adjustment, Authoritarianism and Human Rights in Africa," *Comparative Studies in South Asia, Africa and the Middle East*, 19, 1 (1999): 158–167.

[78] E. Gyiamah-Boadi, "Associational Life, Civil Society and Democratization in Ghana," in *Civil Society and the State in Africa*, John Harbeson, Donald Rothchild and Naomi Chazan, eds. (Boulder: Lynne Rienner), 141.

who championed human rights in the early independence era. Apart from pro-democracy and civil rights advocacy, they took on economic, social and gender rights issues such as the right to education, disability rights, children's rights and women's rights issues, including concerted campaigns against female genital mutilation and forced marriages. Human rights NGO advocacy pressured many governments to introduce specific legislation and policies aimed at protecting women's rights. In Kenya, Tanzania and Uganda, these NGOs have been at the forefront of advancing women's rights issues on political participation as well as economic and social rights initiatives targeting sexual violence against women and discrimination against women in matters of land allocation, access and inheritance.[79]

Although human rights NGOs have been criticized as elitist and for promoting Western-oriented and donor-driven human rights agendas, they have nonetheless been successful in mobilizing popular resistance against state repression and authoritarian rule. In Nigeria, human rights and pro-democracy NGOs such as the Committee for the Defense of Human Rights (CDHR), the Civil Liberties Organization (CLO) and the Constitutional Rights Project (CRP) led a successful opposition movement against the military dictatorship of Ibrahim Babangida and Sani Abacha in the 1990s. They also led resistance against the exploitative activities of multinational oil companies and their environmental impacts in the Niger Delta. NGOs framed local struggles against oil companies in terms of economic and social rights by drawing attention to the environmental impacts of oil pollution and destruction of ecosystems on the health and livelihood of local people.[80] NGOs and faith-based groups played a similar role in Kenya's pro-democracy movement. The National Council of Churches of Kenya (NCCK) spoke out against government corruption, repression and human rights violations. The Anglican bishop Alexander Muge emerged as a leading opponent of the government's encroachment on civil liberties and political freedoms, playing a role similar to that of Archbishop Desmond Tutu in South Africa's anti-apartheid struggle.

The "second liberation" movement also swept across North Africa, albeit with limited long-term impact. Although the region remained

---

[79] Makau Mutua, *Human Rights NGOs in East Africa: Political and Normative Tensions* (Philadelphia: University of Pennsylvania Press, 2009), 5–7.

[80] For example, Environmental Rights Action (ERA), an advocacy NGO, was founded in 1993 to deal specifically with environmental human rights issues in Nigeria.

characterized by authoritarian rule, by the late 1980s there was evidence of a growing tension in the relationship between political rulers and the ruled. In Egypt, associational life expanded and the concerns of intellectual critics increasingly found voice in new civil society organizations. Within the greater Middle East, democratization seemed to stand its best chance in the Maghribi states of Morocco, Tunisia and Algeria. The forced departure of Tunisia's President Habib Bourguiba in 1987 focused attention on political problems in that country. Economic crisis culminating in an increase in the price of bread resulted in labor conflicts and political violence, which pitted the main labor union, the Tunisian General Labor Union (Union Générale Tunisienne du Travail, UGTT), against the government. Several UGTT leaders were arrested and detained for inciting workplace strikes and attending illegal meetings. Government repression and harassment ultimately led to the disbanding of the UGTT and other civil society groups. The government also made concerted efforts to round up and silence those vocally critical of its policies, including unionists, human rights leaders and Islamists, who constituted the only viable political opposition.[81]

In Algeria, political turmoil provoked by economic crisis called into question the viability of a divided and ideologically factionalized Algerian state. Political liberalization in 1989 resulted in renewed interest in democratic political participation and access to power. In Morocco, where multiparty politics had long been constitutionally enshrined but the role of political parties circumscribed, organized labor pressed for political change. Many instances of state-instigated disappearances and torture resulted from a legal system that set no limits on police power. By the 1990s, labor demands had shifted away beyond economic demands to broader concern for the political rights to organize, strike, and criticize government policies without fear of reprisal.[82]

Human rights organizations played key roles in popular movements for political and social reforms in North Africa. The Tunisian League of Human Rights (TLHR), founded in 1977, was one of the first politically independent human rights groups in the region. Like most human rights organizations that emerged in this period, the TLHR drew membership from the country's professional classes and political

---

[81] Waltz, *Human Rights and Reform*, 68–69, 71.
[82] Susan Slyomovics, *The Performance of Human Rights in Morocco* (Philadelphia: University of Pennsylvania Press, 2005), 14.

elites who sought greater participation in the political process. By the 1980s, more human rights groups emerged across North Africa despite repressive state policies that restricted political activities. Such groups included the Egyptian Organization for Human Rights (EOHR), established in 1985 as part of the Arab Organization for Human Rights (AOHR), which was founded in Tunisia two years earlier. The establishment of the AOHR signaled growing recognition that human rights abuse underpinned many problems shared across the Arab world and that the promotion and protection of individual liberties was a solution to these abuses. These NGOs shared a vision of democratic reform centered on free elections, non-discrimination, due process and legal equality. The TLHR and the EOHR forged transnational linkages with international human rights groups on advocacy campaigns focused on state atrocities including extrajudicial killings and torture, disappearances, prison conditions, restrictions on civil liberties and arbitrary detentions by state security agencies.

Given the restrictive political conditions in the region, North African human rights NGOs had to make careful strategic choices about their activities and how they dealt with the two sectors of society that they sought to influence: government and public opinion. On one hand, governments held real power, and disregard for the way human rights advocacy was perceived by the government was likely to exert costs. On the other hand, advocacy methods that pandered to government interests tended to cultivate public criticism and raise questions about the legitimacy of human rights organizations. Human rights activists also had to contend with critics who questioned the compatibility of Western-based notions of rights pushed by NGOs with local Arab-Muslim cultural heritage.[83] Under these circumstances, human rights activists often had to walk a fine line between upholding human rights principles and acquiescing in violations arising from politically and culturally sensitive issues.

Faced with criticisms of their record of repression and human rights violations, some North African governments made tentative concessions toward political and social liberalization. In Tunisia, the government of Habib Bourguiba initiated a gender equality campaign, advocating for women's rights including universal education for girls, women's admission to employment under the same conditions as men

---

[83] Waltz, *Human Rights and Reform*, 161.

and free consent to marriage. Despite strong opposition from conservatives, Bourguiba enacted the Code of Personal Status, a major reform of family law that gave women the right to divorce and consent to marriage. The law also decreed equality between fathers and mothers, and between children irrespective of gender.[84] Bourguiba's successor, Zine Ben Ali, similarly endorsed human rights and pledged his commitment to uphold them following pressure from local and international human rights organizations. However, legal and rhetorical commitment from political leaders did not always translate into substantive improvement in human rights conditions.

In regard to women's rights, family law reform has been the key to human rights in North Africa because it stands at the intersection of kinship and state.[85] Family law legitimizes the extended male-centered patrilineage that is the foundation of kin-based solidarities within tribal groups. It sustains the patriarchal power of men and the kinship system over women. By remaining faithful to Islamic law, many independent North African states retained the model of the family as an extended patrilineage. Family law therefore largely determines the scope of rights enjoyed by women in both the private and public spheres. These laws set out the legal rights and responsibilities that men and women have in the family and, by extension, in the society at large. Such laws regulate matters of legal personhood, the rights and obligations of spouses within marriage, polygamy, divorce, custody of children and inheritance. In many North African countries, the central question has been whether traditional Islamic family law should prevail unchallenged, or whether legal reforms are necessary to alter the balance of power that the law gives to men and women. Also at issue is the fundamental organization of society and the place of individual and kin-based collectivities within it. In promulgating the family law of the newly sovereign country, each Maghribi state presented its vision of individual rights, kinship and the family. The Algerian Family Code adopted in the immediate post-independence era was firmly grounded in traditional Islamic law. In contrast, the Tunisian legislation included significant reforms centered on individual rights and obligations within a nuclear family system.[86]

---

[84] Béji Caïd Essebsi, *Bourguiba: le bon grain et l'ivraie* (Tunis: Sud Éditions, 2009), 63.
[85] Mounira Charrad, *States and Women's Rights: The Making of Postcolonial Tunisia, Algeria, and Morocco* (Berkeley: University of California Press, 2001), 5.
[86] Charrad, *States and Women's Rights*, 5–6.

In many parts of Africa, human rights reforms and pro-democracy movements have been sustained. Within the first two decades of the new millennium, democratic states, even if flawed, have become the norm in Africa. Most African governments today are elected, usually in contested elections. These elections may not always be free or transparent, but they point to popular expectation that governance should be democratic, inclusive and participatory. As we have seen, a key factor in this development is the emergence of vibrant civil society sectors that include NGOs, activists, lawyers and other engaged parties who are increasingly able to hold governments accountable to their domestic and international human rights obligations.

These developments in human rights activism in Africa bring new perspectives to the history of international human rights. The rise to prominence of international human rights NGOs such as Amnesty International, Article 19 and Helsinki Watch (later renamed Human Rights Watch) in the 1970s and 1980s has led some scholars to the conclusion that this period marked the breakthrough moment in the history of international human rights. To be sure, human rights captured global imagination from the 1970s onward due to the activities of international human rights NGOs. Human rights activism expanded internationally, and through local civil society networks it evolved into a global movement. In Africa, this reach is demonstrated by the emergence of local human rights and pro-democracy movements that were at the vanguard of the continent's "second liberation." However, as I have argued throughout this book, the human rights movement in Africa has a deeper history that goes beyond the narrative of NGO activism to which international human rights history has been reduced. The era of NGO activism marked an important phase in the development of human rights in Africa, but so too did earlier anti-colonial movements and political opposition struggles.

Human Rights Abroad

As the politicization of the human rights program at the UN intensified in the late 1960s, African diplomats, along with delegates of newly independent Asian countries, played decisive roles in shaping the development of international human rights.[87] They contributed to

---

[87] Burke, *Decolonization and the Evolution of International Human Rights*, 148.

framing self-determination as a human right in key documents such as the International Covenant on Civil and Political Rights and the International Covenant of Economic and Social Rights, which were adopted by the UN in 1966. The first article of both covenants asserts the right of all peoples to self-determination and the freedom to determine their political status and pursue their economic, social and cultural development. African diplomats at the UN and other international forums, however, tended to push a state sovereignty-based notion of self-determination. African leaders who championed the right to self-determination in anti-colonial struggles often could not countenance extending this right to subnational groups demanding autonomy within existing states.

When the Organization of African Unity was created in 1963, member countries expressed commitment to international human rights and, specifically, the UDHR. The OAU Charter affirmed the commitment of African member states to "the inalienable rights of all people to their own destiny" and recognized freedom, equality, justice and dignity as essential objectives for the achievement of the legitimate aspirations of African peoples.[88] However, the OAU Charter also strongly affirmed the principles of national sovereignty and non-interference in the internal affairs of member states. This effectively limited the organization's capacity to hold member states accountable for human rights violations, thereby reinforcing the view that the OAU was more interested in protecting state sovereignty than protecting human rights.[89]

With more African states gaining independence, there was less focus on human rights except as a tool in the fight against vestiges of white minority rule in Rhodesia, Namibia and South Africa.[90] Leaders of newly independent African states frequently used the platform of the OAU and the UN to decry human rights abuses in external sites even as they resisted attempts by Western nations and organizations to police the suppression of civil liberties and political rights in their own countries. Such external pressures for human rights reforms were generally perceived as neo-colonial interventions and violations of national

---

[88] Preamble, Charter of the Organisation of African Unity, 1963.
[89] Killander, "African Human Rights Law in Theory and Practice," 391.
[90] Magnus Killander, "African Human Rights Law in Theory and Practice," in *Research Handbook on International Human Rights Law*, Sarah Joseph and Adam McBeth, eds. (Cheltenham: Edward Elgar, 2010), 390.

sovereignty. At its first assembly of heads of state in Cairo in 1964, the OAU condemned continuing racial bigotry and racial oppression against black citizens of the United States and urged the US government to ensure the total elimination of all forms of discrimination based on race, color or ethnic origin.[91] Throughout the 1970s and '80s, the OAU pushed for UN sanctions against South Africa for its apartheid policy even as it turned a blind eye to the atrocities of African leaders like Mobutu, Bokassa and Idi Amin, the latter of which was elected chairman of the OAU in 1975. African leaders often failed to make connections between human rights abuses at home and oppression abroad. To take one example, the government of Ahmed Sékou Touré in Guinea had a record of political repression and domestic human rights violations; yet Conakry, Guinea's capital, was the external headquarters of the African Party for the Independence of Guinea and Cape Verde (PAIGC), whose struggle for independence from Portuguese rule rested on the right to self-determination.[92]

The OAU's adoption of the African Charter on Human and People's Rights (ACHPR) in 1981 brought human rights into renewed focus at a time when many African countries were under military dictatorship or one-party rule. The stated objective of the drafters of the ACHPR, also known as the Banjul Charter, was to "prepare an African human rights instrument based upon an African legal philosophy and responsive to African needs."[93] The ACHPR echoes universal individual-based human rights but also promotes communal solidarity. The Charter departs from the formulations of other regional and international human rights documents in that it codifies a broader scope of rights that includes both individual rights and the collective rights of peoples. In language that harks back to the cultural nationalism of Nyerere's African socialism, Kwame Nkrumah's consciencism and Kenneth Kaunda's Zambian humanism, the ACHPR affirms the "virtues" of African historical tradition and the "values of

---

[91] "Resolutions of the First Assembly of the Heads of States and Government of the Organization of African Unity, Cairo, July 1964," reprinted in Gideon-Cyrus Makau Mutiso and S. W Rohio, eds., *Readings in African Political Thought* (London: Heinemann, 1975), 407.

[92] George M. Houser, "Human Rights and the Liberation Struggle: The Importance of Creative Tension," *Africa Today*, 39, 4 (1992): 13.

[93] James Silk, "Traditional Culture and the Prospects of Human Rights in Africa," in *Human Rights in Africa: Cross-Cultural Perspectives*, Abdullahi Ahmed An-Na'im and Francis M. Deng, eds. (Washington D.C: The Brookings Institution, 1990), 308.

African civilization," which should characterize African reflection on the concept of human and peoples' rights.[94]

The ACHPR also outlines the duties of states and individual members of society. It asserts the collective duty to achieve the total liberation of Africa and to achieve "genuine independence."[95] It specifies a wide range of individual duties, including the obligation to respect fellow human beings and treat them with respect and tolerance, the duty to preserve and strengthen positive African cultural values, the duty to preserve the harmonious development of the family and the duty to respect and support one's parents. The Charter further outlines individual obligations to the state, including the duty to serve one's national community and not compromise state security, the duty to preserve and strengthen national solidarity and independence and even the duty to pay taxes imposed in the interest of the society.[96]

The distinctive provisions for collective rights and individual duties in the ACHPR have attracted both praise and criticism. Critics point to the apparent tension between inalienable individual human rights and the collective rights of peoples, suggesting that the emphasis on collective rights risks undermining the individual-centered character of traditional human rights norms. Criticism has also centered on the wide range of duties outlined in the ACHPR and the concerns that they weaken universal human rights, understood as unconditional rights that people have simply as human beings. However, supporters of the ACHPR point out that the Charter strikes the right balance between individual rights and collective rights in ways that reflect African norms and values.[97] There is some merit to this claim. Individual-centered rights are part of a broader spectrum of rights that constitute universal human rights as we understand them today. Several international human rights documents stipulate the collective rights of communities alongside the obligations of rights-holders.[98]

---

[94] Organisation of African Unity, "African Charter on Human and Peoples' Rights 1981" (hereinafter ACHPR). Available at www.achpr.org/instruments/achpr/. Accessed September 13, 2016.

[95] ACHPR, preamble.   [96] ACHPR, articles 28–29.

[97] Makau Mutua, "The Banjul Charter: The Case for the African Cultural Fingerprint," in *Cultural Transformation and Human Rights in Africa*, Abdullahi An-Na'im, ed. (New York: Zed Books, 2002), 68–69.

[98] For example, the International Covenant on Economic, Social and Cultural Rights, which affirms that the individual has duties to other individuals and to the community. Similarly, the UDHR asserts the rights of peoples and states to economic and social development.

The ACHPR's language of collective rights and corresponding duties is an acknowledgment of the functional complementarity of individual and state/society relations. While people have rights, they also have duties. This provides a useful framework for balancing the complex web of individual and communal rights claims in contemporary African societies. In addition to the ACHPR, the OAU and its successor, the African Union, have adopted treaties and established institutions dealing with specific human rights issues. These include the African Charter on the Rights and Welfare of the Child and the African Court on Human and Peoples' Rights, which represent regional responses to international human rights and an attempt to ground universal human rights norms in African political and social realities.

★★★

The history of human rights in independent Africa mirrors the broader global history of human rights in the twentieth century. It reveals the dynamism of human rights ideas as reflected in the transformative moments of social and political struggles. The global history of human rights shows that human rights ideas and language have rarely been deployed in normatively objective ways. Human rights doctrine has not been immune from the self-interested considerations that animate local and international politics. Nationalist leaders who strategically invoked human rights and self-determination in anticolonial struggles moved away from human rights once they attained power, speaking instead a language of sovereignty, national solidarity and the collective rights of peoples. In contrast, marginalized opposition politicians and activists continued to find relevance in the discourse of individual-centered human rights and civil liberties. This would constitute the foundations of human rights NGO activism and pro-democracy movements across the continent.

But this is not a uniquely African story. Mark Mazower has noted correctly that while the rise of human rights in the twentieth century can be written as a triumph of civilization over realpolitik, it must also be seen as imbued with politics, cynicism and state interest.[99] To be sure, the human rights doctrine has not solely been an instrument of political or ideological self-aggrandizement. Human rights laws and norms, and the advocates who promote them, have brought about real

---

[99] Mark Mazower, *No Enchanted Palace: The End of Empire and the Ideological Origins of the United Nations* (Princeton: Princeton University Press, 2009), 149.

positive changes in Africa and elsewhere in the world. They have empowered oppressed individuals and marginalized groups, legitimized struggles against tyranny and domination and alleviated human suffering by facilitating transformative movements. But the human rights language has also been used to insulate power and to further parochial political and social agendas. Political leaders and activists have interpreted human rights in politically convenient ways at different historical moments: European statesmen seeking to exclude self-determination from the UN human rights agenda in order to protect imperial interests; anti-colonial activists stressing the collective right to self-determination to facilitate independence; opposition dissidents asserting democratic rights to challenge state power in the independent state; and Western and Eastern bloc countries selectively invoking human rights principles in Cold War–era ideological politics.[100] In all these situations, human rights language was invoked in ways that served specific political and ideological agendas. In this regard, the story of human rights in Africa reflects the complexities and contradictions of the global human rights movement.

[100] For most of the Cold War period, human rights discourse was a propaganda tool in the ideological war between the Soviets and the Americans. For a discussion on the impact of the Cold War on human rights debates at the UN, see Normand and Zaidi, *Human Rights at the UN*, 197–200.

Old Struggles and New Causes

The story of the human race is a recapitulation, from age to age, of the struggle of man to enjoy fundamental rights.

– Nnamdi Azikiwe[1]

At the height of the African anti-colonial struggle in the 1950s, Aimé Césaire, the Martinique writer and co-founder of the négritude movement, was asked about the interplay between radical particularism and cosmological universalism in his writings on black consciousness. Césaire responded that for him, black consciousness was not a rejection of universalist idealism. With the négritude movement, his objective was to formulate an alternative universality grounded in black humanism. "The universal is not the negation of the particular because one moves toward the universal through a deepening of the particular," Césaire explained. "I do not enclose myself in a narrow particularism. But nor do I want to lose myself in a lifeless universalism. There are two ways to lose oneself: through walled segregation within the particular and through dilution within the universal. My conception of the universal is of a universal enriched by every particular."[2] This view, which Césaire expressed in the context of the black consciousness movement, also eloquently captures the central question in contemporary philosophical, legal and policy debates

---

[1] Nnamdi Azikiwe, "Essentials for Nigerian Survival," *Foreign Affairs*, 43, 3 (1965): 455.
[2] Gary Wilder, *The French Imperial Nation-State: Negritude and Colonial Humanism between the Two World Wars* (Chicago: University of Chicago Press, 2005), 290.

about human rights in Africa. This question centers on the place of universal human rights in Africa and the reciprocal place of African particularism in universal human rights.

One of my main arguments of this book is that despite its claims to universality, the human rights movement has not always been inclusive or equally ardent about the rights of all peoples. In fact, the history of human rights that I present in this book is a story of persistent tensions between movements for the expansion of human rights protections for more people and simultaneous counter-impulses for exclusion and restrictions of human rights protection. If the story of international human rights is one of the progressive expansion of rights to an increasing number of marginalized groups through a series of successful struggles, it is also one of cynical manipulation of rights language to maintain privilege and insulate power.

To be sure, the human rights movement has largely been a project in expanding political and social inclusivity. This is evident in the work of nineteenth-century antislavery campaigners, who, spurred by religious beliefs and enlightenment notions of natural rights, pushed governments to make the suppression of the slave trade a focus of international diplomacy. They demanded that governments take legal action to extend certain basic rights and liberties, already enjoyed by free citizens, to enslaved Africans. But their appeals for rights inclusion and expansion often came up against counter-arguments for exclusion by those who sought to maintain the status quo. The language of rights was used by both sides. The defense of transatlantic slavery rested partly on a perverse notion of the *property rights* of slaveholders. To free the slave without due compensation to the slave owner or without restitution to slaveholding communities, some claimed, was to replace one injustice with another. Abolitionists countered with moral and legal arguments about the primacy of human dignity and the liberties of those enslaved over the property rights of slaveholders. Arguments for rights inclusion ultimately triumphed over the voices of exclusion with the global abolition of slavery. The conceptualization of the slave trade as a crime against humanity, and of slave traders as *hostis humani generis* (enemies of mankind), helped lay the foundation for twentieth-century international human rights law.[3] These developments challenged the

---

[3] Jenny Martinez, *The Slave Trade and the Origins of International Human Rights Law* (New York: Oxford University Press, 2012), 149.

political and social exclusions of the enslaved and served to affirm their inclusiveness within the human community.

Like antislavery, anti-colonial struggles for self-determination were, at their core, demands for rights inclusion and expansion. Independence activists in Africa as elsewhere in the colonized world demanded that the full rights of citizenship and political participation enjoyed by colonists at home be extended to colonial subjects abroad. Their struggle for independence rested on the framing of self-determination as a fundamental human right. This interpretation of human rights extended beyond individual-centered liberties to include the collective political rights of those disenfranchised by colonialism. European powers whose colonial interests were threatened by the inclusion of collective self-determination under the rubric of international human rights strongly opposed this expansion of human rights doctrine. Imperial interests were better served by keeping human rights narrow and confined to individual claims against state intrusion.

At the early UN, European imperial powers saw the inclusion of self-determination in the human rights framework as a challenge to national sovereignty. They resisted the prospects of dismantling their colonial empires or extending the right of self-determination to colonized peoples on the basis of the new universal human rights order. By insisting on a narrow individual-centered interpretation of human rights, they could prevent anti-colonial struggles stirring up in imperial outposts from being legitimized as a global human rights cause. This could reveal moral and legal contradictions of colonialism. However, as with antislavery, the voices for rights expansion ultimately triumphed over the forces of exclusion and restriction. The collective right to self-determination would become an integral part of the international human rights order with the emergence of a more globally representative UN. The affirmation of the right to self-determination set the tone for significant expansion of the boundaries of the international human rights system in the 1960s and '70s. The more inclusive the international human rights system became, the more it became a patchwork of standards and concepts relating to an increasingly varied range of human situations.[4]

In Africa, as elsewhere in the world, the trajectory of rights inclusion has not always been linear or progressive. Many individuals and

---

[4] Eva Brems, *Human Rights: Universality and Diversity* (Leiden: Martinus Nijhoff Publishers, 2001), 21.

communities continue to suffer grave human rights violations on grounds of race, gender, ethnicity, sexual orientation, religion or political affiliation. Although some human rights violations occur because of the lack of state capacity to protect rights, others result from the lack of political will to challenge entrenched abuses and inequities. In independent Africa, arguments for collective rights and national solidarity rights have often been used to justify violations of individual civil liberties and minority rights. The most notable contemporary examples of political and culture-based rights exclusions are the continued restrictions imposed on women's rights and the rights of sexual minorities.[5]

Sexual orientation discrimination and violence against sexual minorities are widely viewed as acceptable in many African countries. Apart from South Africa where sexual minority rights have witnessed rapid progress since the end of apartheid, there has been strong resistance elsewhere in Africa to the expansion of human rights doctrine to include sexual minority rights.[6] Many African states sanction sexual orientation discrimination to varying degrees, and until recently, even international organizations resisted the idea that sexual minorities should be included in the frameworks of fundamental human rights protection. For this reason, political homophobia, sexual orientation discrimination and violence against sexual minorities has been described as "one of the last frontiers for advancing the idea that all human beings have fundamental rights."[7]

In this concluding chapter, I examine contemporary questions about the role of the African state in human rights protection. Human rights are typically defined as inherent entitlements that individuals hold against state power. Under international law, states are considered the primary duty bearers of human rights claims within their territories. Yet the history of human rights in Africa shows that the state has been largely ineffective as the primary protector of human rights. If anything, states have been responsible for, or complicit in, some of the most egregious human rights violations in the continent. In some cases, states and ruling regimes have coopted the language of

---

[5] Bonny Ibhawoh, "Human Rights Inclusion and Exclusion," in *The SAGE Handbook of Human Rights*, Mark Gibney and Anja Mihrand, eds. (New York: Sage, 2014), 337.

[6] Marc Epprecht, *Hungochani: The History of a Dissident Sexuality in Southern Africa* (Montreal: McGill-Queen's University Press, 2004), 227.

[7] Debra DeLaet, *The Global Struggle for Human Rights* (Stamford: Cengage, 2014), 130.

human rights to justify political and social interventions that restrict civil liberties. Human rights struggles led by political opposition leaders and civil society groups have often been aimed at challenging abuses of state power. The state, as both protector and violator of rights, remains a central and enduring paradox of human rights in Africa. As human rights language expands to more causes, it is fitting to conclude by examining how African states have grappled with the tensions between universal human rights principles and local socio-cultural realities that test these rights ideals. To return to Aimé Césaire's universalism/particularism dialectic that opens this chapter, I consider how African particularism has been expressed in interpret-ations of universal human rights within the contemporary African state.

In the introductory chapter of this book, I reviewed the universalist claims of international human rights alongside particularistic asser-tions of African human rights values. Assertions of African human rights values have long been made by intellectuals and political leaders, and they provide the philosophical foundations of the African Charter on Human and People's Rights. These assertions of African cultural values continue in contemporary human rights debates across the continent, perhaps nowhere more so than in post-apartheid South Africa. The progressive constitutional human rights framework adopted in South Africa as part of the democratic transition process represents the possibilities of instituting democratic rights-based pol-itical culture in Africa. At the same time, the attempts to interpret human rights in ways that reflect South Africa's unique political history and culture demonstrate the continuing challenges of *vernacu-larizing* or indigenizing international human rights in transitioning African states.

Vernacularizing Human Rights

The notion of vernacularizing human rights has been used to describe the process by which universal human rights norms become grounded in local communities. It is a constructive process that affirms and delineates the scope of human rights in different cultural contexts.[8] Vernacularizing human rights requires seeing human rights in specific

---

[8] Sally Merry, *Human Rights Gender Violence: Translating International Law into Local Justice* (Chicago: University of Chicago Press, 2006), 37.

situations rather than as the application of abstract principles. In this sense, vernacularization refers to the interaction between established international human rights principles and local norms to produce hybridized legal and normative frameworks for human rights protection. This should not be confused with the cultural relativist repudiation of universal human rights, which I discuss in the introductory chapter of this book. Rather, vernacularization is a deliberate process of investing universal rights with local meanings that can potentially strengthen human rights protection and contribute to the normative application of global human rights.

The notion of vernacularizing human rights has also been described in terms of the "culturalization of human rights law," which involves the reconceptualization of international human rights law through a culturally based approach. The goal is to improve the effectiveness of human rights through cultural acceptance and legitimation, leading to a better balancing of conflicts of rights.[9] The notion of vernacularization opens new analytic space for conceptualizing and theorizing human rights. It acknowledges that forging a universal human rights culture is necessary and perhaps even desirable in our globalizing world, but insists on attuning universal human rights principles to local conditions. Even though the universal is often construed in opposition to the local, the notion of vernacularized universal human rights is not an oxymoron. Universal human rights have intrinsically local dimension since they gain meaning when applied to local contexts.

Political and legal developments in post-apartheid South Africa have included efforts to indigenize or localize universal human rights norms. *Ubuntu* as a traditional African ethical concept deployed to legitimize the Truth and Reconciliation Commission (TRC) represents a distinctive vernacularization process aimed at legitimizing a human rights culture in South Africa.[10] Ubuntu was first prominently asserted in South Africa's 1993 interim constitution and later became a central theme in the work of the TRC, established to deal with

---

[9] Lenzerini Federico, *The Culturalization of Human Rights Law* (Oxford: Oxford University Press, 2014), 44.

[10] Bonny Ibhawoh, "From Ubuntu to Grootboom: Vernacularising Human Rights through Restorative and Distributive Justice in Post-Apartheid South Africa," in *Domains of Freedom: Justice, Citizenship and Social Change in South Africa*, T. Kepe, M. Levin and B. von Lieres, eds. (Cape Town: University of Cape Town Press, 2016). The discussion here draws on my arguments in this paper.

human rights abuses perpetrated under apartheid and to help the country come to terms with its past through national reconciliation. The role and relevance of Ubuntu as the philosophical basis of the TRC and transitional justice project from apartheid to multiracial democracy has been well studied.[11] Our limited concern here is with the articulation of Ubuntu as a human rights paradigm founded on African ethics and its deployment to legitimize the restorative justice agenda of the TRC. Ubuntu, as invoked in the context of the TRC, can be read as a vernacularizing process and uniquely African normative contribution to an expanding international human rights system.

The South African TRC was conceived as part of a bridge-building process that would help lead the country away from its deeply divided past to a future founded on the recognition of human rights and democracy. As a national transitional justice project, the mandate of the TRC centered on truth-finding and national reconciliation.[12] Apart from its mandate to investigate the gross violations of human rights committed under apartheid, however, the TRC was also mandated to recommend measures to prevent future violations of human rights. The hope was that this would allow the country to leave behind the past of a divided society characterized by strife, conflict and injustice, and commence the journey toward a future founded on the recognition of human rights, democracy and peaceful coexistence. In establishing the TRC, the African National Congress (ANC)–led government of Nelson Mandela hoped that uncovering the historical truths about apartheid abuses and injustice would provide a foundation for building a new human rights culture. As Archbishop Desmond Tutu, who headed the TRC, put it, "We need to know about the past in order to establish a culture of respect for human rights. It is only by accounting for the past that we can become accountable for the future."[13]

---

[11] Richard Wilson, *The Politics of Truth and Reconciliation in South Africa: Legitimizing the Post-Apartheid State* (Cambridge: Cambridge University Press, 2001); Lyn Graybill, *Truth and Reconciliation in South Africa: Miracle or Model?* (Boulder, CO: Lynne Rienner, 2002); Drucilla Cornell, *Law and Revolution in South Africa: Ubuntu, Dignity, and the Struggle for Constitutional Transformation* (New York: Fordham University Press, 2014).

[12] Transitional justice here refers to judicial and non-judicial measures implemented to redress legacies of human rights abuses in the aftermath of conflict and repression.

[13] Truth and Reconciliation Commission of South Africa Report, vol. 1. Available at www.justice.gov.za/trc/report/finalreport/Volume%201.pdf. Accessed September 12, 2016.

Ubuntu, as defined by its chief proponent Archbishop Tutu, represents an indigenous African philosophy of justice centered on healing, forgiveness and reconciliation aimed at restoring the humanity of both victim and perpetrator.[14] To be sure, the meaning of Ubuntu and its correlation or congruence with international human rights and restorative justice remains deeply contested. Scholars and commentators have challenged the notion that Ubuntu is an indigenous African justice system with deep historical roots in South African cultures or that it reflects principles of restorative justice. Some critics have suggested that Ubuntu was reinvented by ANC ruling elites to legitimize the TRC by presenting a romanticized but ahistorical vision of rural African community based on reciprocity, community cohesion and solidarity.[15] Other critics have argued that Ubuntu, deployed as a nation-building philosophy, mandates conformity and a form of social cohesion that denies individual "participatory difference." In other words, Ubuntu as a human rights paradigm reaffirms the statist and collectivist notion of human rights, preferred by ruling elites, rather than an individual-centered notion of human rights.

The debate over the authenticity of Ubuntu as expressed in the post-apartheid transitional justice and its relevance to human rights remains unsettled. What is clear however, is that Ubuntu was asserted frequently in the work of the TRC and provided the basis for its restorative justice mandate. This followed earlier constitutional invocations of Ubuntu as the "grounding ideal of the black population" of South Africa, which made possible the post-apartheid Interim Constitution of 1994 that guided South Africa's first democratic elections.[16]

Central to the TRC's mandate was ensuring respect for victims and their experiences.[17] In the TRC process, apartheid perpetrators were offered conditional amnesty if they could show that their individual acts of gross violations of human rights, for which they sought amnesty, were politically motivated. Amnesty applicants also had to disclose the full truth about their violations, normally during public hearings. The TRC sought to balance the victims' need for justice with the fair and respectful treatment of perpetrators. By most

---

[14] Desmond Tutu, *No Future without Forgiveness* (New York: Doubleday, 2000), 50–52.
[15] C. B. N. Gade, "Restorative Justice and the South African Truth and Reconciliation Process," *South African Journal of Philosophy*, 32, 1 (2013): 10.
[16] Cornell, *Law and Revolution in South Africa*, 121.
[17] Truth and Reconciliation Commission Act (South Africa), Section 11.

accounts, this balance was largely achieved through the public's involvement in the process and the recurring appeal to Ubuntu as a guiding philosophy behind the Commission's work.[18]

The question has often been raised whether the South African TRC was a transitional justice "miracle" or model for the rest of the world: Can it serve as a model for other countries in the aftermath of serious human rights abuses? Or was it a miracle of the sort that occurs but rarely in the life of nations, dependent solely on the compelling personalities of extraordinary leaders?[19] The global interest in the South African TRC brought new focus to the possibilities and limitations of the restorative justice approach to addressing the legacies of gross human rights abuses at a national level. Although the granting of amnesty was contentious, the international community largely favored the South African TRC as a model and as a compromised middle way forward for societies in transition where amnesty is the pragmatic choice.[20] The TRC came to symbolize a vision of human rights promotion and accountability founded on universal standards and reinforced with local norms.

The South African TRC, and the role of Ubuntu within it, represents a uniquely South African normative contribution to the universal human rights idea and, specifically, the discourse on human dignity and transitional justice. Notwithstanding its well-documented shortfalls, the TRC brought visibility and some level of domestic and international legitimacy to the restorative paradigm of transitional justice. The TRC and the philosophy of Ubuntu mobilized to support it offered an alternative to the dominant retributive transitional justice paradigm. Rather than orchestrating Nuremburg-style legal prosecutions, South Africa's post-apartheid leaders opted for a process that addressed rights violations through public-truth telling, contrition and reconciliation. This restorative justice process was necessitated by South Africa's unique challenge of democratic transition: the quest for accountability for past human rights violations and the simultaneous need for collective healing. Ubuntu, as deployed within the TRC, therefore represents a distinctive human rights vernacularization

---

[18] Jennifer Llewellyn, "Truth Commissions and Restorative Justice," in *Handbook of Restorative Justice*, Gerry Johnstone and Daniel Van Ness, eds. (Portland: Willan, 2007), 363.

[19] Graybill, *Truth and Reconciliation in South Africa*, xi.

[20] Jeremy Sarkin-Hughes, *Carrots and Sticks: The TRC and the South African Amnesty Process* (Antwerp: Intersentia, 2004), 6.

process informed by local cultural sensibilities, histories and political exigencies. Besides serving to validate South Africa's transitional justice project, Ubuntu was also framed as an African-inspired contribution to the discourse on human dignity and as legitimation of restorative transitional justice.

Ubuntu has also provided normative and philosophical grounding for judicial enforcement of human rights. This is most evident in South African's jurisprudence on economic and social rights. Several cases decided by the Constitutional Court of South Africa have laid the groundwork for an emerging jurisprudence of economic and social rights globally. South African courts have taken the lead in tackling problematic issues of distributive justice and provided useful directions for developing the jurisprudence on constitutionally guaranteed economic and social rights.[21] Judicial interpretations of South Africa's constitutional guarantees of social and economic rights have rested on the notion of human dignity expressed in Ubuntu. In one prominent case dealing with the right to shelter, Justice Albie Sachs emphasized the importance of interpreting and applying constitutional rights provisions on access to adequate housing in light of historically created landlessness in South Africa. He stressed the need to deal with homelessness in a sensitive and orderly manner, and the special role of the courts in managing complex and socially stressful situations. Invoking Ubuntu, Justice Sachs stated: "The spirit of Ubuntu which is part of the deep cultural heritage of the majority of the population, suffuses the whole constitutional order. It combines individual rights with a communitarian philosophy. It is a unifying motif of the Bill of Rights, which is nothing if not a structured, institutionalized and operational declaration in our evolving new society of the need for human interdependence, respect and concern."[22] Based on this and similar rulings, some legal scholars have argued that South Africa's groundbreaking social and economic rights jurisprudence offers models that should be exported to other countries.[23]

---

[21] Such landmark cases include *Soobramoney v. Minister of Health* (Constitutional Court of South Africa, 1997) and *Government of RSA v. Grootboom* (Constitutional Court of South Africa, 2000).

[22] *Port Elisabeth Municipality v. Various Occupiers*, Constitutional Court of South Africa, 2004.

[23] Eric Christiansen, "Exporting South Africa's Social Rights Jurisprudence," *Loyola University Chicago International Law Review*, 5, 1 (2007): 28–43.

The role of Ubuntu in the South African TRC and the legal enforcement of constitutional human rights represents a vernacularization
process that holds the potential of instituting a uniquely South African
human rights culture founded on universal principles and local cultural norms. Ubuntu sheds light on the importance of promoting
human rights through the principles of reciprocity, inclusivity and a
sense of shared destiny between peoples. It points to the possibilities
of establishing culturally grounded legal and normative human rights
regimes in Africa. It offers a model for legitimizing international
human rights in local contexts and imbuing them with cultural relevance. But perhaps most significantly, Ubuntu marks a distinctive
African normative contribution to the discourse on human dignity in
international human rights.

New Causes

The mid-twentieth-century rights revolution, I have argued, held
three distinct human rights promises: the promise of self-
determination, democracy and equality. Although independence from
colonial rule fulfilled the promise of self-determination, it did not
immediately fulfill the human rights promise of democracy and equality. Rather, the immediate post-colonial period ushered in an era of
anti-democratic authoritarian rule and repressive "big men" dictatorships. With the end of the Cold War, however, a wave of political
liberalization and democratization swept across Africa from the 1990s
into the new millennium. Although some experiments at democratic
governance have faltered, the general trend suggests Africa's gradual
but sustained movement toward civil democratic rule. In one
"Democracy Index" measuring the state of global democracies on
the criteria of electoral pluralism, political participation and civil
liberties, the ranking of several sub-Saharan countries rose progressively from 2006 to 2015.[24] Does this signal the beginnings of the
fulfillment of the human rights promise of democracy in Africa? It is
perhaps too early to say. Fulfilling the final human rights promise of
equality will likely prove most challenging. The promise of equality
remains largely aspirational in Africa as in other regions of the
developing world where deep social inequalities and inequities persist.

---

[24] "The Democracy Index," The Economist Intelligence Unit, 2006–2016.

The twentieth century marked the age of the human rights revolution, but it remains everywhere an incomplete revolution.

As international human rights guarantees expand to include more marginalized groups, the list of human rights grows. New human rights have been recognized through the signing of new international treaties or protocols, as well as through domestic legal reforms. For example, the Charter of Fundamental Rights of the European Union includes several new human rights that were not envisioned in the UDHR or early UN human rights covenants. These include the right to protection of personal data, the right to protection of linguistic diversity, the freedom of the arts and sciences and even the "right to good administration." The European Charter also includes provisions to protect the rights of the elderly to lead a life of dignity and independence.[25] In some countries, the debate over the right to human dignity has extended to voluntary euthanasia, or the "right to die," which is founded on the belief that a human being is entitled to end his or her own life. Courts have considered whether the fundamental human right to life should also include the fundamental human right to die with dignity.[26] Rights traditionally reserved for humans have also expanded to include non-human entities such as corporations, animals and the natural environment. In 2008 Ecuador became the first country to establish the "rights of nature" in its national constitution. This provision protects the inalienable rights of ecosystems, gives people the authority to bring legal petitions on the behalf of ecosystems and requires the government to remedy violations of these rights. These "rights of nature" provisions mark a paradigmatic expansion of the scope of traditional human rights.

The growing list of human rights has prompted concerns about rights inflation and the "overproduction of human rights." If every entitlement claim becomes a human right, critics argue, the human rights idea loses its normative power. Critics of the expansion of human rights caution against a tendency toward framing every human and social problem in terms of rights. Like currency, the value of human rights lies in its restricted use to signify the most fundamental of human entitlements qua humans, and like currency, human rights lose value when overproduced or invoked too often.

[25] Nigel Foster, *Foster on EU Law* (Oxford: Oxford University Press, 2013), 107–108.
[26] Nihal Jayawickrama, *Judicial Application of Human Rights Law: National, Regional and International Jurisprudence* (Cambridge: Cambridge University Press, 2002), 252.

Concerns about the overproduction of human rights mirror related anxieties about the end of the age of human rights and shift toward a "post–human rights world."[27] With an increasing number of states seemingly reluctant to honor international human rights treaties and fulfill domestic human rights obligations, we might be heading toward a post–human rights world characterized by repudiations of established human rights norms and the roll-back of international humanitarian law. The clearest indication of this trend is the global rise of reactionary populism, xenophobia and the growing tolerance of torture even in Western liberal democracies. Another example is the growing list of African countries that have opted to withdraw support for international human rights organizations, such as the International Criminal Court, on the grounds of the Court's perceived lopsided focus on African cases.

Challenges to human rights centered on concerns about the overproduction of rights and the specter of a post–human rights world invite reflections on old questions about the relevance and legitimacy of universal human rights. Notwithstanding the claims of global inclusivity, universal human rights continue to be challenged on multiple fronts by proponents of varying degrees of cultural relativism and by the fact that legal and normative universality hinges more on possession than enforcement. International human rights remain unevenly recognized, promoted and protected around the world. This raises pertinent questions about the future of human rights in Africa as elsewhere. Given the challenges to international human rights, what will universality mean in local contexts where primary obligations for rights implementation and enforcement reside?

The recent history of human rights in Africa indicates that the question of legitimacy continues to pose a major challenge to the work of human rights advocates. From Algeria to Zimbabwe, human rights activists across Africa confront questions about the legitimacy and indigeneity of their rights agendas. Pro-democracy campaigners and women's rights activists are often accused of building alliances with external agents to promote Western agendas at the expense of African, Arab, Islamic or other religious values. Authoritarian governments and oppressive non-state actors have used this line of argument to

---

[27] Imogen Foulkes, "Are We Heading towards a 'Post Human Rights World'?," British Broadcasting Service. Available at www.bbc.com/news/world-europe-38368848. Accessed December 30, 2016.

undermine movements for political liberalization, civil liberties and socioeconomic rights. Securing local legitimacy is therefore crucial to the prospects of human rights promotion and protection in Africa. Human rights norms are likely to be more effective and relevant when they are intelligible in local idiom and vernacular.

★★★

In the writing of this book, I have been guided by the calls for a counter-hegemonic approach to human rights history. Such an approach draws attention to the role of subaltern actors to balance traditional emphasis on dominant and powerful actors. It also recognizes that interpretations of human rights are neither fixed nor settled, but are dynamic and constantly changing. Counter-hegemonic approaches to human rights are necessary because hegemonic intellectual frameworks in and of themselves contribute to the mystique of hegemonic dominance.[28] Hegemonic approaches to constructing human rights histories promote narratives that place powerful actors at the center of the human rights story while consigning subaltern actors to the footnotes. Such one-sided narratives not only reinforce and reproduce systems of dominance, they also have the effect of undermining the underlying egalitarian claims at the core of human rights doctrine. A counter-hegemonic approach is particularly relevant to understanding the place of Africa, and the "Third World" more generally, in the global human rights story.

The counter-hegemonic history of human rights that I have attempted to tell in this book is a story of longstanding struggles by marginalized communities for rights inclusion within systems of rights exclusion. From antislavery to pro-democracy struggles, rights movements have confronted the reactionary impulse to maintain dominance and oppression. The struggle for rights inclusion is a continuing one. It continues in oppositional political struggles against authoritarian rulers, in women's rights movements and in ethnic minority rights struggles. The struggle for rights inclusion also manifests in new social movements for women's rights and the rights of sexual minorities.

In response to economic crises and the failure of male-dominated politics, Africa has witnessed the rise of a new wave of feminism since the 1980s. Women, who have borne the brunt of economic hardship and political upheaval in the post-colonial state, have mobilized to

---

[28] Waltz, "Universalizing Human Rights," 68.

assert their influence in local and national politics. The emergent African feminism has not taken the path of radical Western feminism and the debates about female autonomy, sexual liberation and contested gender identities. Rather, African feminism has been described as being "distinctly heterosexual, pro-natal, and concerned with bread, butter, culture and power issues."[29] In Côte d'Ivoire, women mobilized to assert their voices in politics and to influence national laws that affect their status as wives and mothers. In Ghana, women's groups that were allied with religious organizations and traditional authorities successfully pressured the government to enact intestate succession laws to redress discrimination against wives and children in property inheritance. Along with other laws affecting marriage and divorce and family economic accountability, Ghanaian women have led the movement for legislative reform of unjust and repressive patriarchal customary practices. In South Africa, women have continued with the crucial role they played in the anti-apartheid struggle, in new struggles for social equity and economic empowerment that include the constitutional right to education, health and housing. The net result is that across Africa, women have become more visible in political and economic life despite the persistence of some patriarchal traditions. Perhaps the clearest example of this progress is Rwanda where in 2013 women secured 64 percent of seats in parliamentary elections, making it the country with the highest proportion of women in Parliament in the world.

However, similar progress has not been made with the rights of sexual minorities. As with other minority rights, the central issue with lesbian, gay, bisexual, transsexual and queer (LGBTQ) rights protection is the internationally recognized right to non-discrimination. The main obstacles to the inclusion of LGBTQ rights are typically religious, sociocultural and institutional. These exclusionary barriers exist in every region of the world but have become especially pronounced in Africa. Amid state-sanctioned homophobia, discrimination and violence, efforts to extend human rights protection to LGBTQ people has emerged as the latest frontier in the struggle for rights inclusion. Demands for equal rights for sexual minorities has faced stiff opposition. Governments have rejected calls for equal rights

---

[29] Gwendolyn Mikell, ed., *African Feminism: The Politics of Survival in Sub-Saharan Africa* (Philadelphia: University of Pennsylvania Press, 2016), 4.

protection for sexual minorities and in many cases have responded with legislation that criminalizes homosexuality and restricts the rights of LGBTQ people. Across Africa, states have enacted draconian punishments for homosexuality, ranging from death sentences to long-term imprisonment. Advocates of LGBTQ rights face familiar accusations of promoting a "decadent" Western agenda that is at odds with indigenous cultural and religious values. International interventions aimed at protecting LGBTQ people from violence and discrimination are criticized for treating their sexuality in isolation from the local conditions in which they are embedded.[30] Old cultural relativism arguments have been marshaled against attempts to frame sexual minority rights as a universal human right.

Paradoxically, many of the new anti-homosexuality laws ostensibly enacted to promote African moral values and to repress supposedly "un-African" sexual tendencies are in fact the legacies of past religious and political colonialisms. Nineteenth-century European penal code systems extended to Africa during colonial rule included the criminalization of homosexuality and so-called sodomy laws. British officials, for example, introduced sodomy laws in their colonies in the belief that indigenous cultures did not sufficiently punish immorality and "perverse" sex. They believed that draconian sodomy laws and other "immorality laws" would inculcate European morality into resistant native masses.[31] Many of these colonial immorality laws have been retained and reinforced in the independent state. The persistence of these homophobic social and legal traditions poses the greatest impediment to LGBTQ rights protection in Africa as elsewhere in the ex-colonial world.

In 2011, the UN Human Rights Council (UNHRC) passed a groundbreaking resolution recognizing LGBTQ rights and issued a report documenting violations of the rights of LGBTQ people, including hate crimes, criminalization of homosexuality and discrimination. A subsequent resolution on "Human Rights, Sexual Orientation and Gender Identity" expressed grave concern at acts of violence and discrimination, in all regions of the world, committed against

---

[30] Robert Lorway, *Namibia's Rainbow Project: Gay Rights in an African Nation* (Bloomington: Indiana University Press, 2014), 3.
[31] Alok Gupta, *This Alien Legacy: The Origins of "Sodomy" Laws in British Colonialism* (New York: Human Rights Watch, 2008), 5.

individuals because of their sexual orientation and gender identity.[32] The report acknowledged that governments have too often overlooked violence and discrimination based on sexual orientation and gender identity. It called upon countries to bring LGBTQ people within national human rights protection by repealing laws that criminalize homosexuality, abolishing the death penalty for offenses involving consensual sexual relations and enacting comprehensive anti-discrimination laws and policy reforms.

The UNHRC resolution was a significant first step in the inclusion of LGBTQ people within the international human rights system. It marked an important milestone in the struggle for LGBTQ inclusion and equality. It affirmed that LGBTQ people are endowed with the same inalienable rights and entitled to the same protections as all human beings within the framework of international human rights law. However, as with previous movements for rights inclusion, the UN's move to extend universal human rights protection to LGBTQ people was met with stiff exclusionary opposition. Strident reactionary calls were made to exclude affirmations of LGBTQ protection from the universal human rights agenda to preserve national social and cultural autonomy. Some of the strongest voices both for and against LGBTQ rights inclusion at the UN have come from Africa.

South Africa co-sponsored the 2011 UNHRC resolution that affirmed the rights of LGBTQ peoples. South Africa also voted in favor of a related resolution in 2014 and went on to enact national legislation against discrimination on the grounds of sexual orientation.[33] When the LGBTQ resolution was put before the UNHRC in 2011, it passed only narrowly, with 23 votes in favor and 19 against. The 2014 resolution also passed with a narrow margin. Apart from South Africa, every other African country on the UNHRC either voted against the resolution or abstained.[34] One opposing African

---

[32] United Nations, Report of the United Nations High Commissioner for Human Rights, "Discriminatory laws and practices and acts of violence against individuals based on their sexual orientation and gender identity," A/HRC/19/41, November 17, 2011.

[33] Suzanne Graham, *Democratic South Africa's Foreign Policy: Voting Behaviour in the United Nations* (New York: Palgrave Macmillan, 2016), 77.

[34] United Nations Human Rights Council Resolution, "Human Rights, Sexual Orientation and Gender Identity," (2011) A/HRC/RES/17/19; Human Rights Council Resolution "Human Rights, Sexual Orientation and Gender Identity" (2014) A/HRC/RES/27/32.

diplomat railed against the LGBTQ resolution as "an attempt to replace the natural rights of a human being with an unnatural right."[35] The language of rights was used both to demand social inclusion and to maintain exclusion. The rejectionist premise of those seeking to maintain exclusion was that LGBTQ rights, unlike other human rights, could not be validated as natural rights.

The strong opposition to extending the protections of international human rights norms to LGBTQ people reflects the continuing tension between inclusionary and exclusionary impulses that underlies human rights history. In many African countries, restrictions on LGBTQ communities, and the toleration of violence against them, continue to be justified on the grounds of the primacy of collective religious and cultural rights over the liberties of LGBTQ people. This is a familiar argument. Contemporary LGBTQ rights struggles indicate that the human rights struggles of the twenty-first century will resemble the struggles of the past – from the anti-slavery campaigns of the nineteenth century to the anti-colonial and pro-democracy movements of the twentieth century. Present-day trends mirror these earlier struggles by oppressed and marginalized communities for human rights inclusion. Like contemporary LGBTQ rights campaigners, abolitionists and anti-colonial activists also came up against strong reactionary counter-movements to maintain exclusion, often also rationalized in the language of rights. The African human rights story is certainly one of transformative political and social change. Ultimately, however, it is as much a story of rights restriction and exclusion as it is a story of rights expansion and inclusion.

---

[35] Saralyn Salisbury, "African Opposition to the UN Resolution on Sexual Orientation and Gender Identity," *Human Rights Brief*, November 10, 2011. Available at http://hrbrief.org/2011/11/african-opposition-to-the-un-resolution-on-sexual-orientation-gender-identity. Accessed June 25, 2014.

Index

Abbas, Ferhat, 146, 179, 188, 201–202
abolition, 55–64
abolitionism, abolition, 61
abolitionists, xii, 2, 63, 65–67, 71–73, 78,
  80, 222, 238
Aborigines Protection Society, xxi, 59,
  71–72, 96
Acheampong, Ignatius, 176, 182
Acholi, 191
Afonso, king of Kongo, 55, 68–70, 74
Africa
  culture, 37
  history, xii–xiv, 4–5, 10, 23, 29, 45, 60,
    160
  North, xv
African Charter on Human and People's
  Rights, Banjul Charter, xxi, 45–46,
  48, 217, 219, 225
African National Congress, 3, 128, 159–163,
  227
Afrikaner, 78, 123, 126–127, 159
Akan, 40, 49–50
Akyem Abuakwa, 74
Al-Bashir, Omar, 3–5, 206
Algeria, 82, 86, 103–104, 108, 122, 134,
  142–143, 145–146, 164–165, 175,
  179, 187–188, 190, 201, 212, 214,
  233
Algerian National Liberation Front, FLN,
  103, 188, 201
Al-Qaeda, 208
Al-Shabaab, 208

American Anti-Slavery Society, 1–2, 59
American Colonization Society, 77
American Declaration of Independence,
  11, 26
Amin, Idi, 175, 190–192, 196, 198, 217
Amnesty International, 16, 162, 191–192,
  194, 201, 203, 215
Angola, 69, 102, 104, 108, 110, 126, 165,
  196, 198, 203
Anti-apartheid movement, 159–163
Anti-colonial activists, 15, 23, 92,
  134–136, 143, 152, 156, 170–171,
  174, 178–179, 199, 238
Anti-colonialism, xvi, 5, 9, 15, 21, 23, 25,
  27, 51, 60, 92, 104, 112, 120, 122,
  125, 130–135, 140, 146, 148, 154,
  157, 170–171, 173, 179, 183–184,
  186, 201, 216
  as human rights movement, 134–139
Antislavery, xii, xv, 1, 5–6, 9–10, 21,
  27–28, 54–64, 68, 70–77, 79–88
  links with human rights, 61
Antislavery Convention, 60, 75
Anti-Slavery Society, 1, 71
Apartheid, 3, 26–27, 31–32, 35, 52,
  125–129, 156, 159–163, 203, 211,
  224–229, 235
Apartheid Convention, 163
Arab, 4, 82, 84, 145, 156, 168, 189–190,
  208, 213, 233
Arusha Declaration, 34, 185
Asante, 2, 74, 148

Ashanti, 74, 114
Asia, 15, 37, 78, 100, 128, 134, 145, 153,
    164, 168, 176, 178, 197, 210, 215,
    See also Asian values
assimilation policy, 100
Atlantic Charter, 25, 92, 130–133, 135,
    137–138, 141, 146–148, 150, 160
authoritarianism, xvi, 92, 129, 141, 179,
    189, 192
Azikiwe, Nnamdi, 131, 133, 145, 147–149,
    171, 174, 182–183, 221

Baba, Ahmed of Songhai, 43
Bamba, Amadou, 77
Banda, Hastings, 50, 192, 194, 201, 209
Bandung Conference, 164
Bantu Education Act, 128
Bantustans, 161
Belgium, 85, 142, 153, 156
Benin, 88, 119, 198, 209
Berlin Act, 95
Berlin Conference 1884, 84, 95
Biafra, 183, 197, 202
Bible, 10, 63
bill of rights, 11, 26, 92, 149, 166–170,
    174–175, 182, 184
bisexual, 235, *See* LGBTQ
Bokassa, Jean-Bedel, 175, 192–195, 198,
    217
Boko Haram, 208
Botswana, 168
Bourguiba, Habib, 188, 212–213
Bourne, Fox, 96
boycott, 60, 72, 159, 163
Brazil, 76
British and Foreign Antislavery Society,
    59, 71, 83
British Church Missionary Society, 73
British South African Company, 98
British West Indies, 2, 140
Buganda, 86, 114, 120, 124, 151
Bulgaria, 158

Cairo Declaration on Human Rights in
    Islam, 34, 46
Cameroon, 112, 150, 152–153, 155, 165
Canada, xix, 9, 205
Cape Colony, 78, 80, 123
capital punishment, 2, 104
Césaire, Aimé, 221, 225
Chad, 190, 195

Chamberlain, Joseph, 107
child soldiers, 204, 207–208
China, Chinese, 128, 158
Chirwa, Vera, 179, 201–202
Christianity, christians, 1, 5, 21, 26–27,
    44, 63, 65, 71, 73–74, 77, 86, 147,
    167, 183
Churchill, Winston, 120, 130–132, 141,
    149, 160
citizenship, 19–20, 88, 93, 121, 160, 175,
    197, 223
civilization, 10, 84, 91, 94–95, 97, 99, 115,
    124, 126, 218–219
civilizing mission, xii, 84, 90, 92, 94–95,
    97–98, 108, 129, 154, 164
Clarkson, Thomas, 71–72
Cold War, 16, 18, 158, 195–196, 203, 208,
    220, 231, *See* also Western bloc,
    See also Eastern bloc
collective punishment, 102–103, 114
collective rights, 17, 38, 47–48, 56, 89, 93,
    98, 114–115, 137, 171–172, 175,
    177, 190, 217–219, 224
colonial rule, 91, 101, 105, 129, 164
    Belgian, 51, 96–97, 102, 109–110
    British, 75, 78, 94, 98–99, 113, 115, 118,
        123, 125, 131–132, 143, 158, 174,
        183, 201
    France, 55, 80, 100, 106, 126, 139, 146,
        169, *See* also French
    French, 51, 80–81, 99–100, 103, 111,
        114, 121, 137, 164, 169, 193
    German, 79, 86, 102
    labor issues, 112
    land issues, 108
    law and legal systems, 119
    pacification, 101–105
    Portuguese, 102, 104, 109–110, 126
    reistance to, 119–122
    violence, 101–105
colonialism, xii–xiii, xvi, 2, 5–7, 9, 25,
    27–29, 60, 83, 86, 89–93, 100, 103,
    144, 163–164, 176
    treaties, 98
common law, 75, 114–115, 169
Congo, 69, 84–86, 89, 96–97, 102, 110,
    192, 196, 203
Congo Free State, 84, 96
consciencism, 33
Côte d'Ivoire, 235
Crowder, Samuel Ajayi, 73–74

Cuba, 76, 203
Cugoano, Ottobah, 71–72

Dallaire, Roméo, 205
Danquah, Joseph, 173–174, 179, 182, 199,
    201–202
decolonization, xiii–xiv, 5, 18, 26, 102,
    104–105, 120, 135–136, 152–154,
    158, 164–166, 169–171, 174, 178,
    182, 203, See also anti-colonialism
democracy, 27, 32–33, 51, 88, 141, 144,
    169, 175, 180–181, 190, 198,
    201–202, 208–211, 215, 219, 227,
    231, 233–234, 238
Denmark, 158
Diagne, Blaise, 2, 5, 42, 121–122, 139–140
dignity, 32–33, 36, 38, 49, 52–53, 55, 63,
    68, 80, 99, 127, 156, 160, 165, 186,
    216, 232
distributive justice, 15
divorce, 92, 115, 117–119, 214, 235
Du Bois, W.E.B, 2, 140
duties, 38–39, 45–48, 51, 98, 101, 151,
    180, 186, 218
    relationship with rights, 45

Eastern bloc, 195–196, 220, See also
    Cold War
Ecuador, 232
egalitarianism, xiii
Egypt, 14, 33, 82, 114, 164, 188–190, 198,
    208, 212
emancipation, 1, 56, 60–61, 64, 71, 73–74,
    78–81, 83, 88–89, 91, See also
    abolition
emergency, 61, 103–104, 166,
    173
Emergency Powers Act, 181
Enlightenment, 9–11, 18, 47, 53, 61–62,
    66, 72, 147, 150
enslavement, 43, 57, 63–64, 66–67, 69–72,
    81, 89
Equiano, Olaudah, 1, 5, 63, 71–72
ethics, xi, 1, 31, 34–35, 44, 46, 49, 57, 62,
    64–65, 69–71, 82, 227
    indigenous, 35
Ethiopia, 14, 44, 78, 111, 164, 180, 195–196,
    198
Europe, Europeans, 12, 83–84, 89–91,
    94–95, 97–102, 106, 108, 110,
    115–117, 120, 122, 124, 129, 131,
    134–135, 137–139, 141–142, 144,
    155–157, 161, 165, 172, 232
European Convention on Human Rights,
    15, 142, 166
Ewe, 153

Fabian Society, 131
feminism, 234
forced labor, 108–112, 193
Forced Labor Convention, 109
forced marriages, 92, 115–116, 118, 211
Four Freedoms, 132, 148
Fourteen Points, 139, 149
free trade, 99
Freedom Charter
    Uganda, 151
French Declaration of the Rights of Man
    and Citizen, 11

G77, 164
Gacaca Courts, 207
Gaddafi, Muammar, 189–190, 197
Gandhi, Mohandas, 139
gay, 235, See LGBTQ
gender, 40–41, 47, 51, 167, 171, 205–206,
    211, 213, 224, 235, 237–238
gender identity, 236
genocide, 4, 102, 202, 204–205, 207
    Rwanda, 204–205
Ghana, 32, 40, 72, 107, 112, 141, 145–146,
    155, 164, 171–175, 179, 181, 190,
    197, 199, 201, 210, 235
globalization, 20, 50
Gold Coast, 74, 80, 107–108, 116, 121–122,
    139, 141, 146, 164, 173, See also
    Ghana
griot, 30
Group Areas Act, 127–128
guerrilla war, 103–104
Guinea Bissau, 165

Habré, Hissène, 195–196
Habyarimana, Juvénal, 204
Haile Mariam, Mengistu, 195–196,
    198
Haiti, 2
Hatata, 44–45, See also Yacob, Zara
Hayford, Casley, 90
Herero, 102
historiography, xii, 7, 20, 29, 53, 56, 66
honor, 39, 41–42, 233

human dignity, 32–33, 39–44, 47, 49,
    52–53, 222
human rights
    activists, 4, 57, 60, 86, 213, 233
    African concept of, 8, 31, 36–39,
        49, 51
    Asian values, 37, 176
    chronology of, 5
    codification, 19, 22, 27
    collective, 18
    communual, 39
    concept of, xix, 5–6, 8, 10, 16, 18–19,
        25, 35, 39, 41, 49, 52, 59, 138, 143
    cultural legitimacy of, xv, 36, 52
    debates at the UN, 14
    discourse, 5, 20
    empirical and ideological constructs of,
        xiv
    essentialism, essentialists, 16–17
    evolutionists, 8
    genealogy of, xi, xv, 9–10, 37, 53, 56
    generations of, xiii
    historiography, xii, 20
    inalienability of, 6, 47–48, 50, 92
    invention of, 12–14, 36
    legitimacy, 36
    links with antislavery, 61
    movement, xii–xiii, 6, 14–18, 21–22,
        25–26, 37, 53, 57–60, 93, 105, 129,
        132–135, 138, 143, 147, 169–170,
        178, 201, 215, 220, 222
    positivism, 8
    pre-history, xv
    presentism, xiii
    universality of, xvii, 6, 11, 29, 35, 47, 50,
        55, 92, 94, 142, 221–222, 233
    vernacularization of, 52–53, 226, 229,
        231
Human Rights NGOs
    Amnesty International, 192
    Article 19, 192, 215
    Human Rights Watch, 192, 194,
        204–205, 215, 236
    International League for Human Rights
        and the Human Rights, 192
humanism, xv, 5, 10, 31, 33, 41–42, 47, 50,
    63, 187, 217, 221
humanitarianism, humanitarians, 4, 58,
    60–61, 65, 71, 83, 85, 89, 96, 123,
    154, 192, 202, 206–207, 233
Hutu, 204

Igbo, 42, 50, 88, 125, 183, 197, 202
Immorality Act, 128
India, 113, 144, 158, 164
Indians, 80, 83, 86, 107, 123, 128, 139,
    145, 156, 161, 164
indigenous traditions, xii
individualism, xiii, 8, 17, 33, 35, 38–39,
    93, 137, 187
International Criminal Court, 3–4, 206, 233
International Labor Organization, 109–111
international law, 8, 62, 75, 84, 96–97,
    138, 155, 163, 224
International Monetary Fund, 209
Islam, 34, 43–44, 46, 81–82, 167, 214, 233

Jaja of Opobo, 114

Kabaka of Buganda, 114, 120
Kaunda, Kenneth, 32, 145, 187, 197, 217
Kenya, 32–33, 81, 103–104, 108–109,
    116–117, 122, 134, 139, 141–143,
    145, 165–166, 168, 175, 179,
    184–185, 191, 200–201, 211
Kenyatta, Jomo, 32–33, 145, 151, 175,
    184–185, 200
Kérékou, Mathieu, 209
Kikuyu, Gikuyu, 33, 104, 106, 151, 184,
    200
Kingsley, Mary, 100
Kongo, 55, 68–70, 74
Korea, 158

labor, xvi, 50, 65, 69, 75, 78–81, 83–84, 91,
    95, 100–101, 105, 108–111, 124,
    126, 129, 143, 153, 157, 167, 178,
    184, 193, 209–210, 212
Lancaster House Conferences, 168
Lango, 191
League of Nations, 2, 60, 75, 87, 95,
    110–111, 139, 141, 153–154, 158
    Covenant, 95
    Mandates Commission, 153
Leopold, King, 84–85, 89, 96, 102,
    See also Congo
lesbian, 235
LGBTQ, 235–237
liberalism, xii, 9–12, 18, 47, 53, 65, 100,
    113, 147
Liberia, 1–2, 14, 66, 77–78, 111, 140, 149,
    164, 206–207
    Declaration of Independence, 77

Libya, 189, 197, 208
Lockerbie bombing, 190
Lord's Resistance Army, 192, 208
Lugard, Frederick, 78, 94
Luo, 184, 200

Machel, Samora, 177
Madagascar, 141, 198
Magna Carta, 11, 14, 120, 142
Malawi, 50, 179, 192, 194, 201, 209
Mandel Decree, 118
Mandela, Nelson, 3, 5, 160, 162–163, 227
Manden Charter, Manden Oath, 42–43
Mandingo, 67
manumission, 57
Margai, Albert, 185
Massai, 185
Mau Mau, 103–104, 142–143, 184
Mboya, Tom, 165
Mixed Commission Courts, 62, 76
modernity, 50, 97
Morel, Edmund, 85, 96–97
Morocco, 43, 114, 187, 212, 214
Mozambique, 104, 110–111, 126, 165, 177,
    180, 196, 198, 203
Mubarak, Hosni, 189
Muslim Brotherhood, 189
Muslims, 43–44, 81–82, 146, 167, 183,
    189, 213
Mwalimu, 30

Naguib, Mohammed, 189
Namibia, 102, 153, 165, 196, 198, 203,
    216, 236
Nasser, Gamal Abdul, 33, 188–189
National Patriotic Front of Liberia, 206
nationalism, 130–134
Native Courts, 117, 119
native rights, xvi, 91–92, 94–95, 97–98,
    100–101, 108, 122, 124, 129, 139,
    154, 161
Natives Land Act, 126
Nazism, 141
Nehru, Jawaharlal, 139
neo-colonialism, 196
Nevinson, Henry, 110
Nigeria, 51, 65, 72, 78, 87–88, 102, 107, 112,
    114, 118, 121–122, 125, 131, 139, 141,
    145, 147, 149, 157–158, 165, 167, 171,
    182–183, 197, 202, 210–211
Nimeiry, Gaafar, 175

Njinga, Queen of Kongo, 68–70
Nkrumah, Kwame, 33, 130, 145–147, 164,
    171–174, 181, 196–197, 199, 201, 217
Non-Governmental Organizations,
    NGO, 10, 27, 58, 155, 189, 198,
    201, 210–211, 213, 215, 219
Nuremburg trials, 229
Nyasaland, 156, 166, 168, 178, *See* also
    Malawi
Nyerere, Julius, 32–33, 35, 145, 151, 172,
    175, 185–187, 196–197, 217

Obote, Milton, 190, 192
Odinga, Odinga, 179, 200–202
Ojukwu, Chukwuemeka, 183
Orange Free States, 126
Organization for African Unity, 216–217,
    219
Organization of African Unity, xxii, 45–46,
    163, 176, 216–217
Ottoman Empire, 81, 83, 153

Padmore, George, 148
Pakistan, 164
Pan-African Congress, 2–3, 140, 148
pan-Arabism, 33, 188–189
Pasha, Urabi, 114
patriarchy, 115
personhood, xiv, 5, 7, 39, 42, 214
Petition of Rights, 11
Poland, 158
political revolutions, xii, 9, 11, 26
    American, 11
    French, 11, 115
Portugal, 55, 69, 109, 163
Preventive Detention Act, 173, 181
primitive, primitivism, 93, 177
Privy Council, 97–98, 107
Prohibition of Mixed Marriage Act,
    128
property rights, 80–81, 111, 123, 160, 168,
    188, 222

queer, 235, *See* LGBTQ
Quran, 10

Ransome-Kuti, Funmilayo, 157–158
Rawlings, Jerry, 210
repugnancy doctrine, 75, 115–116
Revolutionary United Front, 206
Rhodes, Cecil, 90, 123

Rhodesia, 98–99, 109, 112, 127, 141, 159, 165–166, 216
right to die, 232
rights of nature, 72, 232
Roosevelt, Eleanor, 142, 149
Roosevelt, Franklin Delano, 14, 130, 132, 148, 160
Ruanda-Urundi, 153
Rwanda, 165, 204–205, 207, 235
Rwandan Patriotic Front, 204

Sadat, Anwar, 189
salongo, 50, 193
Savimbi, Jonas, 203
segregation, 26, 124–129, 144, 147, 159, 187, 221
Selassie, Haile, 78, 195
self-determination, xvi, 5, 7, 15, 18, 21, 23, 84, 89, 92, 95, 105, 112, 122, 129–135, 138–142, 172, 175, 178, 182, 199
Senegal, 32, 80, 121, 165, 172–173, 195, 210
Senghor, Senghor, 32, 172–173, 176
Sese Seko, Mobutu, 50, 175, 192–196, 203, 209, 217
settlers, 104, 106, 108–110, 122, 124, 126, 165, 168
sexual minorities, 224, 234–235
sexual orientation, 236, *See* LGBTQ
Sharp, Granville, 71
Sharpeville massacre, 129, 161
Sierra Leone, 66, 73, 76–77, 168, 185, 206–207
slave trade, 12, 44, 55–57, 59–62, 65–74, 76–78, 81–84, 86, 99, 222, *See* also slavery
slavery, slaves, 1, 6, 14, 29, 43, 56–57, 61, 63–64, 71, 75–76, 78–79, 82–84, 86, 88, 109–110, 222
rebellion, 68, 102, 141
resistance, 56, 64, 67
Smuts, Jan, 127, 143–144
social movements, xii
South Africa, 14, 31–32, 35, 50–51, 80, 109, 123–126, 128, 159–160, 162, 165, 203, 224–230, 235, 237
South African Communist Party, 161
South African Native National Council, 128

South West Africa, 102, 153, *See* also Namibia
Southern Rhodesia, 98
Soviet Union, 158, 196, 203
Sri Lanka, 164
Sudan, 3–4, 40, 78, 81, 112, 164, 175, 206
Surinam, 76
Switzerland, 158

Tanganyika, 34, 79, 151, 153, 155–156, 169, 185–186, 197
Tanganyika National Union, 34, 169
Tanzania, 32–33, 108, 145, 156, 165, 172, 175–176, 185–186, 190, 197, 207, 211
Taylor, Charles, 207
Thuku, Harry, 139
Togoland, 153, 155
Touré, Ahmed Sékou, 145, 217
Touré, Samori, 77, 114
transsexual, 235, *See* also LGBTQ
Transvaal, 126
TRC. *See* Truth and Reconciliation Commission
trial by ordeal, 115
Trinidad, 158
trusteeship, 154
Truth and Reconciliation Commission, 31, 51, 160, 226–230
Liberia, 208
Sierra Leone, 208
South African, 31
Tse-tung, Mao, 158
Tunisia, 82, 112, 146, 187–188, 208, 212–214
Tutsi, 204
Tutu, Desmond, 31, 211, 227

ubuntu, 31–32, 34–35, 51, 226–231
Uganda, 114, 151, 165, 168, 175, 177, 185, 187, 190, 192, 197–198, 208, 211
Uhuru, 25, 138
Ujamaa, 33–34, 185, *See* also Nyerere, Julius
UN Covenant on Civil and Political Rights, 48
UNITA, 203
United Kingdom, 104, 131, 163
United Nations, 8, 10, 13–14, 16–20, 25, 56, 87, 127, 137, 141–145, 151,

153–157, 162–165, 172, 177–178, 180, 189, 192, 205, 207, 215–216, 220, 238
Charter, 8, 92, 127, 141, 143, 151, 155, 162–164
covenants, 8
    Convention on the Prevention and Punishment of the Crime of Genocide, 205
    Covenant on Civil and Political Rights, 13, 143, 162, 166, 216
    Covenant on Economic, Social and Cultural Rights, 143, 162, 166, 218
General Assembly, 8, 14, 127, 137, 162, 165
Human Rights Council, 4, 236
peace keeping missions
    Assistance Mission to Rwanda, 205
Trust Territories, 136, 155
United States, 1–2, 14, 77, 85, 124, 130–131, 140–141, 145, 147–148, 157, 163, 196, 203, 217
constitution, 77
Declaration of Independence, 77
Universal Declaration of Human Rights, 3, 8–10, 13–16, 18–19, 25, 34, 56, 60, 92, 127, 133, 137, 141–142, 145, 149, 152, 155–156, 162, 164, 166, 180, 185, 205, 216, 218, 232
Universal Islamic Declaration of Human Rights, 34
Upper Guinea Coast, 67

Versailles Peace Conference, 2–3, 140
Verwoerd, Hendrick, 161
Vienna Congress of 1814, 75
Vietnam, 158

Western bloc, 158, See also Cold War, See also Cold War
widows, 117, 192
Wilberforce, William, 71
Wilson, Woodrow, 139
women, 8, 27, 42, 44, 47, 51, 56, 66, 70, 73, 92, 115–119, 124–125, 129, 132, 151–152, 155, 157–158, 203, 206, 211, 213–214, 224, 233–234, See also gender
World Anti-Slavery Convention, 72
World Bank, 209
World War I, 2, 87, 139–141, 144, 153
World War II, xi–xiv, 6–8, 10, 15–16, 18, 20, 53, 87–88, 92, 100, 105, 108, 112, 130, 132–134, 137, 141, 143–144, 153–154, 166, 170, 202, 205
Wright, Joseph, 73

Yacob, Zara, 44
Yoruba, 41–42, 50, 69, 73, 118

Zaire, 50, 175, 192, 209
Zambia, 32, 145, 165, 185, 187, 197, 210
Zanzibar, 77, 81, 86, 112, 156
Zimbabwe, 159, 198, 233
Zong slave massacre, 65
Zulu, 50